CW00502817

ROUTLEDGE LIBRARY EDITIONS:
ARTIFICIAL INTELLIGENCE

Volume 5

ARTIFICIAL INTELLIGENCE

ARTIFICIAL INTELLIGENCE
Its Philosophy and Neural Context

F.H. GEORGE

Routledge
Taylor & Francis Group
LONDON AND NEW YORK

First published in 1986 by Gordon and Breach Science Publishers

This edition first published in 2018
by Routledge
2 Park Square, Milton Park, Abingdon, Oxon OX14 4RN

and by Routledge
711 Third Avenue, New York, NY 10017

Routledge is an imprint of the Taylor & Francis Group, an informa business

© 1986 by Gordon and Breach, Science Publishers

All rights reserved. No part of this book may be reprinted or reproduced or utilised in any form or by any electronic, mechanical, or other means, now known or hereafter invented, including photocopying and recording, or in any information storage or retrieval system, without permission in writing from the publishers.

Trademark notice: Product or corporate names may be trademarks or registered trademarks, and are used only for identification and explanation without intent to infringe.

British Library Cataloguing in Publication Data
A catalogue record for this book is available from the British Library

ISBN: 978-0-8153-8566-0 (Set)
ISBN: 978-0-429-49236-5 (Set) (ebk)
ISBN: 978-0-8153-6336-1 (Volume 5) (hbk)
ISBN: 978-1-351-10959-8 (Volume 5) (ebk)

Publisher's Note
The publisher has gone to great lengths to ensure the quality of this reprint but points out that some imperfections in the original copies may be apparent.

Disclaimer
The publisher has made every effort to trace copyright holders and would welcome correspondence from those they have been unable to trace.

Artificial Intelligence
Its Philosophy and Neural Context

F.H. GEORGE
Brunel University, U.K.

GORDON AND BREACH SCIENCE PUBLISHERS
New York London Paris Montreux Tokyo

Copyright © 1986 by Gordon and Breach, Science Publishers, S.A., P.O. Box 161, 1820 Montreux 2, Switzerland. All rights reserved.

Gordon and Breach Science Publishers

P.O. Box 786
Cooper Station
New York, NY 10276
United States of America

P.O. Box 197
London WC2E 9PX
England

58, rue Lhomond
75005 Paris
France

14-9 Okubo 3-chome
Shinjuku-ku
Tokyo 160
Japan

Library of Congress Cataloging in Publication Data

George, F.H. (Frank Honywill), 1921–
Artificial intelligence: its philosophy and neural context.

(Studies in cybernetics, ISSN 0275–5807; v. 9)
Bibliography: p.
Includes index.
1. Artificial intelligence. 2. Information science.
I. Title. II. Series.
Q335.G385 1984 001.53′5 84–10253
ISBN 2–88124–009–7 (Switzerland)

ISBN 2–88124–009–7. ISSN 0275 5807. All rights reserved. No part of this book may be reproduced or utilized in any form or by any means, electronic or mechanical, including photocopying, recording, or by any information storage or retrieval system, without permission in writing from the publishers. Printed in the United Kingdom by Bell and Bain Ltd, Glasgow.

Introduction to the Series

The subject of cybernetics is quickly growing and there now exists a vast amount of information on all aspects of this broad-based set of disciplines. The phrase "set of disciplines" is intended to imply that cybernetics and all the approaches to artificial (or machine) intelligence have a near identical viewpoint. Furthermore, systems analysis, systems theory and operational research often have a great deal in common with (and are in fact not always discernibly different from) what is meant by cybernetics, as far as this series is concerned: inevitably, computer science is bound to be involved also.

The fields of application are virtually unlimited and applications are discovered in the investigation or modelling of any complex system. The most obvious applications have been in the construction of artificially intelligent systems, the brain and nervous system, and socio-economic systems. This can be achieved through either simulation (copying as exactly as possible) or synthesis (achieving the same or better end result by any means whatsoever).

The range of applications today has become so broad it now includes such subjects as aesthetics, history and architecture. Modelling can be carried out by computer programs, special purpose models (analog, mathematical, statistical, etc.), and automata of various kinds, including neural nets and TOTES. All that is required of the system to be studied is that it be complex, dynamic, and capable of 'learning' and also have feedback or feedforward or both.

This is an international series.

FRANK GEORGE

Contents

Preface

In this book I have attempted to place Artificial Intelligence (AI) in the context of cybernetic thinking and information science. This involves giving some consideration to philosophical, behavioural and neurophysiological matters. It is this contextual issue that is my main interest although at the same time I hope to consider the AI approach to cognition in a fair amount of detail.

I have had the benefit of reading the following important works: Patrick Winston and Richard Brown's *Artificial Intelligence: An MIT Perspective*, Margaret Boden's *Artificial Intelligence and Rational Man*, R.W. Sampson's *Adaptive Information Processing*, the various and considerable writing of Donald Michie, L. Johnston's and E.T. Kervanou's *Expert Systems Technology* and Alex Andrew's *Artificial Intelligence* — as well, of course, as all the books and papers listed in the references. This book is in no way intended to compete with all these excellent books — without which I would know much less about AI; it is though intended to provide a link between AI and the worlds of philosophy, logic, neurophysiology and the like: to provide a sort of context for AI.

Inevitably when writing such a book, especially in a field such as AI which is developing very quickly, there are many different ways one could place the emphasis. I considered saying a great deal more about the tools for building expert systems (expert system builders such as AGE and EMYCIN) and more on Knowledge Elicitation, Knowledge Representation and expert systems themselves. Instead I chose to concentrate on expert systems and in particular on two consultative expert systems — PROSPECTOR and INTERNIST, thanks especially to the careful and painstaking guidance of Drs. Johnston and Kervanou. I am planning in the future to provide a more detailed analysis of expert systems.

The term "expert system" is somewhat ambiguous since the work on GPS by Newell, Shaw and Sinom, Checkers by Samuel and GT by Donald Michie are all expert systems as I see it, but they are not consultative in that they do not interact with the user or explain (justify) the advice given — the title "consultative expert system" is often though identified with "expert system".

I profoundly believe that AI, and rather especially expert systems, are going to play a major part in the future of both science and business and in a way this is something of a triumphant justification for the originators of such thinking — particularly Norbert Wiener and Warren McCulloch.

FRANK GEORGE

BOOK 1

The Basic Issues of Information Technology

Preface to book 1

In Book 1, I shall try to set down what I conceive to be the most central and most basic issues of information technology, which I shall take to include cybernetics and artificial intelligence.

These basic issues will include some discussion of the distinction which is increasingly made by some people between cybernetics and artificial intelligence (AI), although I personally still think of cybernetics as including AI. It is perhaps though a matter of no great importance how we make such classifications.

The other main considerations include some statement, in the form of guidelines, if not precise definitions, as to what is to be regarded as a cybernetic problem; I shall call it this if only for brevity's sake. This leads to a consideration as to which systems can, or should, be studied cybernetically, and also to the realisation that cybernetics is, in some measure, *a point of view*. It is a methodology on its own, has a philosophy of its own, but its systems and their modelling, it takes from wherever it finds them. This entails a considerable overlap with other disciplines both as a source of systems to analyse and models to construct as well as in terms of methodology.

There are many special questions of a philosophical kind that arise and these, in one way or another, surround the mind–body problem problem. We shall examine all these matters in Book 1, and they lead on to a more detailed analysis in Book 2.

1

The Nature of the Problem

In this book I hope to achieve a certain number of reasonably clear-cut goals. The first is to outline what I believe to be the principal problems of cybernetics, especially with respect to artificial intelligence (AI). Herein lies the first important issue.

When Wiener and his associates (1948) first introduced the notions of cybernetics, and Shannon (Shannon and Weaver, 1949) first drew attention to the importance of information theory, and the group of scientists and philosophers in North America in the 1940s first held discussions on philosophy of science and cybernetics, there was an upsurge of interest in "man as a machine". McCulloch and Pitts (1943) in America, and Turing in Britain (1951), among many others from various disciplines, further stimulated that interest. Out of their work came renewed efforts in the modelling of nervous systems and the development of particular modelling methods such as neural nets, leading both to and from automata theory in general and such methods as TOTES in particular.

At the same time as this was happening, there arose a new interest in purposive behaviour and teleological explanation. Furthermore, thanks to the interest of Gregory Bateson, Margaret Mead and others, the ideas of cybernetics were seen to be capable of being used to model social, anthropological, economic, indeed almost any sort of system in which scientists were interested.

There were underlying themes (which we shall discuss later in more detail) regarding feedback and feedforward, adaptation, and so on. All this lay within the general context of the belief that, despite the semantic difficulties involved, there was a sense in which "machines could be made to think".

Since these early days, a great deal has happened. The hugely over-optimistic forecasts that progress would, in the fifties and sixties, be electrifying, did not materialise. This is fairly typical historically, since a "breakthrough" often stirs up enthusiasm and over-statement, however well intentioned. However, my theme here is more concerned with one particular aspect of the subsequent history of cybernetics. What is now regarded as

AI, and workers within their field think of it as separated from (broken away from) cybernetics, did indeed emerge in a separate form. Rather as a liberal party, having done its job of liberalisation, may cease to exist, so cybernetics having persuaded other disciplines to look at themselves "cybernetically" was in danger of disappearing. This disappearance being encouraged by the unwanted presence of a lunatic fringe (much the same thing has happened to psychology).

So in writing now about cybernetics *and* AI, I am conceding that the two have in some measure parted company, even though I shall think of the latter as being largely included in the former. (*pace* AI—folk). In his recent book, Alex Andrew (1983) has quoted me specifically as "identifying cybernetics and AI", and reasonably so.

Historically, the basic idea that "machines" *could* be made to "think" required interpretation and evidence by implementation. This meant following up modelling methods such as neural nets, but it was soon realised that in practice the only universal model capable of realistic use was the suitably programmed computer. Noughts-and-crosses (tic-tac-toe), NIM and other games were quickly tackled and soon came the cascade of ideas and programming methods (LISP, heuristics, etc.) which led to the division of labour between those who programmed computers and those who did other things. "What are those other things?" is the first question. But before we attempt to answer it let it be said that there is an important distinction (of degree no doubt) between the *simulation* of human behaviour (of special interest to psychologists and physiologists) and the *synthesis* of cognitive activities which has great value in the field of control engineering and many other fields besides.

The distinction between simulation and synthesis cuts across the current cybernetic-AI distinction, since many cyberneticans are interested in computer modelling and many AI people are concerned with how their work helps in understanding human behaviour, both "normal" and "abnormal".

If however we admit, however temporarily, the cybernetic-AI distinction, we might ask what is left when the AI work has been subtracted. The answer is (or should be) of special interest, I think, to both parties. The remainder includes all other model making methods such as automata, information theory, TOTES and the application of formalisation. The fields of activity to which these other methods can now be addressed is everything and anything at all (e.g. history, economics, the arts) in just the same way as AI methods could apply to anything at all. Because the "other" methods are less easily demarcated, their use can often be buried in the field to which they are applied. It does appear though that this is now happening to AI as well.

The actual situation that then pertains is that all too often AI people will regard cybernetics as an empty subject. This picture, which is characteristic of the sort of absurd extremes that arise in science and philosophy, is wholly ridiculous. It is reminiscent of Russell's outright condemnation of Wittgenstein's second phase philosophy and Wittgensten's subsequent loathing of *Principia Mathematica* and the formalism it stood for. Such formalism was baptised the Augustinian viewpoint (Baker and Hacker, 1980) and presented as the rigid and the backward looking. Such feuds abound and are doubtless the result of fervant enthusiasm and dedication, but none the less fatuous for all that.

For my own part I think of AI as part of the spearhead of cybernetics and a field of immense potential. Indeed in this book I would lay no claim to describing AI in and of itself, since this has already been excellently done by many writers including Margaret Bowden, E. Charniack and Y. Wilks, R. Sampson, Winston and Brown, Nilsson, Slagle and many others. These are works mainly by people currently active in the field of AI and I would not for a moment suggest this book is an attempt to compete with their work. Similarly it is no function of any book, least of all this one, to attempt to compete with those two excellent sources of papers on AI, the series of books on *Machine Intelligence*, from Edinburgh and edited by Donald Michie and his associates, and the equally excellent journal *Artificial Intelligence*, edited by Daniel Bobrow; there are also other journals that are springing up like mushrooms. I have drawn extensively on all these sources to try to give a picture of AI at work, in the general context of cybernetic thinking.

If cybernetics is concerned with precision and effectiveness in modelling complex, interactive adaptive feedback and feedforward systems, this in practice will entail supplying a formalised account of fields of activity as varied as history (Chandler 1984) and art (Rosenberg 1983) or business science (Strank 1983). I believe this sort of approach entails looking carefully at the philosophical and semantic aspects of the development; the behavioural fields could also entail looking in turn at the neurophysiological evidence. I hope to do just that, but only with a view to providing guidelines to AI work in their simulatory role.

Marr's work (1974, 1975, 1982) in characteristic of those AI researchers whose primary interest in simulation of the nervous system. He saw visual sensation and visual perception as starting with the formation of a "primal sketch" which is rather like the primitive and important features of a scene. These, for Marr, include shading-edge, extended edge, line, contrast, lighters, size, etc. All this is in the periphery of the visual system and therefore primarily retinal (i.e. mechanisms of detection).

This is followed by the central processes (mechanism of construction) which group and organise (e.g. prints) figures-ground data and generally provide an interpretation of the primal sketch. This is similar to (but not quite the same as) Price's (1953) distinction between primary and secondary recognition. In fact, it is rather like the distinction sometimes made between *sensing* (visually) and *perception*. But in any case there may be many stages which are more or less separable in the total visual activity.

The great virtue, or so it seems to me, is that AI provides a powerful tool which goes beyond traditional experimental psychology and neuropsychological modelling and theorising (e.g. Hebb, 1949; Palm, 1982) and this should be recognised by all those parties interested in the function of the senses. Dr Marr's (1975) own words are worth quoting here:

> The situation in modern neurophysiology is that people are trying to understand how a particular mechanism performs a computation that they cannot even formulate, let alone provide a crisp summary of ways of doing so. To rectify the situation, we need to invest considerable effort in studying the computational backgrounds to questions that can be approached in neurophysiological experiments.

He goes on to emphasise, quite rightly, that this work is an indirect approach to neurophysiology, but a direct approach to vision. This is the synthesis coming first, but with the simulation in mind and with a thorough awareness of the great complexity involved. He makes the point that until you have tried to suitably program a computer to perform even relatively simple looking tasks you cannot have any feel for the complexity of the problem. His words again:

> The power of this approach is that the knowledge one obtains concerns facts that are inherent in the task, not in the structural details of the mechanism performing it.

With all of this, I would readily and unconditionally agree, but would like to add a caveat. It is all too characteristic of philosophers that they will support a viewpoint: Wittgenstein's constructivism, Peirce's pragmatism, Russell's atomism or Ryle's natural language approach, and see them less as alternatives and acceptable (even if not equally acceptable) approaches to the philosophy of language, say, and more as the one single correct approach (theirs) and the others as incorrect approaches (all those that are not theirs). This same attitude has often pervaded science and one remembers experimental psychologists of the 1930s, 1940s and 1950s, with their love of apparatus and statistical analysis, and their loathing of theory. The danger is that the enthusiasm of AI people could similarly carry them so far that they could see absolutely no virtue at all in any other approach. For example, to take a philosophical approach and try to carefully analyse one's language, in order among other things, to try to decide whether a problem is a "real" one or not. So the nativist-empiricist controversy in perception was wasteful and absurd since it was a totally semantic issue and could be resolved by almost immediately a little linguistic — philosophical consideration. It was time wasted when one might be writing and testing programs.

It is not being suggested that AI people see it in this extreme light any more than cyberneticians outside AI see AI people as wasting their time. There are doubtless minority groups in both camps though who do think this, but it would be sad to see this parochiality go too far. Another example which is closely parallel is the feelings that often exist between logicians — mathematical on one hand and non-mathematical on the other. That there are various possible approaches to logic is obvious but it is not easy for people wholly involved in the more extreme removes of axiomatics and recursive functions to see much use in the "limpid world" (Quine's words) of those like Strawson or Austin.

It has also been said against the AI group that they claim for their work a case for simulation that could never in fact go beyond synthesis. I know of no case personally where excessive claims have been made but I would guess that the vast majority of people in the field must know that as long as we are in doubt about the way human mechanisms function, we cannot be sure that we possess a precise simulation model. It seems virtually certain in cases such as visual perception that template models, PERCEPTRON-like models and the various neural models cannot all be simulations. Similarly in syntactical analysis augmented-transition nets, Marcus type syntax and forms of dependency grammar cannot all be simulations of the way human beings deal with language. Perhaps none of them are simulations or perhaps some two or three are part of a more general simulation; all of this must, at least for the time being, remain uncertain.

I have though, returning to the suggested AI-cibernetics distinction, seen it said (a private communication from a distinguished AI worker) that cybernetics, while worthy enough when originally founded by Wiener and Shannon, "had died but simply refused to lie down". The answer here is that it has changed and evolved and much has rubbed off on other disciplines and been incorporated by those other disciplines, and if you think of AI, not as the central thrust of cybernetics, as I do, but as something now working on its own, there is still a great deal remaining in cybernetics, including the various methods and the application of those methods to any field of activity, but perhaps especially to human behaviour and the human nervous system. From this, I believe, a very valuable association with philosophy is growing up, where the ambitions of modern pragmaticists (e.g. Montague, Stalnaker and Martin), people in cognitive linguistics (e.g. Osgood and Rozeboom) and meaning theorists, (e.g. Quine, Bennett and Grice) can find a valuable trade off. The cybernetician should be greatly involved in such linguistic, logical and behavioural undertakings and add some emphasis to them. At the same time his own models should be built on them to put-it-another-way, the field of overlap here, perhaps the field of (descriptive) pragmatics is part of cybernetics and its models — gradually appearing in automata theoretic or program form — is a bridge to AI.

For my own part I am personally concerned (apart from my work in AI) in research is what is perhaps best called behavioural semiotic. I think of this as a valid field for a cybernetician to work in, but would add that whether or not you call this (or *could* call this) cybernetics is of absolutely no consequence. This raises that other chestnut about the (historically) useful but often misleading distinctions that occur (or can be thought to occur) between disciplines so that one asks "What is a philosophical problem?" "Is that a part of physics or chemstry?" and so on. One reason for the founding of cybernetics, rather like operational research, was to cut across the more obviously arbitrary boundaries of existing success and "slice the cake" differently. It is partly for this reason that we now have so many labels and to tilt at the labels (and their roughly delineated adherents) without too much consideration of the detailed work of some of the people, regardless of the labels, seems foolish.

Trying to classify what AI people do, what cyberneticians do, and their relation to each other is one clearcut aim, another is to try to outline the methods of modelling which are available to scientists — primarily information scientists, as well as outline and evaluate progress both in the wider (cybernetic) and also the narrower (strictly AI) approaches.

I would like also to say something about the present controversy (Searle, 1982) over "strong" and "weak" viewpoints in AI. Searle seems to argue that a simulation (or model) of a human being (or anything at all) is different from the "thing" (human being) itself. A model that is a "complete" duplicate is hardly appropriately called a model. The trouble with these sorts of discussions is that one is often dealing with a "straw man": no one seems to hold the view they are supposed to. But we can at least point to a subsidiary question as to whether the fabric of a system directly affects, or not, the behaviour of a system. This is a familiar argument for which there are no definite answers available. But it comes to this: can an artifically constructed system have exactly the same experiences as a human being?

The traditional philosophical problem of "other minds" rears its head here because there is no way we can be certain that *other people* have the same feelings as we have. It is constantly the case, as far as even cognition is concerned, let alone conation, that we cannot seriously encompass our answers in the Turing Interrogation Game, since the constraints imposed by it are no more than suggestive of the criteria we need. In fact, we can never *know* (if that implies indubitibility) whether "machines" (as defined as "artificially constructed systems") will have the property of consciousness, but we might guess that if they get to the point of holding humanlike conversation with self-reference, etc., then consciousness may prove to be inevitable. It seems likely that for our model to be humanlike in all respects may require that it be made of colloidal protoplasm and be exposed to a similar range of experiences. But this is too fanciful for the moment. What one might contend is that there is no obvious reason why such a state of affairs might not be achieved. However, on the short term, all people interested in AI will be satisfied if we continue to accumulate more and more information about humanlike systems and their behaviour, and continue to compare and contrast the consequent models with the human to see when they are apparently getting nearer to an understanding of the principles upon which the human being functions.

There are a number of people — some even within cybernetics and AI — who are sceptical or appalled, or both, by what is sometimes claimed, or what is anyway implicit in the whole project. Hubert Dreyfus (1965, 1972) stands out as one of these who believes that far too much is claimed for the computer. It does not seem worthwhile to enter in any detail into the argument at this point, since Margaret Boden has adequately dealt with many of the misunderstandings embodied in Dreyfus' other objections such as those which stem from Gödel's theorems. In general, the limitations that apply to the abilities of computers are limitations that apply in much the same way to human beings, and although one should be careful about claims made on behalf of work in cybernetics and AI, most of the objections put forward, in such a form as Dreyfus' arguments, are usually simply incorrect.

The scene is now set in part I of this book to look at cybernetics and modelling methods with some reference to philosophy, neuro-physiology and psychology and then to explicitly discuss AI in part II in terms of the same sort of behavioural context.

2

Some Preliminaries

This book is, as has already been made clear in Chapter I, about cybernetics and artificial intelligence (AI) and we in this second chapter we shall, among other things, outline the relation that I see as existing between these two closely related subjects. In doing so, we shall be following up what we have said already.

In the rest of Book I, I shall be outlining the methods mainly used in cybernetics and also lay some considerable emphasis on their philosophical foundations.

This book has a general (broad-brush) approach, it does not attempt to cover every aspect of the subject, but neither does it avoid the need for detailed examples of each of the samples (they cannot be exhaustive) we show, in order to make clear the compass of the subject.

One facet of our range of interests that could be regarded as a major one is the neurophysiological study of the brain and I have previously written on this subject in *The Brain as a Computer* (1961), but this subject will not be given a major treatment here. It will in fact appear from time to time in Book II as a subsidiary theme.

In Book II we give a detailed treatment of cognition from a viewpoint that is mainly AI and in some measure philosophical, and in some measure psychological.

Two central concepts for us are, as was said earlier, *simulation* and *synthesis*. We shall mean by 'simulation' the construction of models that purport to achieve the same ends as human beings *and* by the same means. We shall, of course, think carefully, especially as to what is meant by "the same means". By contrast, 'synthesis' involves the construction of models that purport to achieve the same, and similar, ends as human beings but not claiming that this is achieved by the same means. The question of the fabric of construction must also be considered since this is in no way claimed to be a part of the present modelling methods. What is vital here is whether the different fabrics make a "real difference" and if so what difference it is that they make.

In the next chapter we shall be describing a range of modelling methods and giving some examples of each application. It also behoves us to consider the extent to which these models are intertranslatable. All of this in turn is bound up with formalisation, which is the extent to which we make our theories precise (Braithwaite, 1953). This too is a matter which requires some discussion, and this we shall attempt straightaway.

Formalisation has a mixed history. In a sense the first major example was that of *Principia Mathematica* which showed that mathematics was capable of being formalised in the sense of being derivable from logic. Although formalisation is a *relative* matter, so that anything can be the model of a theory and any theory can be the interpretation of a model, it most often happens that the "most basic" model of all is logic.

Formalising in general involves translating from one language to a more "precise" language and the translation rules are required to actually carry through the translation. We also need formation rules (incomplete in the case of a natural language) and semantic rules (also incomplete in the case of natural language). Interpretation of a body of discourse A (if better understood and more "precise" than another body of discourse B) is both a translation of B, and in these special circumstances of greater precision, is called a formalisation of B.

This raises the question of "models", and although we have said that logic is, in some senses, a basic model, this would not go without dispute (e.g. Brouwer and the Intuitionists in the case of mathematics) and it may be that if we are hinting at a "foundation" for our subject, many would argue, (e.g. Wittgenstein, 1953) that the subject needed no foundation. Many though will argue that we do quite naturally seek to "reduce" theories and descriptions to more "primitive" and more easily understood concepts than those apparent in the original, so it is that mathematics and branches of science are so often thought of as a special case of a more basic process of association. This latter use of 'logic' refers to the inference-making activity which occurs pre-linguistically. We should not therefore be thinking of logic here as whatever is embodied in symbols or in language.

Those who eschew the idea of "foundations" for mathematics or science will take heart from the fact that models can be constructed without any more ado and are seen as, and used as, "intuitively useful" models of descriptions and easy enough in themselves to understand. Such examples as TOTES, flow charts, block diagrams, maps, etc. spring to mind and these, with many other models, will be our topic in the next chapter. We shall not be discussing hardware models, except insofar as references to servosystems and computers imply the existence of hardware, but it goes without saying that hardware models do exist, and they include wind-tunnel models and a whole range of special purpose models to simulate different processes and activities.

We must now pick up again the points made above which were taken to distinguish, if that is thought desirable, between cybernetics and AI. (I shall not, I say again, in general be wishing to emphasise this distinction and will continue, in general, to assume the latter is included in the former). A cybernetic model involves at least simulation. That is, like a map, it has the same structure as the original (the system or the territory) *and* it has the same function, which is to achieve certain goals or realise certain purposes (more needs to be said about this and will be said later) by the same means. We use 'same' here but can only be sure, even if that, of 'somewhat similar to' or 'not obviously different from' and we must needs accept this as a standard.

So far, in practice, cybernetics has tackled its modelling activities in a piecemeal fashion where the overlapping and often ill-fitting pieces are linked together by a fairly general theory, often as in the case of Wiener's original approach a (fragmented) mathematical theory. But at the modelling level, and therefore of course at the theoretical level too, the pieces are presupposed to be capable of being fitted together to form a complete system; let us call it S. Let S then be a "complete" model of a human being and one that could satisfy *inter alia* the Turing Interrogation Test. It is, of course, not being asserted that S, the model of a human being, *is* a human being, although we must ask ourselves whether there could arise a situation where S and the human would be indistinguishable on one hand, or "identical" on the other. What sort of conditions would this indistinguishability or identity imply, or is it something that is *a priori* impossible, even perhaps absurd? One thing that seems likely now is that we shall run headlong into the mind-body problem and perhaps also the notorious problem of privacy of sensations and language (Wittgenstein, 1953; Ayer, 1968; Cook, 1969; *et al.*).

Let us suppose, what is in fact the case, that we have computer programs that when inserted into the computer cause it to behave "perceptually". This means say, (Rosenblatt, 1958; Rapoport 1950a; 1950b; 1950c; 1950d; Selfridge, 1959; Uttley, 1954, 1955, 1966; *et al.*) that a system has been constructed that "recognises" features of its environment (a pattern recognition system) and probably uses methods of classification, of whatever kind, which involves the interpretation of a set of sensory inputs. Such a recognition system could be extended to deal with novel inputs and the need to *give them* a classification. Now we *could* argue that this seems to be humanlike, and perhaps is an accurate simulation of the human being, so now let us tentatively and temporarily put the program on the shelf.

We then repeat the operation for learning, thinking and this involves language, hence also language and logic. Then when we have a set of programs which all *seem to be* accurate simulations of the human cognitive process (we cannot talk of *acts* at this stage), we set about putting them together into one massive program which perceives-learns-thinks-solves problems (and therefore plans and makes decisions) — speaks and makes inferences. One can argue that you have now *the equal of* (if so, it could clearly then "be better than") a human being in its abilities of a cognitive kind. Such a model would clearly be enormously useful since it would engender a great deal of observation and experimentation to see whether the likeness was "complete", and also further modification if and where it was not. But has our S become indistinguishable from, or identical with, a human being?

In the case of distinguishability, since the model is in the form of computer programs, the test must be of the Turing kind; the fabric is quite different. Now if the Turing test is passed, can we say that the fabric is irrelevant? The answer must be "yes" for some purposes and less obviously (more tentatively) "no" for others.

One of the reasons (not necessarily the only one) why the answer could be "no" is that in the wider experience of S we must be able to find some loophole — perhaps S is too efficient and if so how are mistakes introduced? Perhaps S is non-emotive — how would we simulate emotions in S? Perhaps S is asocial and this would be inevitable if S lives independent of a history and a society. How, in short, does the real world and its influence on human beings reflect itself in S?

Given an S-society living in an environment E, we can, granted that E is similar to a human environment, expect to be able to generate humanlike behaviour, always granted the "emotional mechanism" can get angry, happy, pleased, annoyed, etc. But we still have to show how this can be done and in the end (to *prove* the point) do it. In the meantime we can only challenge the sceptic to say why he believes it cannot be done. What is his evidence? It is difficult not to believe that the "proof of the pie is in the eating".

We can though see one problem clearly. Is it the problem that our S-society has seemingly to evolve over long periods of time, or alternatively can its experience be truncated by supplying it with an "artificial" history (in rather the same way as *drosophila* is vital to genetic studies)? The answer is again that we are not certain but it seems that our experience (our history) is acquired by means of history books and a general agreement as to what has transpired in the past. This implies that we can teach history to S just as we can teach English to S and all we need to do is update our historical studies, and S will become familiar with its own history, one suspects as an offshoot of *homo sapiens*. There is no illusion that such a teaching of history will be an easy matter but it is one that seems to be perfectly possible in principle. One has to say in fact to the sceptic, give me some reason for believing it is not possible, or more strongly give me evidence that it is impossible.

In the absence of evidence to the contrary, we shall assume that the whole undertaking *is* possible and we must in the limit, as cyberneticians, undertake it. It will be borne in mind that this whole undertaking is carried out in order to acquire a blueprint (structural and functional) for a human being and it is by no means intended to construct human beings artificially.

The question to which we must now give preliminary consideration is as to whether there is reason to believe that an S, which is composed of different fabric (e.g. metallic and the like) must necessarily be different from a human being, and also whether, if it was composed of the same fabric, it would still be (and that is our first decision) necessarily different.

An analogy might help us off the ground. An aircraft can have a metallic frame (i.e. most aircraft) or it can be made of wood (e.g. the *Mosquito*). No difference occurs as an aircraft *per se*, even if differences *in degree* of performance arise, due to lighter weight, different skin friction, etc. This simply analogy makes it clear that we are looking for differences that really are differences; this reminds us of the construction of the Turing Interrogation Game. The differences in performance we will look for is in manifesting different languages (we will teach it English), in different processing resulting in different actions, in holding different opinions and so on. In passing we note that groups of people differ among themselves and between cultures even more than individuals among each other in what we would regard as differences which are *not* really differences.

One point we should pick up here and which is fairly central to our interest, is that we would teach S English but not "build it in". It could learn English in its S-society if the society spoke English. There is no requirement that we set up an E so that English necessarily emerges. Our position is always the same in this respect. If asked to program a chess-playing "machine", we would not "build in" our best generalisation and make the machine (doubtless a computer program) play the game; obviously this way it could never improve and would obviously fall foul of Lady Lovelace's stricture that "machines only do what they are made to do"; this is so unless of course we have also built the flexibility to undo the generalisations it is given. Humans also, of course, only do what they are made to do, but we want our S, like humans, to widen the range of "programmers" to include a variable environment. We are concerned with programming a computer to have the ability to learn any game in general, and chess in particular. It can therefore learn new tricks, unlearn old ones and generally have the capacity to outplay its initiator (initial programmer). That this learning might be by acquaintance or description (not wholly in the Russellian sense but by direct experience or by language) is evident.

The point here is that much of what cybernetics has attempted to do so far, has not gone that far, and the question arises as to whether we can effectively construct an S (that meets our current requirement) by, as it were, adding on new constraints. The answer is uncertain, but let us at least see how far we can take our current procedure.

The question of mistakes, errors of judgement, the acquisition (and maintenance) of false beliefs, etc. *requires* no additional "mechanisms", since the very fact that S, like a human being, must make inductions, inductive inferences, etc., based necessarily on incomplete information and even its deductive processes, embedded as they usually are in practical reasoning, are dubitable, we should expect errors to occur "naturally". This is, of course, apart from any error that might occur at the level of the fabric's functioning. That, in practice, some of these errors will occur because of emotive considerations is very likely, but this presupposes what we have not yet acquired — an "emotional" system.

It is not different to imagine the inclusion of emotions in S. This would be necessary for survival for any S which was to be involved in an "open society" — threatened by other species (especially, say, *homo sapiens*) and competing for goal-satisfaction and goal-needs. It would be an alarm system which would facilitate physical activity e.g. fight and flight and would also by virtue of its fabric have all sorts of side-effects. Ss, for most purposes (synthesis), do not need emotions, but to simulate human beings they do. The same sort of argument applies to S being social.

We must then consider collections of Ss, since no one S alone will satisfy our requirements, other than by obviously artificial device of making S behave *as if* other Ss were in its environment.

The holding of opinions depends upon criteria which are subjective in that they are inimitable to the individual and reflect his experience (by acquaintance and description), underlie his wish to repeat a particular experience and avoid another. These are limiting cases which entail preferring one thing to another and which could involve a justifying of one's preferences, by apparently (or actually) objective criteria; "Beethoven is a better composer than Tchaikovsky" and the like. We can then, more or less, adduce criteria which seem to justify our sensations and culminate in explicating terms like "better than". It would surely be the case that any S of the richness we prescribe would be capable of doing the same. But we will be looking at this matter again later.

We have asked about identity, as well as indistinguishability, and here we can simply assert that we can think of no reason at all why there should not — given the appropriate colloidal protoplasmic fabric — be complete "identity" between a "manufactured" S and a naturally occurring human. The sort of extended Turing test which is now apposite is one where you have to be able to say: "I cannot tell S from a human being when I mix with him socially in the fullest sense." If there is a reason (or reasons) why this is *a priori* impossible, let us hear the reason. That it has not yet been done is evident, but that it could not be done is not.

Let us now make reference to important literature which has both fuelled and influenced my present quest, apart from those already referred to in Chapter I. Books on cybernetics which could be regarded as being in the main stream of the subject apart from Wiener's initiating book *Cybernetics*, which heralded the start of the modern movement, are Ashby's *Design for a Brain* (1952) and *Introduction to Cybernetics* (1956), Grey Walter's *The Living Brain* (1953), Lerner's *The Fundamentals of Cybernetics* (1972), and many others which will be listed in the Bibliography.

There is also, of course, apart from the series called *Machine Intelligence* and the journal *Artificial Intelligence,* a vast number of papers, especially in *Cybernetica, Kybernetes* and spread throughout many other journals and collections of conference papers.

3

Model Making

Since our main purpose in cybernetics is to model (in a dynamic, purposive and feedback way) aspects of complex systems which occur in reality, we will expect to make a study of model making methods. There will, in what follows, be no claim to completeness, since new methods of modelling can, in some sense, be developed indefinitely. All that we shall claim is that the models we describe in this chapter (and there are many of them) are all germane.

We can start with a very general claim to the effect that all of mathematics, logic, probability and statistics form a reservoir which we can tap for our purposes. In particular, we should regard logic as basic to our interests, but this has been discussed in many texts so we shall make only a few brief comments on "classical" logic and move directly to "empirical logic". I am also supposing that the reader is already thoroughly familiar with block diagrams and the various forms of flow charts, as these are basic to any sort of model making (George, 1981).

Logic

We shall not, as I have said, provide any *detailed* description of the methods of classical logic, since that has been done before (e.g. George, 1979). Furthermore, we return to logic in Chapter 7 where we consider it, as it were, the other way around, by asking how logic can be formalised, or rather computerised; since ultimately our aim is to simulate "logical" or rational behaviour. Let me simply say that the formal logical systems start with the *syllogism* and the *sorites* and go on, via the propositional calculus, to the higher *functional* and *predicate* calculi. The reason why the word 'formal' is used about these logistic systems is that certain logical relationships, such as the relationship of inference or entailment from one statement to another, depends on a purely formal relationship which exists between those statements. We should say that words like 'term' and 'proposition' are used very frequently in such logics and the word 'proposition' means the same here as when it used to refer to propositional attitudes such as beliefs, doubts and uncertainty.

The bulk of formal logic originated from language and discourse in which inference and entailments were made. These could become complicated and lead to paradoxes, and they could, with the syllogism as the best known example, represent systematic valid arguments. The development of powerful symbolic logics did not immediately change their direction, since George Boole (a founder member of modern symbolic logic) thought of Boolean algebra as representing rational human thinking. Then with the propositional calculus and even more obviously with the functional calculus, the impetus was associated with the foundations of mathematics. This led in turn to the well known theories of Gödel, Post, Church and Turing. That work shows that mathematics could not *show itself* to be both consistent and complete at the same time. Even more important, was the result that showed that "classical mathematics" has no decision procedure. This led some to argue that therefore no "machine" (artificially constructed system) could carry through the manufacture of "classifical mathematics" and since human beings had actually done so, it ruled out the idea of man-as-a-machine. We have dealt with this argument before (George, 1979), but we can say now that the argument from Gödel's theorem is irrelevant to the fundamental themes of cybernetics.

Symbolic logic, on the trail of mathematics led to the development of the Functional calculus. The arguments of metamathematics also require set theory, but all of this takes us beyond our present cybernetic interest. The use of functions and the paraphernalia of the predicate calculus can, though, be given a different interpretation. In other words, ordinary language involving individuals and properties can be analysed logically in a subject-predicate form.

To finish off this brief word on logic, let me look at the word 'logical' again and ask more specifically what we mean by it. It is clear that the word is often used as if it were synonymous with 'reasonable', 'sensible' and 'plausible'. But in fact, we should really use the word 'logical' for what we can infer from something else; it is correct reasoning.

Other angles on logic, which deals with uncertainty can be provided in many ways. One way is demonstrated by Reiter (1979) when he talks of *logic by default.* He quite rightly points out that, in terms of the beliefs we hold, a failure to prove not — A means that A is often accepted. If I am told X is a bird, and no more about X, I will assume X can fly, although there are certain well-known birds like ostriches and pelicans which are non-flying.

I shall not go into detail on Reiter's work, which is still in its early stages, except to say that he provides further evidence for a belief in practical reasoning which is often not in accord with what we might call "classical logic", and yet provides extremely useful information which guides our behaviour.

Turning to "logical behaviour" and therefore to empirical logic, which also entails looking further at practical reasoning, we look at what has sometimes been called "satisfactoriness logic". The crux of the discussion now hinges on the idea of purpose. Whereas classical logic is a permissive discipline and tells us what may follow by virtue of our assumptions, "practical logic" tells us what we *need to do*, or think, in order to fulfill a purpose or attain a new belief.

If I say "I wish to go to Cardiff", and I am presently in Great Missenden, then the first step will take me to High Wycombe, then across the M40 and the dual carriageway to the M4 and so on. The goal determines the steps to be taken. It is not, of course, that there is necessarily a unique or even optimal route to Cardiff; there may be many, but hopefully *one* is optimal. It is clear that to get to Cardiff entails that I do certain things, but equally it does not entail it in the ordinary sense of entailment. Rather it sets constraints on my behaviour.

Let us look at a more heavily constrained situation. I have to get to E, and when I leave A (my starting point) I find a choice of routes B, C and D. If I choose B I go on to F and G and then can go no further. If I choose C I am blocked altogether, whereas if I choose D I go straight on to E. Now I say that to get to E entails taking the route to D. It is the only route. If I am then placed in a *new* situation where I am told to get to E′ from A′ and have choices B′, C′ and D′, I choose D′. This, of course, is an inductive step in which I have to hypothesise (with little evidence) that the structure of territory 2 is much the same as territory 1. So we investigate more territories and build up more evidence. This makes clear that much of practical logic is indeed inductive. The reason my first example was not, and the later ones need not have been, is the possibility of having a map (either from Great Missenden to Cardiff, or A to E, A′ to E′, etc.). Given a map then I only assume the correctness of the map and follow the rules which show clearly what I have to do to achieve a goal.

In a sense this kind of goal-determined logic occurs in the classicial logics. When I wish to show that certain wff is a theorem in P, I need to follow through the truth-table procedures. P though is permissive in that it tells you that given the axiom set for P, a whole set of statements, such as:

IIpIpqIpq

and

Ipp

follow, where I is "material implication" and I have chosen to use Polish notation. It sets out all the things that are logically entailed.

In ordinary linguistic logic, we find that if we say "Harry is in Marlborough," then this entails a whole range of consequences: "Harry is not in Hungerford," "He is in Wiltshire," "He is south of Oxford," and so on.

It is clear that a logical calculus based upon assumptions gives an array of entailments of a kind that is not particularly useful to the scientist or practical reasoner. This leads to an expectation that our scientist and practical man will operate in a manner very different from a desecription in terms of P. It also suggests that the inferences he will draw and use as justification for his behaviour and his beliefs will be different. He will be particularly involved in logics of uncertainty and we should look a little more into what these logics involve.

If I am asked "Is X psychotic?", then I might say "I am not sure," or "to some extent," or "he is 35 per cent psychotic," or simply "yes" or "no". There are two obvious possible reasons for the uncertainty. Either we have no agreed criterion for psychoticism or he satisfies only some of the criteria, or we do not know enough about him to classify him. This goes back to the same difficulties that caused us to introduce many-valued logics. The sort of uncertainty we are now confronted with is not the same as when I assume territory 1 and territory 2 are the same. That was an assumption based on *some* evidence. This situation would be the same if I simply had not carried out enough tests on X and my knowledge is incomplete, but is different because of the two obvious possible reasons mentioned above.

In practice, I will argue that just as we are not certain of the truth of a statement, so we are not always wholly sure what a statement means. We are not certain of the nature of reality or how we know what we know. Similarly, in practice, we can seldom employ the definiteness of classical logic, and where we can we need to add constraints in the form of goals or purposes in almost all cases.

Formalisation and Axiomatisation

I will discuss formalisation in general, as well as axiomatisation. The importance of formalisation lies in the reverse process from providing a full behavioural context for linguistic behaviour. This is, as we have already said, a process of translation from one level of description to a more "precise" level, and entails that we supply the necessary translation rules. It can be carried through in stages. After the first stage of formalisation we can proceed to further stages of formalisation by using suitable models, such as automata, that might be regarded as appropriate as an underlying structural model for the suggested theory.

Braithwaite (1953) has proposed what he called a "zip-fastener" approach to formalisation, where we can zip down from the theory to the model or up from the model to the theory. The idea of using models in science is by no means new, and Braithwaite, among many others, has analysed the use of such models and their relation to theories in science. There is a sense in which almost anything can be used as a model for almost anything else, but as in the use of analogies or metaphors, so models, to have predictive value, must bear some measure of similarity to the structure or process being modelled.

The idea of modelling (cf. analogy) depends upon similarity of structure and/or function, as in the case of a wind tunnel, a painting, even a person who says "let this piece of paper here represent Africa and this South America . . .".

In science we try to make such models explicit and more precise and tie them to the theory they are supposed to clarify and exemplify by some sets of rules which we usually call translation rules. The operations involved frequently include logic and whereas at the level of the "process" modelled (e.g. a scientific theory or the process it purports to represent) the (descriptive) statements may be empirical, at the level of the model the statements (formulae, sentences, etc.) are usually formal. This is of course one of the ways in which the formal and factual sciences meet.

We can also argue that a scientific theory is made up of empirical statements which use terms capable of operational definitions, whereas the model uses logical statements, which are not in themselves verifiable. The opposite interpretative process of going from model to theory is a "zipping up" process. The implication of the zip-fastener theory is that the alternative processes are interlocked at each stage of the translation from model to theory.

An example of formalisation we might mention is that of Whitehead and Russell with respect to the concept of number in *Principia Mathematica.* Another famous example from biology is that of Woodger (1952).

Axiomatisation

Axiomatisation methods are methods for putting a descriptive system into the form of a blueprint, in the sense that we are saying first that some combination of symbols are well-formed (wf) or meaningful and some are not. In English, xyxyxy is obviously not meaningful. We then divide the meaningful statements up into axioms and theorems, where the theorems are the logical consequences of the axioms. They are "true" in the sense that they follow from the axioms, and not in the sense that they necessarily depict "reality". We should add perhaps that the choice of axioms in an AS are influenced by the 'fertility' and relative simplicity of the wff concerned.

We can think of ASs, like Spinoza's ethics, as semi-formalised and purporting to represent some aspects of reality, and these grade over into highly formalised ASs which might have no interpretation at all. In general, of course, ASs are constructed with a particular interpretation in mind, the Propositional calculus being a formalisation of the primitive connectives 'or', 'and' and 'not'.

The idea of ASs goes back a very long time, at least to Euclid, where it was used to describe geometry in such terms, and where the axioms were thought to represent self-evident truths. These were then used as a basis for drawing inferences which in turn revealed (and proved) truths which were far from self-evident.

If we are concerned only with logical descriptions, such as arise in mathematics, say, then there is no question of *external* testing of the axioms or theorems that arise from the axioms. If we are concerned with an empirically descriptive system such as in science, then of course there is the need for such external testing, in the same way as a map must be checked against the territory mapped to ensure sufficient similarity of structure.

In axiomatisation, we are usually also symbolising (representing words and terms by single letters as in Boolean algebra) and we are also usually formalising. This is so because an AS is usually a relatively precise system. Symbolisation, though, is not necessarily involved, because a system for axiomatisation may achieve the necessary precision by axiomatisation alone.

In our pursuit of ASs we need to choose or construct some language L which is to act as the so-called basic language of the AS. This basic language normally contains only logical signs. The axioms and theorems of the AS contain certain constants not occurring in language L, called the axiomatic constants of the AS. Some of them are given without definitions: they are called the axiomatic primitive constants of the AS, while all other axiomatic constants are introduced by definitions on the basis of the primitives. The language L′ obtained from the basic language L by adding the axiomatic constants is called the axiomatic language. L and L′ can both be subsumed, at some levels of description, as being the same language. In other words, from an alphabet we can construct words (using formation rules) and sentences (formulae) from these rules, which are 'true' or 'false' in that they either follow or do not follow from the rules of the language. They are sometimes called simply "valid".

A simple example will suffice to demonstrate what is intended. An alphabet can be made up of X and Y. The formation rules are XX or XY are wf. but nothing else, so then we can say. If X then XX, if Y then XX, etc. Similarly in English, from A, B, C, ..., we can derive such words as 'cat', 'dog', 'sitting on', 'rug', with syncategoromatic terms 'the', etc., so we can say 'the cat is on the mat' and it is meaningful (whether or not it is true). It goes without saying that languages such as English and French are not yet (completely) axiomatised.

The derivations of theorems in our AS must be a matter of purely logical deduction. Nothing may be referred to the intuition and no knowledge of the "objects" of the theory may be utilised except that which the axioms entail. Since the derivation of the theorems is purely logical, it is clearly open to *formalisation.* This means that we may have a syntactical system for L, specifying primitive sentences in L and rules of inference for L, and may extend this system to a syntactical system for L′ with the axioms as additional primitive sentences: the theorems of the AS are then those sentences which are provable in L′ but not in L. By 'provable' we mean of course those statements that follow by a finite number of applications of the rules of inference to the axioms.

There are two ways of testing an AS for consistency, completeness and appropriateness to the intended interpretation. The first is the way just described, where the axioms are contained as primitive sentences, and the theorems are obtained by proofs, i.e. without premises. The second is where the axioms are not counted as primitive sentences, and the theorems are obtained by derivations in which the axioms appear as premises. There is no essential difference between these treatments beyond that of mode of presentation.

We now look beyond the start of our AS and say that with the construction of the language L′ in which an AS is formulated, the following additional procedures may be applied. The language L′ can be *formalised* which means that a syntactical system with explicit formal rules for L′ may be constructed. Furthermore the language L′ can be symbolised. The use of symbols may merely be as shorthand (and for convenience of making deductions) as in algebra, or be a part of the process of formalisation, although neither process is essential to setting up an AS, i.e. artificial symbols used in place of words of the natural language. In general ASs are formulated in words, and rules of transformation are not specified. The rules of the basic language are presupposed, which means that the ways of making deductions in the word language are usually assumed to be familiar. Further, there is presupposed a particular interpretation of the basic language L, the usual interpretation of the logical words of the word language and only the interpretation of the axiomatic constants in L′ is deliberately kept open.

The two procedures of formalisation and symbolisation described above can be independent of each other, as we have seen. To be quite explicit on this point let it be said that whereas English words are symbols, it is the use of shorthand that earmarks symbolisation, e.g. let x stand for "the woman who always stands on the corner of the street on Saturdays". A word language can be formalised by introducing transformation rules phrased with the logical words 'and', 'or', 'not', 'every', 'some', etc., instead of the symbols corresponding to these words. On the other hand, all or part of the language can be symbolised without also formalising it and this means without explicitly laying down syntactical transformation rules. In fact it would be a mistake at this moment to insist that the process of formalisation should itself demand this, since we can accept a certain "contextual vagueness" even *after* formalisation.

When an AS is stated, the basic language used is assumed to be understood. Usually its interpretation is presupposed and only in special cases is it explicitly specified, by semantic rules, or by other more precise definitional means. On the other hand, the interpretation of the axiomatic constants is not fixed. An AS can be interpreted in more than one way, as is obvious by consideration of Boolean algebra and the Propositional calculus, which are two different interpretations of the same symbolic model.

When an interpretation of the primitive symbols is given, the remaining axiomatic constants straight away receive an interpretation through their definitions, and thereupon all sentences of L′ have an interpretation including the axioms and theorems. An interpretation of an AS is called a "true" interpretation if under it all axioms are true, and, moreover, an L-true interpretation, if all axioms are L-true, or "logically true". One of the essential characteristics of axiomatisation consists in the fact that the deduction of the theorems makes no use of any interpretation of the axiomatic constants. Each theorem is L-implied by the axioms. Therefore, under any true interpretation all theorems are true, and under any L-true interpretation they are L-true. In this way, the same AS may serve as a representative of many different theories.

We must have some reservations about what has been said about 'true' and 'L-true'. In the first case, as with explanation, we wish the axioms to be true statements in general, but can in practice only know the extent to which they are confirmed. Nor is this all, since we may include axioms in ASs which we have reason to believe are false, in the hope of providing further evidence for the belief in their falseness, and also perhaps to see what would have been the consequence of their truth. This can also be used as a device for distinguishing "good" from "bad" theories.

We say an interpretation of an AS is a logical interpretation provided all axiomatic primitive constants are interpreted as logical constants, otherwise we say it is a descriptive interpretation. Thus an interpretation of an AS is a descriptive interpretation provided at least one axiomatic primitive is interpreted as a descriptive constant.

By a *model* (and often we mean a logical or mathematical model) we mean a base which is used for the axiomatisation of the constants of a given AS with respect to a given domain D of individuals, such that the model of the AS satisfies all the axioms. D may, for example, be the class of numbers of a certain kind, or in our case a descriptive process, a base that makes for descriptive precision on interpretation. The study of models is in some respects simpler than that of interpretations, since it deals with extensions, not intensions; or, as some would say, with classes, not properties.

Logical interpretations are essentially the same as models. Therefore, if we are only interested in possible applications of a given AS within the "logical" field, the investigation of models is sufficient. However, if we are interested in the use of a given AS in fields of empirical science, such as physics, economics or biology as a formal representation of a given (scientific) theory, then we have to consider descriptive interpretations. This amounts to being sure that the logical structure of both the model and theory are the same, and then asking whether either adequately represents the empirical facts under investigation.

We next investigate the completeness and consistency of our AS, and see if we can discern a *decision procedure*. We should then turn to definitions which can take a whole variety of forms, but since as in certain other cases, this has been described fairly completely elsewhere, I shall not discuss definitions here. For a detailed discussion of definitions see George (1981, Chapter 10). There we considered ostensive, labelling, naming, descriptive, glossary, explanatory and the whole host of other definitions.

This is a much as we shall say about axiomatisation and definition, and I will now devote a few words to one kind of model which is particularly appropriate to the formalisation of purposive behaviour; this model or these models are known as automata in one form or another.

We can represent finite (or non-finite and potentially infinite) automata in a number of different ways, but I shall say the absolute minimum, hopefully consistent with understanding the basic ideas underlying them as their properties, once again, are discussed in great detail in what is now a vast literature.

What is important to us in this context is that they represent one kind of versatile and useful set of models. They are by no means the only appropriate models, since mathematics, decision tables, logic, servosystems, TOTES (Miller, Galanter & Pribram, 1960) and a whole host of other models are available and we shall say a little about both TOTES and various kinds of decision table. We are now simply *illustrating* a method of formalisation by way of the use of Automata as models. We can formalise a whole range of systems that perform operations which start historically with the foundations of mathematics, but carry on to a consideration of other types of problem solving activity.

We can think of a Turing machine (1936) as being a typical automaton made up of a tape ruled off into squares and capable of having a symbol written onto a square, reading a symbol from a square and moving either left or right along the tape. There is also the program which is the set of quadruples (or quintuples) which decide the total behaviour of the Turing machine.

This assumes that the Turing machine is capable of only a finite number of distinct internal states and that the next operation at any time t is a function of its internal configuration at the moment and the finite expression which then appears on the tape. We can define a Turing machine more formally as follows:

$$\begin{aligned} Q(t+1) &= G(Q(t), S(t)) \\ R(t+1) &= F(Q(t), S(t)) \\ D(t+1) &= D(Q(t), S(t)) \end{aligned} \qquad (1)$$

G is some function relating the previous state and the previous input, while F is a function relating the same two functions as G. G determines the change of state, while the output R writes on the square it is scanning, this "writing" may include over-printing the symbol already there, *and* also moving the tape either to the left or the right. The new function D simply tells us which way the tape moves.

Formal mathematical descriptions of Turing machines are available in Turing (1936), Post (1943), Kleene (1952), Davis (1958), Arbib (1965) and Minsky (1967). We are not concerned here with the various notations which are all equivalent to each other, and indeed will assume familiarity with the Turing methods.

A computation on a Turing machine Z is a finite sequence, $A_1, A_2, \ldots, A_n$ of instantaneous descriptions where $A_1 \rightarrow A_{i+1}$, and where $\rightarrow$ means "yields" or "leads to". A_p is the terminal instantaneous description. This then gives rise to the tape and the application of the quadruples to realise a computation.

As far as Turing machines are concerned, we must think of a *function*, as being defined by the Turing machine's behaviour. The argument occurs on the tape before computation starts and the value of the function for that argument is what is left when the computation is complete. So by new conventions, we can investigate a whole range of processes, including the whole of mathematics.

It is important to realise that what is mathematically interesting may not be cybernetically interesting, and vice versa. Thus it is that Turing machines (a *particular* form of automaton) with many channels, as well as having tapes with many rows rather than a single one, are of some cybernetic interest, but of little mathematical interest. They are of little mathematical interest because it can be shown that all problems solvable by multi-channel, multi-tape machines can also be solved by single channel single tape machines. This, however, still leaves a variety of different *methods* for solution, and these differences are of interest to the philosopher as a possible approach to an understanding of our views and how we arrive at them, or at least to methods of formalisation.

We next mention a version of finite-state machines; we are assuming the word 'machine' to be sufficiently understood here in a broad sense as an "artificially constructed" system. We are concerned with a machine or a model or a black box that is interacting with an environment. A stimulus or input to the machine is a response or output from the environment and vice versa.

We need to distinguish between a deterministic and a non-deterministic machine. A *deterministic* machine (and these are the ones we are mainly concerned with) is defined so that its output R, at time t + 1 and is written R(t + 1) is determined by the input at t, and the previous history of the machine. We can write thus:

$$R(t+1) = F(H(t), S(t)) \qquad (2)$$

where H is the previous history and S is the input. F is some function relating the two main features to the output of the system.

A *non-deterministic* machine, which is of special interest, is one where, for example, the input and history determine the probability of some response. This last type of machine is called *probabilistic*, and is a particular case of the class of non-deterministic machines.

The internal state (Q) of the machine is defined as being dependent upon its previous internal state and on the previous input. We write this:

$$Q(t+1) = G(Q(t), S(t)) \qquad (3)$$

When G is some function relating the previous state and the previous input. We can further distinguish between automata that are able to *grow* (and are therefore potentially infinite) and *fixed* automata which includes virtually all those that have been referred to so far. It seems that automata that can grow but cannot do so beyond some specified size can do no more than an automaton that is fixed. We shall call these last automata *growth automata*, and the potentially infinite ones we shall call *growing* automata.

Turing machines can be thought of as being either "growth" or "growing" automata according to their definition.

It should be noted in passing that when we say that a growth automaton can do no more than a fixed automaton we are thinking in terms of computations and not in terms of methods, a point we have already made with respect to Turing machines. This therefore does not mean that, from a cybernetician's viewpoint for example, growth automata are of no interest. There is some good reason to suppose the human brain, for example, comes precisely into this group of automata. We can further classify automata as *continuous* or *discrete* (McNaughton, 1961); they can also be classified as *synchronous* or *non-synchronous* according to whether or not their input and output history can be described completely as occurring during certain discrete moments of time. They may, of course, have any combination of these various properties so far described. In general, we shall say that automata are devices of finite size at any particular time such that the defined output is a function of what has happened at the defined input. Our equations (1), (2) and (3) make this concept more precise.

The basic notion of a finite automaton is that by its present and future behaviour only some finite number of classes of possible histories can be distinguished or recognised. These histories are what we have called the internal states ($q_1, q_2, \ldots, q_n$) of the machine.

The theory of automata, we must remember, is abstract as it stands and is concerned with the logical and mathematical consequences of precisely formed concepts. In fact, while this is true, we can at the same time make the point that the full adder, for example, which is very much part of an existing digital computer design, is a finite automaton whose hardware realisation is precisely the full adder used in digital computers; *our* primary interest for the use of automata is in the modelling of pragmatic systems.

We should, of course, distinguish between the structure and behaviour of an automaton. The structure is precisely what we would expect the anatomy of the system, while its behaviour is the observable change of activity with respect to its input and output. Clocks are typical of the sort of black box we have in mind. They may have many different mechanisms (structures or anatomies) but the behaviour of one clock is equivalent to that of another. At least, to put it more carefully, there are whole sets of clocks with equivalent behaviour, however different their anatomy.

Neural or logical networks (or nets) are another form of automaton (McNaughton, 1961) and provide an alternative description of a finite automaton to that of the tape variety of automaton. They can also be regarded as representing either *fixed* or *growth* processes, and could therefore be regarded as offering an alternative description of either a finite or an infinite (non-finite) automaton or, to quote the best-known example of this category of automaton, the Turing machine.

Neural nets are composed of elements combined into nets by connecting fibres, according to specific rules, and these form what are to be interpreted, at least in some cases, as idealised nervous systems.

Warren McCulloch and Walter Pitts (1943) were the first people to construct such neural net models, and they were the first people to call such models 'neural nets'. The name obviously stems from the intended interpretation of the basic elements and their connections. What they had in mind was an artificial nervous system, which could be constructed theoretically, in a well-defined way, and from which models could actually be constructed.

It is possible to construct neural nets in "hardware", and there are various ways of doing so by the use of transistor or micro-minaturised methods, and they can also be represented by matrices (George, 1977b), and this is especially useful for the computerisation of neural nets.

Neural nets were designed by McCulloch and Pitts as blueprints for the special senses (the senses of sight, hearing, touch, taste and smell) as well as the central processes of the human brain which involves the ability to learn, think and solve problems. We will now describe briefly how neural nets are constructed.

The points of resemblance to the human nervous system are obvious in each case from the way the nets are drawn up. It should be added that there have been many other contributors to neural net theory, although we shall merely refer to them by references to their work. (George, 1956, 1957; da Fonseca, 1966; Culbertson, 1950, 1952, 1956; Blum, 1960; Verbeek, 1960; Cowan, 1962; Lofgren, 1942, 1962; Von Neumann, 1951). I shall assume the reader is in fact already familiar with neural nets (George, 1977b, 1979b) and say no more about them here.

Let us mention next a particular equivalence which exists between every finite-state machine and a neural net. If a machine exists with m inputs, p internal states and n outputs, the equivalent neural net has m input fibres, n output fibres and an $m \times p$ array of inner elements, each cell of threshold 2, where there are m cells for each of the p states. It remains to connect up the neural net to simulate the behaviour of the machine, whatever that behaviour may be, and this can always be done. This argument which is illustrated in more detail in Minsky (1967, p. 55 *et seq.*) does not purport to provide an *efficient* equivalence: it merely shows that the equivalence exists.

We will now proceed to a rather different type of modelling, which has been quite explicitly associated with computers; it is the use of Decision Tables.

Decision Tables

The basic idea of a decision table is that all branches of the decision tree respond to questions answered by "yes" (Y) or "no" (N). Let us look at a table which deals with four questions and therefore has 2^4 (16) possible answers.

In ordinary flow charting terms this decision table would look like Figure 2 where each diamond represents a question (Q1-Q4).

Question 1	N	N	N	N	N	N	N	N	Y	Y	Y	Y	Y	Y	Y	Y
Question 2	N	N	N	N	Y	Y	Y	Y	N	N	N	N	Y	Y	Y	Y
Question 3	N	N	Y	Y	N	N	Y	Y	N	N	Y	Y	N	N	Y	Y
Question 4	N	Y	N	Y	N	Y	N	Y	N	Y	N	Y	N	Y	N	Y
Action	X															
Action		X														
Action			X													
Action				X												
Action					X											
Action						X										
Action							X									
Action								X								
Action									X							
Action										X						
Action											X					
Action												X				
Action													X			
Action														X		
Action															X	
Action																

FIGURE 1 A decision table.

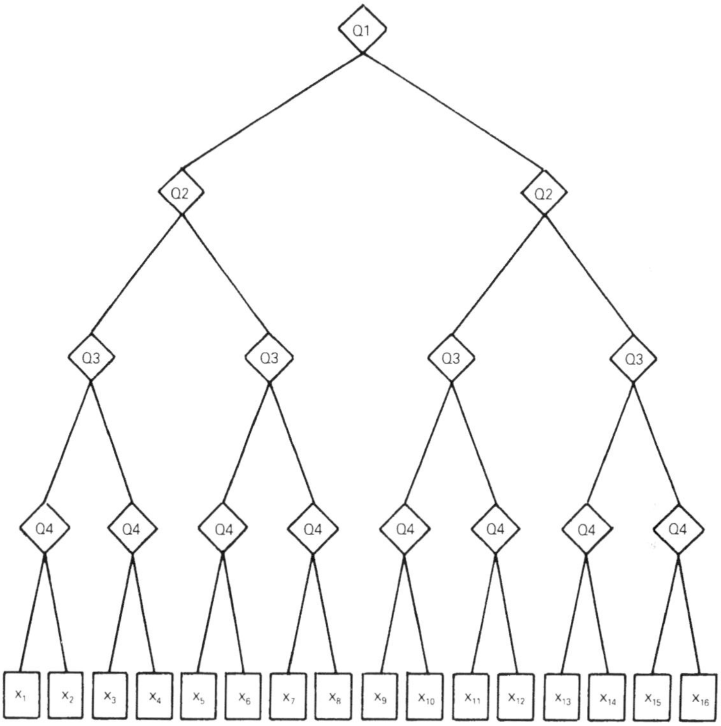

FIGURE 2 Decision table in flow charting terms.

There are two clear characteristics involved. One is that the growth of such nets is exponential, where four questions lead to 2^4 (16) outcomes, and 10 questions would lead to 2^{10} (1024) outcomes, and such rapid growth is hard to contain. Against this is the other characteristic which is that all the outcomes or actions may not be different. Given 1024 possible actions, the decision table may, in fact, only have four different actions.

Decision Charts

This charting process is simple and provides speedy and accurate reference to systems in use. We take an imaginary pension scheme as an example and simplify its logic. The material is approached through seven charts, but I will show only three of the charts (1, 5 and 6).

Eligibility for membership and contribution — Use Chart 1

Death benefit — lump sum — Use Chart 5
— dependents — Use Chart 6

Each chart will lead to a particular outcome in a particular situation. The situation is described by starting with a pointer on the entry spot at the top. You then follow a path down through the tree, your choice at each branch-point depending on the appropriate answer to the question at that level. Form the last decision point (you may not be required to answer every question) the path leads to a particular outcome.

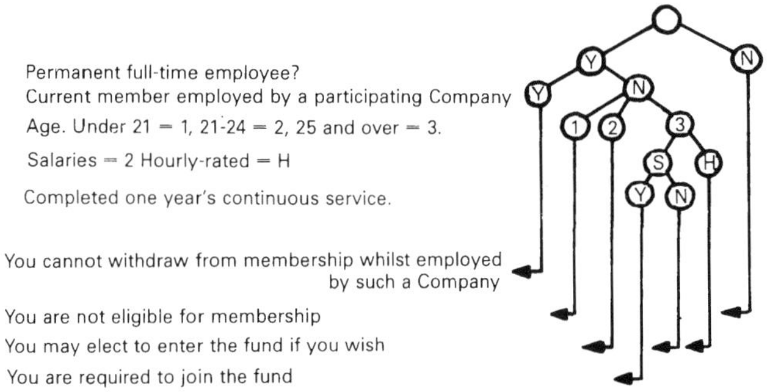

FIGURE 3 Chart 1 for eligibility and contributions.

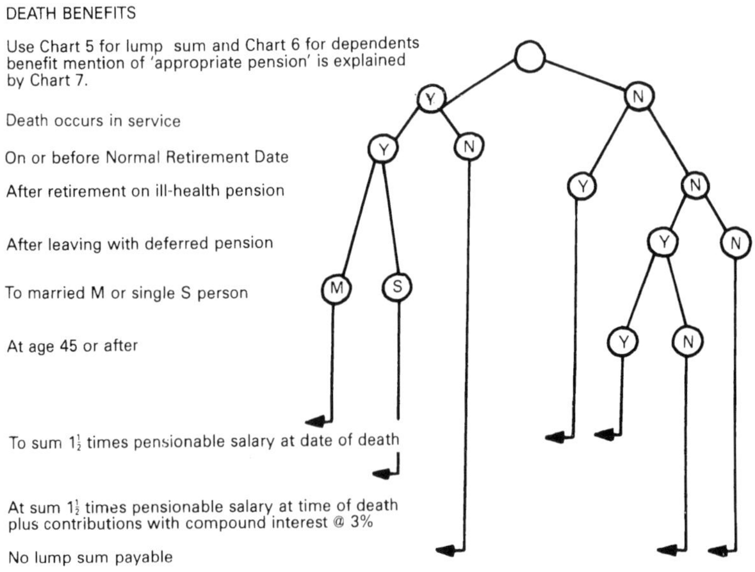

FIGURE 4 Chart 5 for death benefits — lump sum.

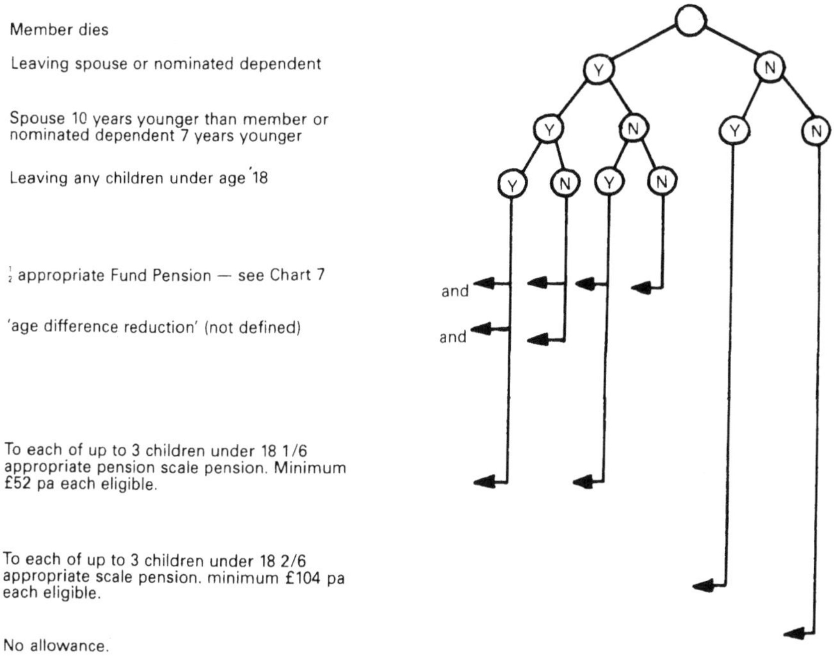

FIGURE 5 Chart 6 for death benefits — dependents.

I will now outline a very specialised type of decision table known as testrologic (*Test*ing, Storing and *R*etrieval *of Logic*). Such programs are called testrolog programs.

Testrolog Programs

First of all I will adopt the method of using single interrupted lines (yes), single continuous lines (no) and both together (meaning either yes or not; it does not matter), and a series of x's (for Y and N, i.e. 'Yes' or 'No'. Let me take a very simple example (Figure 6) and then look at its flow chart (Figure 7). This is for an ordinary decision table which becomes a testrolog tree if the answer to question 2 has no significance if their answer to question 1 was N.

Question 1	N	N	Y	Y
Question 2	N	Y	N	Y
Action 1			X	
Action 2				X
Action 3	X	X		

FIGURE 6 A simple example of a decision table.

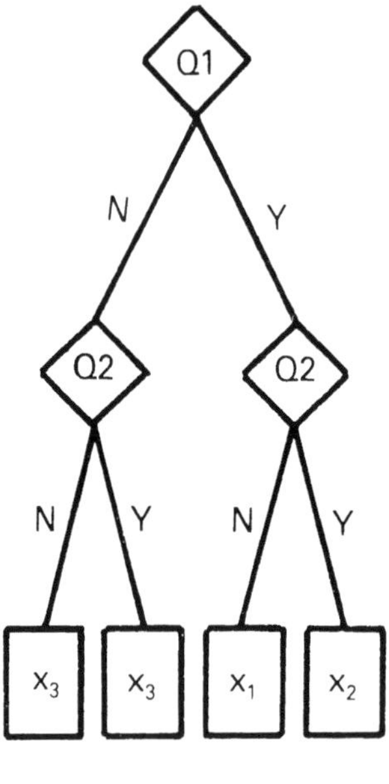

FIGURE 7 Flow chart of the decision table.

This decision can be re-drawn as a testrolog program with | for no, ¦ for yes and ¦| for either Y or N, and we do not care which (Figure 8). Two such questions could be question 1 = 'Are you married?' and question 2 is 'Do you live with your wife?'

We shall now provide an interpretation of a testrolog program to bring out its practical applications. I will select one aspect of a total testrolog

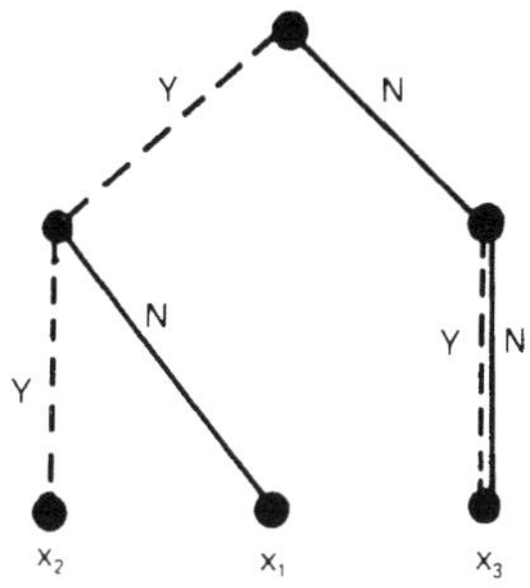

FIGURE 8 A testrolog program.

Now look at a slightly more complicated testrolog program.

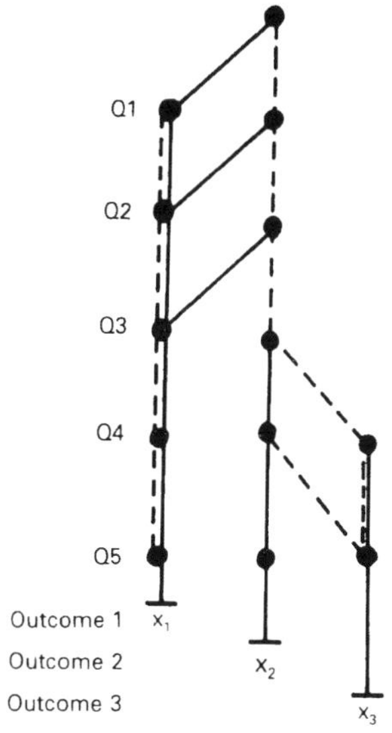

FIGURE 9 Another testrolog program.

system for dealing with business acquisition and this particular part deals with forecasts with respect to the business which is to be considered for acquisition. For this purpose testrolog is partitioned into a set of testrologs and the *modus operandi* will be demonstrated by the two stage coupling between the forecast sales, profits, etc. and the risk likely to be involved with the whole plan to date (George, 1984).

First of all the testrolog *T6* (the sixth in the set used for acquisition testing:

After the forecast we divide the outputs up into A, B, C and D for those continuing, while E stands for Eliminate and we see no more of such a project when it finishes there. Now the outputs A, B, C and D become inputs testrolog T5; but to take account of the weighting from T6, the evaluations would now be different where A's have the endings given in the text, A, AB, B; BC, C; CD, D, E. But should the output from T6 be B, then (though the same net, the outputs are AB, B, BC; C, CD; E, E; and if the output from T6 were C, the output would be B, BC, C; D, E, E, E E and from output we get BC, C, CD; D, E; E, E, E.

This means that we gradually upgrade the proposed company right through to the end of T7 when the final decision must be taken.

No doubt if a single company is involved then some further discussion takes place, indeed it would anyway, even if there were, say, three companies involved, where ordinarily you would take the one with the best final output, especially if it was A. But AB or B become possible acquisitions according to the particular context in which the whole project is reviewed.

The very construction of such testrolog models is extraordinarily helpful, but if such problems regularly occur, they will be actually used again and again. There should, of course, be feedback so that weightings (or questions) are changed in the light of experience. The use of such models is very much (or could be) the core of an expert system (see chapter 5).

We have also the advantage with testrolog of being able to trace back our path to the start and in what manner in the case of acquisition, a particular company has come unstuck (been discarded).

Testrolog programs can, of course, be computerised, and when they are we can, according to the size of screen display, always "roll over" from T1 to T7 and back, at will.

Of all tree-searching methods (see Book 2 for further discussion) it seems likely that, for many purpose testrolog trees are the most general, the most useful and the most exciting.

Finally we return to a discussion of automata and introduce what are called TOTES.

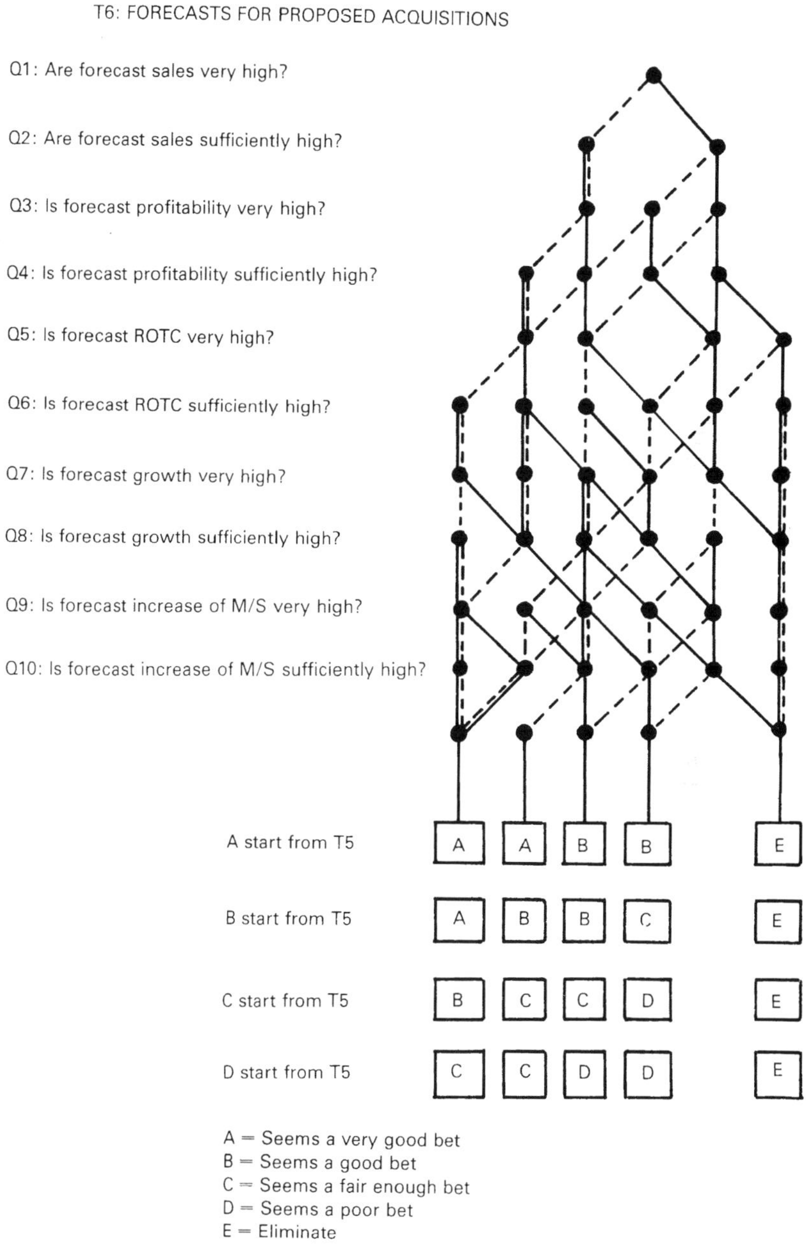

FIGURE 10 A testrolog for acquisition forecasting.

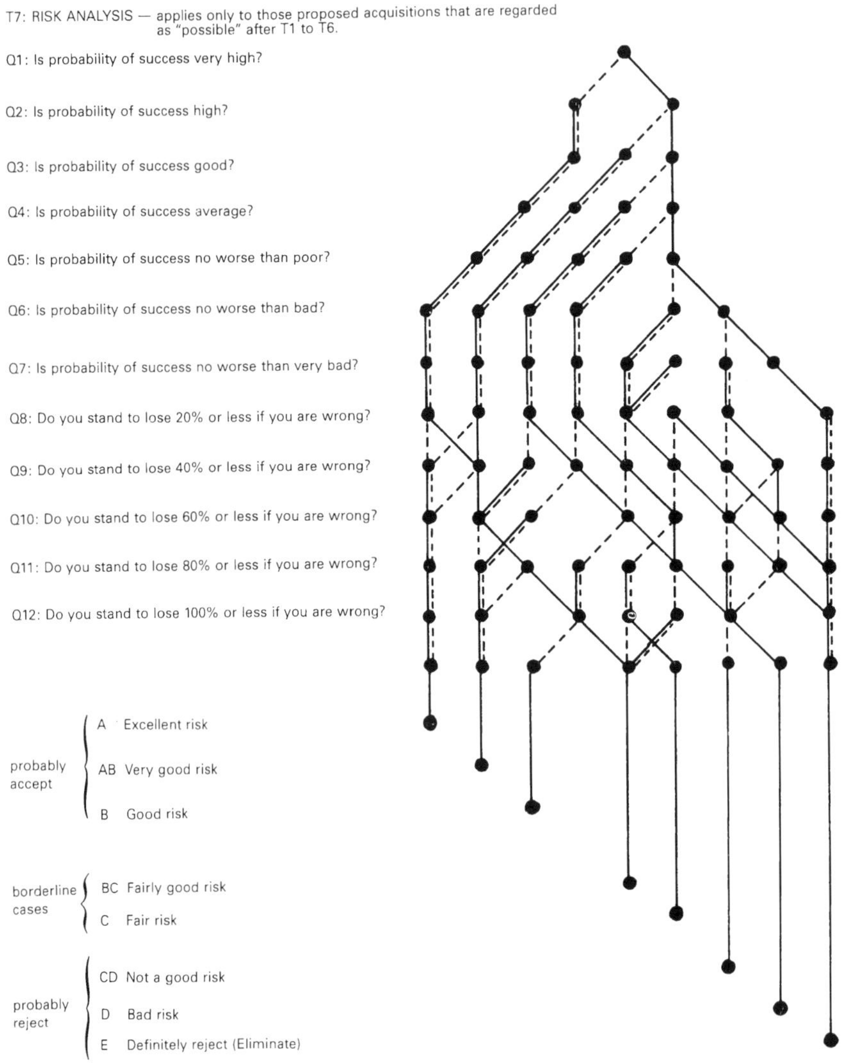

FIGURE 11 A testrolog for estimating risk (risk analysis).

TOTE-type Models

We now suggest modelling techniques, rather along the lines that were envisaged by Deutsch (1955) and used by others e.g. Pribram (1967) in an attempt to provide suitable interactive models. The basic concepts are those of the servosystem and the finite automaton. The servo system is a feedback control system of the kind used by automatic control systems and, partly to divorce it from its engineering origins, we represent it as a TOTE. A simple TOTE (Test-Operation-Test-Exit) is shown in Figure 12. The input could be a rubber used to erase a mark, the operation is the erasing of the mark, the second test is to ensure the mark is erased, which, *if* it is, causes an exit.

A more complicated TOTE is one with feedforward as well as feedback characteristics and this in essence means the ability to anticipate (predict or forecast) future events as well as respond to events that have already taken place. (Figure 13 shows this "anticipatory" TOTE.) The process now is one where we anticipate that the rubber needed must be both for pencil *and* penmarks.

The next type of TOTE is one which stores and remembers, as in Figure 14. This is really a modelling of the mechanism (which could have any number of levels) of memory to be stored and recalled.

We now come to the possibility of "nested" TOTES, where a whole set of inputs and outputs can be made conditional on each other. We take up a rubber and try to remove the pencil marks and fail and then try an ink rubber "on the suspicion" (this would in fact be a feedforward) that the marks are ink and that fails. So ink eradicator is used and it removes the marks. Figure 15 shows the operation. This TOTE sets up a series of

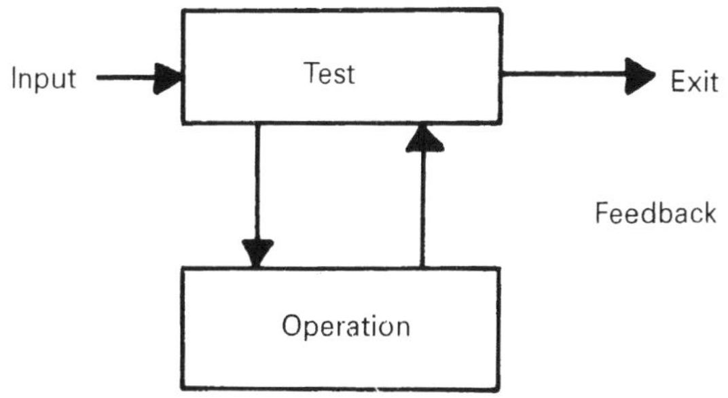

FIGURE 12

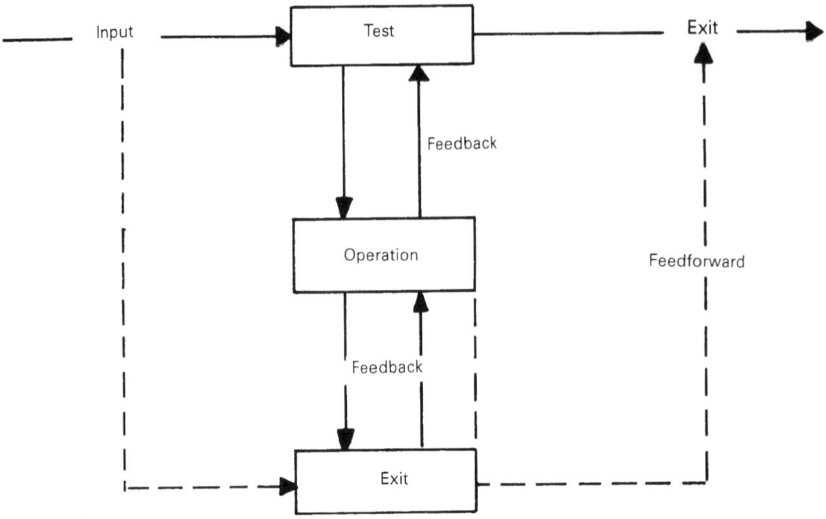

FIGURE 13

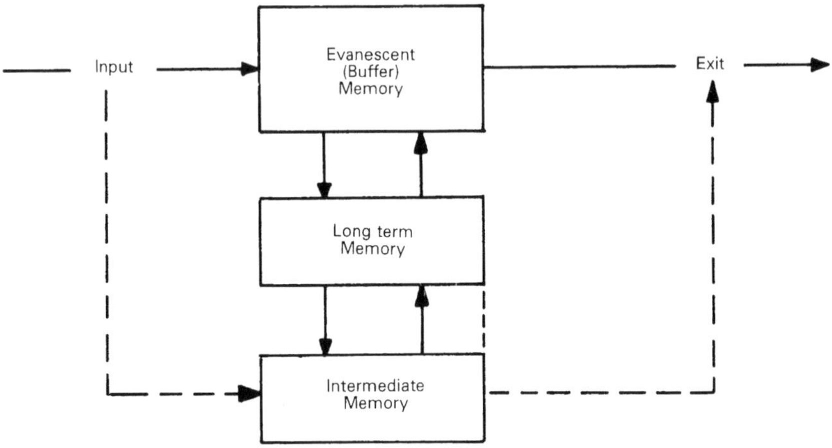

FIGURE 14

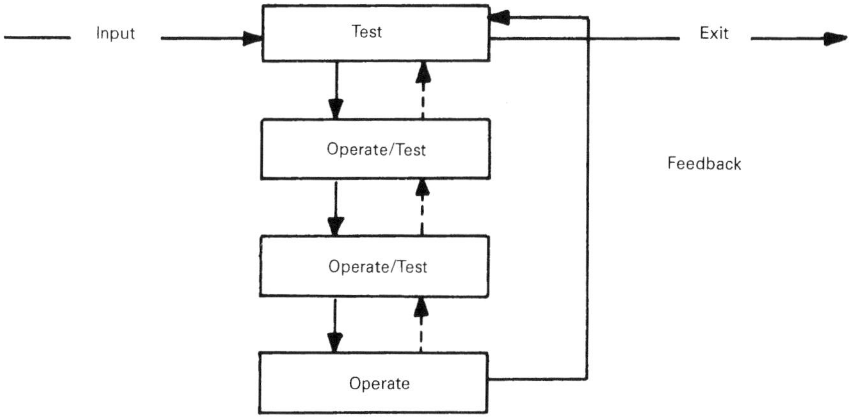

FIGURE 15

operations. If we conjoin Figures 13, 14 and 15, we have a fairly powerful modelling device for adaptive mechanisms.

But now let us look at what can be regarded as equivalent models which can be represented by state transition diagrams, but before doing so we should depict (Figures 16 and 17) interactive TOTES.

This brings us almost to the end of the chapter devoted to cybernetic modelling. It has no pretentions at being complete, but at least covers most of the principal models in use, except for the vast field of computer programming. It is because there are so many that the discussion of each was necessarily brief, in some cases a mere passing reference. In spite of this the chapter was long and anyone with the need for greater detail should follow up the references supplied in the text. We shall in the last section talk briefly in terms of a philosophical approach to our subject.

Behavioural Semiotic

We must now take up a philosophical stance but not so much in a traditional sense, rather from the point of view of a behavioural analysis of epistemological questions (George, 1981). In talking of knowledge and how we know, and what we think we know, we should conclude that we cannot obtain certainty regarding knowledge (empirical facts), if we are talking of what is public or communicable knowledge: this indeed perhaps being all that qualifies for knowledge as opposed to conjecture. We can achieve a

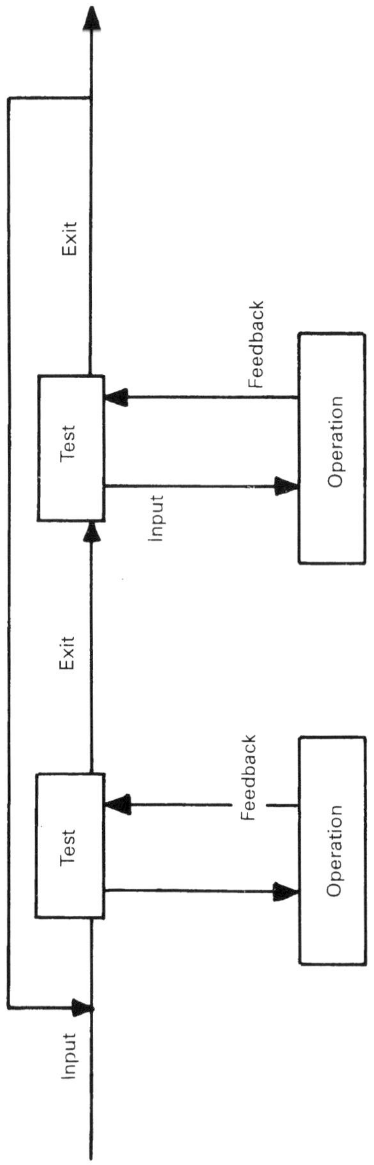
Input
Test
Feedback
Operation
Exit
Test
Input
Feedback
Operation
Exit

FIGURE 16

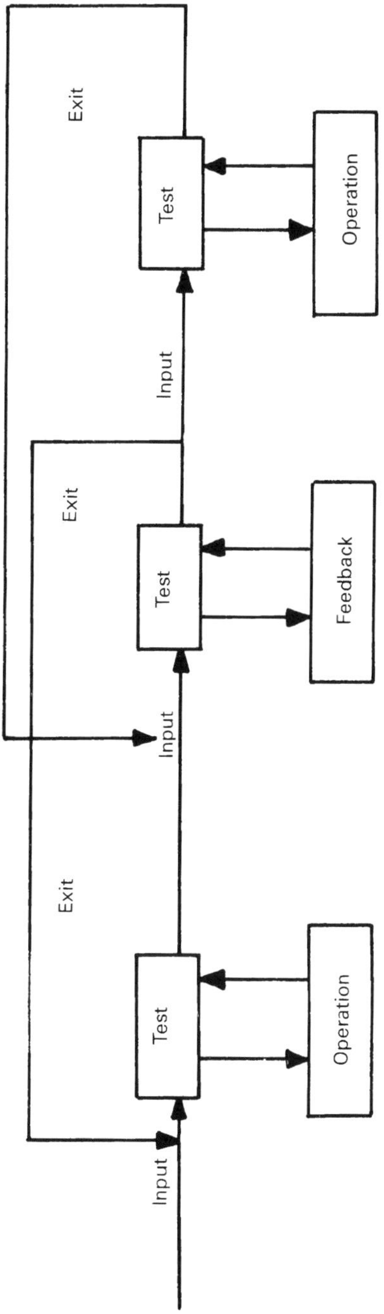
Input
Test
Operation
Exit
Input
Test
Feedback
Exit
Input
Test
Operation
Exit

FIGURE 17

kind of certainty only about our feelings and impressions and these are, to the extent that they are certain, private and uncommunicable, or at least difficult to communicate.

The observer is certainly in some sense imprisoned by his private experience, although as Wittgenstein has emphasised, that privacy is largely illusory and certainly does not justify (as he saw it) a private language. He is though certainly limited by his own private world. He can still derive much from his contact with reality. In talking this way we are maintaining a realistic ontology, even though we may still accept that what we are aware of, or capable in principle of being aware of, is a sufficient basis for much of science and scientific discourse. We should also bear in mind that science is thought by us to be mainly concerned with trying to answer specific questions about specific issues in a specific context, and not merely being a seeker after (universal) truth. We are therefore asserting that the epistemologist should consider what the scientist is asserting in so far as it may help his own case. We also believe that a scientific approach to our epistemology, based on assumptions and known to be dubitable, could throw light on attempts to explicate questions such as those concerned with meaning and truth. Pragmatics is the study of the inter-behavioural responses within which discourse occurs. Semantics is a special case of pragmatics concerned with meaning and syntax is a special case of semantics concerned with formation rules, or whatever is acceptable in grammatical terms. These three disciplines are closely interrelated, and pragmatics is in one aspect a study of psychology and in another aspect a study of cybernetics. What primarily distinguishes these two aspects is whether the approach is simulatory or synthetic.

Behavioural semiotic is in essence a theory of signs, which for C.S. Peirce was virtually the whole of philosophy. We are certainly concerned with sign behaviour and ask what effect linguistic signs (X) will have on an audience (A), when uttered by subject S. It seems that X needs to be interpreted by A (possibly just one particular person) who recognises the interpretation of the signs X and S's purpose in uttering X and A's response, which if overt will involve an action or a new utterance X′, or if covert, may merely involve a change of state (a change in propositional attitudes) sometimes involving a change in some belief and sometimes forming, or strengthening, a disposition-to-respond, which may indeed be precisely a belief. The above beguilingly simple description of sign (especially language sign) activity conceals an enormous degree of complexity which stems in part from the enormous range of language signs, and the considerable range of statement types (Austin, 1962) which takes us well beyond the indicative statements with which we are nevertheless primarily concerned.

As to signs which are not linguistic, we have the range of gestures, perceptions, etc which are appreciated by acquaintance (as opposed to description, in the case of the language signs), this adds to the complexity of the needed theory of signs, and leads to the question of meaning where we need to know how to regard the relation between language and other signs.

Embodied in what has just been said is nothing less than a complete philosophy, the consequences of which I hope to work out elsewhere. The point here, is to recognise that when we consider the AI approach to cognition in Book 2 we shall be involved in logic and language and although most of AI work hardly yet gets to grips with a full scale semiotic, it is that which is ultimately needs to achieve. This is the reason for drawing attention however briefly to what is required to achieve something like philosophical acceptibility.

In using the words "philosophy and acceptibility" it might be supposed that the realist view, coupled to a correspondence theory of truth (perhaps partly in the Tarski form as a Semantic theory) and with the belief that "meaning" at least for us *in this particular pilgrimage* is best viewed as from a pragmatic, or even behavioural, standpoint, necessarily entails wide philosophical acceptance. This is surely not always seen so, especially by those such as Wittgenstein, or more recently, say, Davison, Chomsky and many others who are inclined to carefully separate philosophical from scientific questions. Our hope is that least those who disagree philosophically will know that thought has been given to the philosophical aspects of the problem. Indeed any AI approach to the problem of simulating human behaviour will necessarily (eventually) have to explain how artefacts ("machines that think") will themselves not only use successfully, but develop for themselves, logical and philosophical capabilities. There may be little doubt in many behavioural scientist's minds that there is some universal associative process from which all else springs. This leaves though an enormous gulf of complexity leading to the point where logical and philosophical behaviour can be explained (or explicated) in associationist terms. Work by Osgood, Fodor, Rozeboom and others is just such an attempt, but there is a lot to be done to fill the gap, and many philosophers see any attempt to fill such a gap is, *a priori*, an impossibility.

We shall in Book 2 make some reference to the philosophical or semantic aspects of the immediate problem (however brief) prior to following up the AI approach in detail and finally a brief word on the neurophysiological, which is at the other end of the gap (as we see it) from the philosophical.

BOOK 2

Artificial Intelligence

4

Vision and Perception

The first subject of Book 2 is that of perception. This seems a natural way to start our analysis of cognition, since it is concerned with the input and the initial stages of the processing of information in either the human being or the automaton (our machine artefact with humanlike potential).

The first point to make is that perception overlaps learning and the other features of cognition, and it should be made absolutely clear that such cognitive terms do not fit together like pieces of a jigsaw puzzle, but overlap in a somewhat "fuzzy" way.

Our plan of campaign throughout Book 2 will be to give a brief general statement of our subject, a brief word on the philosophical and the psychological aspects, then a brief cross reference to the nervous system will be made and finally, and this is the main point, an attack on our subject from an artificial intelligence (AI) point of view, involving some sample models which are by no means exhaustive, but are hopefully representative of the manner in which the subject has been handled. The references will attempt to deal with something more like a complete survey of the now extensive literature.

Basic Concepts

By the word 'perception' I shall mean the process of interpreting stimuli impinging on all or any combination of the sensory modalities and stemming from the environment. This involves the *classification* of novel stimuli or combinations of stimuli, and the *recognition* of familiar stimuli, or sets of stimuli, where the interpretation of the input is now clearly connected with the processes of memory.

It is assumed that we cannot recognise other than by *some form of* comparison between the input and what has previously been experienced (perhaps stored) in whatever manner. This is also true (though less obviously so) of perception (that little of the interpretation of stimuli which is not recognition). In other words no perception and, as a result, no intelligent behaviour can occur in any automaton which is not able to store information from the past. This enables the process of *recall* to occur as well as perception, and that part of perception which is recognition. This is not to say that the *innate* structures of the organic systems do not play a significant part in the actual process of perceiving (Gestalt Theory), but whilst this structural consideration is a relevant factor, the more significant factor is the *method* of perceiving which must lie in a comparison between the present and the past.

From the philosophical viewpoint we will often wish to talk about perceptual *acts*, where we say we perceive a shape without "identifying" it (what Price (1953) calls *primary recognition*) or we perceive (identify a shape as) a dog (what he calls *secondary recognition*) and where we wish to think in terms of a "logical" theory of perception, whether phenomonalist or realist, and where it is hoped to analyse perception, and cognition generally, in terms that do not depend upon the underlying behavioural and physiological processes.

Some philosophers (Wittgenstein, 1953) have argued against perception involving any interpretation such as Price has implied and talks of a single process which we can consider as an act; this may or may not be of importance to us in the context of this book; we must though bear it in mind. It is primarily another way of talking (semantics) which can be a matter of great importance, since many disputes (e.g. the well known Empiricist-Nativist dispute) hinged precisely on the interpretation placed on the key cognitive terms used — in this case primarily perception'. This is a matter of considerable importance (Hamlyn, 1961; Warnock, 1967) and we may later need to return to discuss this in relation to the other cognitive terms.

The basic perceptual processing method suggested by Hayek (1952) and Uttley (1954) is that of *classification.* If one could label all the "primitive stimuli", or sense data, that the human being is subject to, it could then be argued that every physical object and every sensory occurrence can certainly be built up by classification. We can expect to build a system indeed which could recognise anything whatever; the logical argument for a complete classification system being capable of *complete* recognition seems unanswerable.

There is though, as far as simulation is concerned, the danger of the "combinatorial explosion". The number of neurons which would appear to be needed for such a "complete" recognition model is astronomical, and far in excess of the number available in any human nervous system, regardless of the method of estimation used. The problem of dimensions could be overcome by the manner in which the human classification system is conceived. It is possible for example that a neuron does not play a single role in one single neural network, but may be capable of playing a part in various different networks as a result of different states of the nervous system prevailing at any particular time. Furthermore the classification in the nervous system cannot be complete, but must be *partitioned, partial* and *adaptive.* By 'partitioned' we mean the system must be built up in modalities as in a decision tree; by 'partial' we mean simply incomplete and by 'adaptive' we mean subject to change as a function of changing circumstances. These two considerations of the versatile neuron's role and the multiple classification can both occur together.

We should next mention two types of model called "genotypic" and "monotypic" (George, 1965). In a genotypic model it is supposed that the detail of the structure of the recognition model is not to be specified with full anatomical detail. Instead, mathematical and statistical operators are used to specify the function, rather than make any attempt to complete detailed structures. The monotypic system supplies (anatomical) detail with as much structural precision as is required. The networks of Uttley (1955) are an example of a monotypic system.

As has been pointed out elsewhere (George, 1965, 1970b) there is another consideration which cuts across the distinction between a monotypic and a genotypic system and that is whether a model is "special purpose" or "general purpose". Arguments have been advanced in favour of specific special purpose receptor systems whereas other arguments have been put forward in favour of general purpose principles. It seems reasonable to argue that a monotypic system is desirable (for most purposes) as long as it is feasible, and a genotypic system is acceptable when a monotypic system has ceased to be feasible. There is indeed no absolute distinction between these two types of modelling procedure; a final consideration is always *the purpose of the enquiry* and the context. As far as the labels 'special purpose' and 'general purpose' are concerned it seems again that both are possible and although the human visual system, for example, seems to have specialised receptors with certain characteristics (and this is one of the points that Gestalt theorists are making) in the form of eyes (as well as ears and the specialised sensory endings of touch and taste etc.), the principles on which information is processed more centrally seems capable of being stated in general terms. Thus, it seems likely that the distinctions which have been made in the past about such models are not as important as they may have seemed at the time.

First Steps in Pattern Recognition

Our basic problem in all cognition is that of *pattern recognition*; it occurs at all levels, including the conceptual levels of human behaviour, we are considering it here in the narrower context of visual pattern recognition. We are suggesting that the basic method by which this is possible, is one of classification of information where that classification does not take place primarily at the actual retinal level. The classification is partial and hierarchical and takes place at the first stage, second stage, and perhaps at a third and fourth stage in the visual cortext and even areas anterior to this in the human brain. Complete classification must be replaced by adaptive classification, although it looks as if an argument can be made out for maximum flexibility occurring in the early years of the life of the organism and as time goes by the classifying system loses a great deal of its adaptivity. This is plausible on purely "logical" grounds since as you fill up all the vacant spaces in a filing system or any other sort of classification system so the number of spaces for new information diminishes. This implies, probably correctly, that the human nervous system finds it more difficult to reorganise combinations of stimuli than it does to organise them in the first instance.

The importance of partial self-classification lies in the following consideration. Whereas a complete classification caters for every conceivable possibility, the vast bulk of possibilities which could be recorded but never occur are not used; a partial classification system classifies only those events which actually occur, say, in the visual field. We will think in terms of the visual sense, but the argument seems to be perfectly general and applies to other senses too. This means that every possible set of properties, i.e. every event or physical object, is either recognised by comparison with an existing record, assuming still that we are depending on "stored" information, which is by no means certain. It may of course be classified as "new" and put into an existing but general and tentative classification. Alternatively, a new classification may be set up as a result of the properties it possesses. No doubt such classification are complex and "cross associative" but we shall not discuss that here.

It is classification (initially no doubt fixed by maturation) with later reorganisation in the light of further experience that we call self-classifying, and this is really a form of adaptation. If the picture at this stage seems too symmetrical and too well organised, let us say that we are concerned here with simulating brainlike methods. This entails starting with idealised models such as neural networks (McCulloch and Pitts, 1943). These models with standard sets of artificial neurons working in a highly systematic and symmetrical way can be built. In practice, human beings have sets of neurons which vary enormously in their sensitivity and in other properties, and operate in part by chemical as well as by physical stimulation and transmission of stimuli, even, though they do so on rather generalised principles of combination which are subject to a considerable amount of error.

It seems likely in fact that the actual neural classification system available in a human being, is an approximation to the sort of abstract and idealised conceptual model we have in mind at this moment. All this we accept as a necessary part of the evolution of any simulation model, and represents a part of the link between cybernetics and AI.

Another point about the perceptual model we have outlined so far is that the partial self-classifying system must take place in a series of stages, involving special purpose receptors, the transmission taking place through partial hierarchical classification to the cortical centres. At the same time information is passed to other control centres in the brain, and this is followed by further visual classification, followed in turn by further (possibly many) stages of conceptual classification and re-classification. But let us leave any further more serious attempt at physiological comment until later in the chapter, and think next of the relation of perception to other aspects of cognition, such as problem solving.

Perception and Problem Solving

Perception is the starting point for all problems, since it is the process of perception which allows us to know anything at all of what goes on in the world around us. We then perceive problems and may also perceive solutions to those problems. Imagination is a major determinant of our ability to arrive at a solution to a problem, and this is a matter to which we must return from time to time. So also is the manner in which the problem is presented to us, or is perceived by us. But the connection between perception and imagination should be noticed here again. Any method of solution to a problem is closely bound up with the manner in which the problem is posed, so that one technique important to problem solving is the translation of a problem from one form to another (Amarel, 1962).

In general, we shall say that perception and conception together provide the whole of what is required in order to solve problems of every kind. If perception is thought of, indeed we have thought of it so far as the process of classifying and possibly reclassifying (and recognition is thought of as comparing an existing input with a previously stored input) then the process of recall may be involved in this latter stage. This is not to say, of course, that recall is concerned only with the remembering of names of physical objects or events, it can involve the complex matter of imagery, which in turn in the human being is closely bound up with consciousness: this is another matter which will crop up again.

Imagery is also a difficult and complicated matter. We shall say, indeed, that one of the properties of the human nervous system is to be able to recall (retrieve) things from memory ("storage"), which has an effect at least *similar to* that of the original stimulation, and this also has some of the "conscious feelings" associated with the original stimulation. This is perhaps because some, usually small, percentage of the original input fibres are reactivated and one has almost a reconstructed picture of events from the past. It is well known that people cannot "see" again (with the apparent exception of those few who are said to have eidetic imagery) the actual details of a building or a face, but many persons have the feeling that they (almost) can. We feel that this is the basic feature which underlines the process of imagery, and is essential to the process often called imagination. It is not at this moment being asserted that this is what must happen, only what seems to happen, or at least seems sometimes to happen.

In spite of what has been said about images being essential to the imagination, this is, from one point of view, not the important aspect of imagination. What is, as it were 'logically', important is that one can foresee the consequences of one's assumptions or decisions (George, 1981). A person without imagination could never solve a problem because he would be unable to imagine what certain unattained states would be like. It is probable (but not absolutely certain) that images are involved here, but that does not seem to be the vital point. The vital point is illustrated by someone who is deciding on his tactics and strategies for some game, say. He has to *imagine* different kinds of conditions such as the state of the ground, weather, etc. In the case of a game he has to imagine how his opponent(s) will approach the game: what tactics will he (or they) use? We could clearly go on and list many more considerations. In this, imagination is a vital part of thinking and thinking is a vital part of problem solving. These various cognitive terms seem in fact merely to draw attention to various properties of the total thought process. Part of the point was brought out by Wittgenstein (1953) when he said:

> Suppose I give someone the order 'imagine a red circle here' — and now I say: understanding the order means knowing what it is like for it to have been carried out — or even being able to imagine what it is like . . .

We have already emphasised the overlap of meaning of the terms used in describing cognitive functions, and there is an overlap here between 'perception' and 'learning', hence the term 'perceptual learning', which should be emphasised as characteristic of this overlap. This represents the fact that we can in some measure fractionate the world at the verbal level in a manner which does not represent the actual possible fractionation of the facts described.

It is clear that we are thinking of perception as a complex process which *can*, for some purposes, be thought of (narrowly) as concerned with input identification and classification, or it can be thought of (broadly) in complex terms, as closely related to (or integrated with) learning, thinking, problem solving and decision taking (George, 1970b) and the rest of the cognitive process. The only difference between the two views is one both of emphasis and of the semantics which represents such emphases. Let us, for a moment, think of the perceptual process strictly in the problem-solving context (George, 1980). We talk about "seeing through" a problem and we could cite Köhler's ape Sultan, as a paradigm of what we mean. It is literally the case that the perceptual phase of problem solving can be not only quite vital to, but virtually the whole of the achievement of a solution. In the game-playing type of problem (see chapter 6), it is inconceivable that the perceptual processes should not play a major part. All attempts to program a computer to play noughts-and-crosses, checkers, chess and other such games without visual scanning are made much more difficult. The interesting point is that in programming the computer to learn the game (and then play it successfully) even under a range of changing circumstances, we map the pieces, by use of symbols, onto the "decision tables" which are used for processing. Such tables are probably the relational statements (conditional probability or stochastic tables) of the relational data base. It is supposed that this is precisely the sort of relationship which exists between perception, or perceptual learning, and thinking. We shall see this technique represented later in the chapter by Clowes' methods.

When we think, we usually symbolise events and then manipulate or process the symbolised representation which is usually linguistic. If we now separate the perceptual part from the thinking part we make the problem a great deal more difficult, since we are asking a man to play games like chess without the visual advantage of seeing the chess-board, and although a blind man can learn to play chess, he finds it very difficult to do so. He lacks the most effective maps (Ramsey, 1931, Armstrong, 1973) for "steering through his surrounding space". What perception provides is a short-circuiting process since it presents essential relationships in a form which is easy to absorb. All this should not obscure one important point which is that both concepts and percepts are eventually mappings on the nervous system; or so we shall think of them, whether or not such a thought is helpful; and Wittgenstein (1953) clearly thought it was not.

The point we have to make in answering this question takes us back to the notion of a partitioned classification system. This meant that visual inputs, recorded originally in the retina of the eye, were classified and symbolised in the visual classification system which presumably constitutes at least the bulk of the occipital lobe of the cerebral cortex. This location is where the "encoded percepts" first appear (at least in terms of our proposed model). They are then fed into the central classification system, which involves all the senses, and is where the "encoded concepts" occur. One way out of our hesitancy in talking this way is to add that the word 'classification' is being used as a theoretical term and not necessarily to be thought of in an Uttleyan manner.

We have, of course, to avoid asserting too much that is hypothetical and often analogical in form. A typical example is the one which we have hinted at. One analogy for storing information in the human brain is to talk to a conceptual model and also a symbolic model and think of them as being in some sense equivalent: the word 'X' makes me think of X and seeing Y makes me think of 'Y'. This is something that can be set up in a computer and by which we can synthesise a good deal of the word-concept thought process. Now to argue that this is the same as the way the human brain operates is clearly a risk, since we do not know (exactly) how the brain operates.

Something, we *have* to say, is clearly 'stored' in the brain. It cannot be an accident that electrical stimulation of the temporoparietal areas of the brain can "bring back memories", or a blow on the head can cause retroactive amnesia. But a different set of processes could still occur where language and concepts are conflated and are not to be thought of as *internal symbols*, but some sort of configuration (of electrical states) working in a much more dynamic interrelated manner than we have hinted at. This is reminiscent of the early brain models of Köhler, and the work of Goldstein, and more recently, Karl Pribram (1971). All this may not be vital to us here because we are talking about (perceptual) problem solving and not about cortical activity in the brain, but the analogies we use could still be very misleading.

The notion of analogy is itself of great importance to problem solving (Hesse, 1956, Meletis, 1978) and it is widely realised that we can often solve a problem by pretending the situation A is like some other situation B. The only danger here is if either the apparent similarity between A and B is in error, or, perhaps more dangerous, when we fail to limit the use of the analogy to the extent of the similarity. This though is the manner in which heuristics often seem to be used by the human, and certainly by our automata.

Languages are like maps or pictures, logics are like geometries, as Wittgenstein often remarked. Memory stores are like files, or computer data bases, and this is assumed (although often questioned) by AI research workers. Such analogies can be enormously helpful. (We should mention here ANALOGY, a programming system for analogical procedures which has been written by Evans, 1970). Let me return to my analogy of thought as capable of being simulated by (or analogous to) a computer processing system. Embedded in such a processing system is (must be) the ability to use inductive and deductive logic (in the widest sense), and it is the use especially of inductive logic, which is such an important part of the classification activities of the brain at the more abstract levels of its activity. It also explains how our memory systems lose information because of the need to classify and generalise. This is much like Reichenbach's Context of Discovery, or Peirce's Abduction in Action.

A major feature of the classificatory process which directly links sensory messages from the environment with the interpretation we place on the environment is precisely that of perception. We are particularly sensitive to the way such visual information is presented and related to the non-visual features of a situation. This situation is likened to that of a mathematician who, in trying to solve a problem such as proving a theorem, will often represent his problem in visual terms, such as by geometrical drawings, and this helps "the conceptual process". It is axiomatic of mathematical analysis that the geometrical representation of the problem cannot be a proof, or even part of the proof, but is a mere aid to the problem solver. Another mathematical example is the difficulty experienced in going from three-dimensional space to space of higher dimensions, because of the inability to draw suitable drawings or even envisage the problem in spatial terms. A clear example is that of going from vectors to tensors.

Any construction set such as a jig-saw puzzle, which is accompanied by a picture of the finished article is infinitely easier to complete than one that does not have such a picture. The reason is obvious enough, in that a picture allows you to make continual comparisons against a standard yard-stick which feeds back information regarding success and clues as to likely solutions (knowledge by acquaintance). That such clues could be linguistic as in the case of hunt-the-thimble, with 'getting warm' etc., is equally obvious. (Knowledge by description — even if sometimes of a rather simple kind). Problem solving is greatly facilitated if we can provide as much sensorily-determined information as possible, and over and above that, we want to try to provide such information in the most suitable manner; this may be relative to the actual problemsolver. This last point touches again on the manner in which we represent problems. As we have already mentioned Saul Amarel (1962, 1965) has devoted a lot of thought to the mode of representation of problems and we should always bear it in mind. If we pick up some sort of visual problem picture, by rotating it we might hit on a position where the solution becomes obvious. If we take a symbolic problem and translate it into a new language or a new form, then the solution of the problem becomes obvious. The mathematical 'trick' of reducing a problem to one already familiar is but one of many examples of what is meant.

Pattern Recognition Models

Let us now start our pilgrimage into the AI type models of pattern recognition and following Sampson (1976) I will assign pattern recognition efforts to three somewhat arbitrary (and overlapping) stages, as shown in Figure 1).

In the first stage, *image processing*, the input signal is preprocessed (cf. the role of the retina with respect to the cortex) to make subsequent tasks easier. This preprocessing may take many forms, from sharpening of edges and elimination of "noise" to normalisation of an image through the application of transformations which give it some standard position, orientation and size. We will look at just one example of image processing due to Culbertson (1950). We shall look briefly at his methods.

Culbertson's Model

Culbertson used neural nets for his modelling; he was concerned with the way in which our visual patterns are recognised. He compiled a 'retina' from many layers of neurones (neural nets) which have the properties such that any figures projected on to the retina were processed by taking them through all transformations necessary to provide a comparison with a set of "templates" (standard set of figures). The following neural (logical) net diagrams show how a figure may undergo all sorts of transformations which allow it to be tested in all possible positions.

The first transformation is simply a linear one (Figure 2), the second is for dilation (Figure 3) and the third for expansion (Figure 4), and the last for rotation (Figure 5).

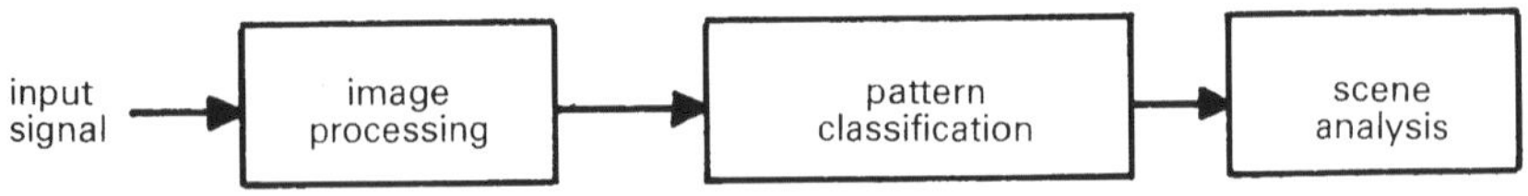

FIGURE 1 The main stages in pattern recognition.

So the process continues, so that if a figure is, for example, a triangle, then sooner or later, under transformation, it will appear in a particular standard position and be recognised as such. This is the essence of image processing, at least of the main kind.

We will not have much more to say about image processing since this is not the most central issue for AI. We shall however return to some models of vision in a later section where *image processing* is included.

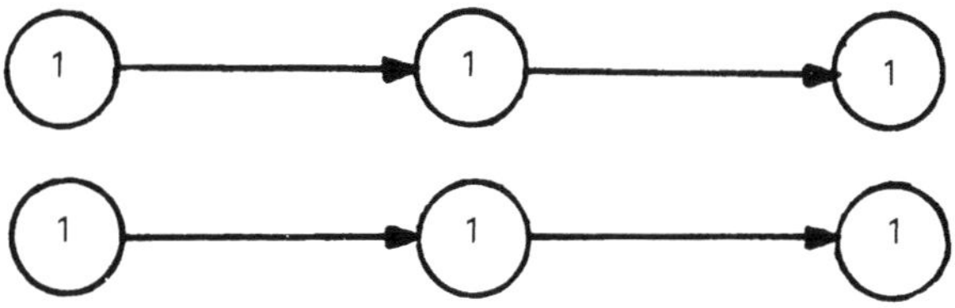

FIGURE 2 Simple linear translation.

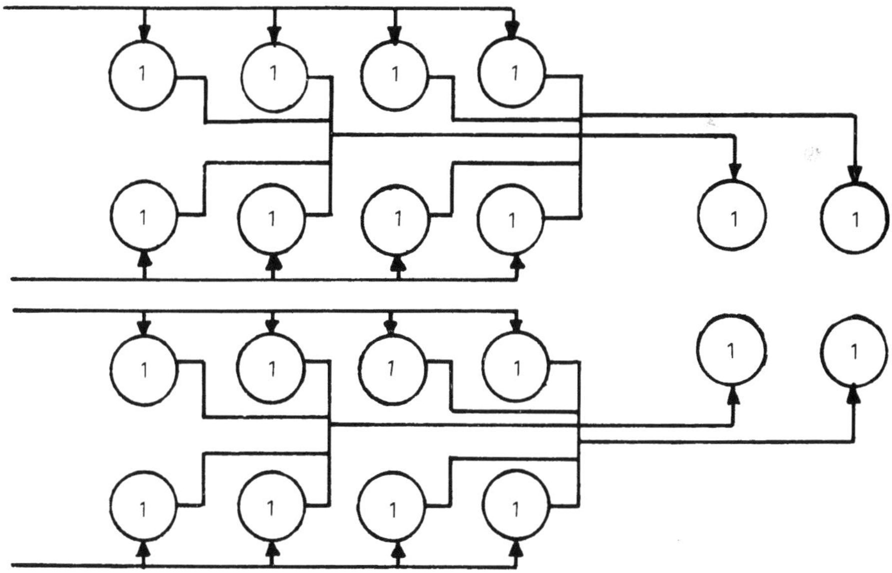

FIGURE 3 Dilation from four sets of four elements onto one set of four elements.

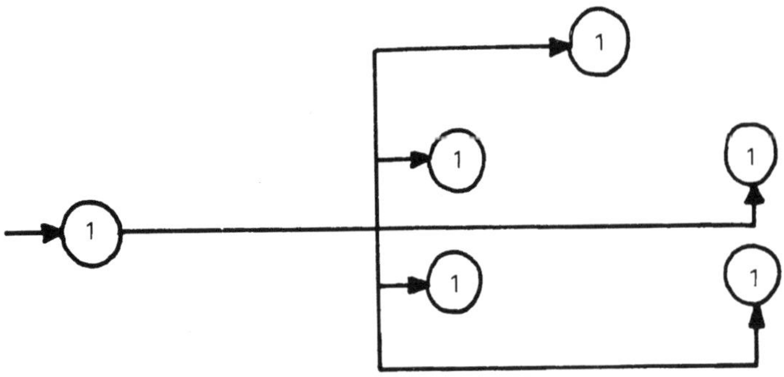

FIGURE 4 Expansion from one to five elements.

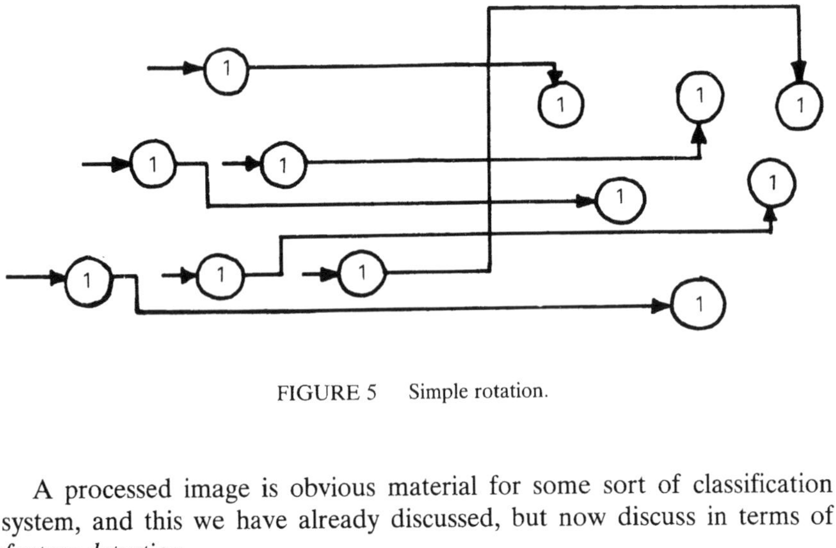

FIGURE 5 Simple rotation.

A processed image is obvious material for some sort of classification system, and this we have already discussed, but now discuss in terms of *feature detection.*

By contrast with template matching of the Culbertson type, we have the *feature detection* approaches. These methods take a number of "measures" on the input pattern and attempt to integrate the resulting values in order to reach a decision. The features can be simple, such as the presence (or not) of a light source, or complex, as in a geometrical figure. The way in which the values of the features are combined may also be complex, although a simple weighted sum of values has frequently been used.

Feature detection schemes may work either *sequentially* or in *parallel.* Sequential methods use information from the evaluation of some previous feature to decide which feature to evaluate next, and although sequential methods are more powerful than parallel ones, they are also more complex. For this reason they have been used very much less.

We next consider an early example of an unusually versatile pattern recognition system: PANDEMONIUM (Selfridge, 1959).

Pandemonium

PANDEMONIUM is a pattern recognition system which *learns* to recognise patterns. It has not therefore a fixed pre-processed range of patterns it can recognise but can develop its range as it experiences new patterns. Indeed PANDEMONIUM can be taught the names of patterns (cf. NAMER, Chapter 7), and can quickly be taught to say what the name of a pattern is before it is told; this is reminiscent of avoidance training within conditioning theory.

The method used is in the first idealised version of PANDEMONIUM is that of minimising the difference between a received message and a set of transmitted messages; in other words, ensuring the nearest thing possible to an exact match is obtained.

Figure 6 shows the idealised version of PANDEMONIUM and Figure 7 shows the amended version.

The amendment is necessary because the demons are not always able to discriminate sufficiently to allow of a clearcut solution to the problem in hand.

The problem is that given a received message M_r^i and a range of transmitted messages, n

$$\sum_{t=1}^{m} M_t^i$$

then to choose an M_s^i such that the difference between M_r^i and M_s^i is minimal.

The difficulty is that the demons often need the support of the sub-demons, and it is now easy to see that the data demons are supplying information to the sub-demons, and they in turn are supplying it in partially classified form to the demons; this is a system which is essentially a classification system. We now consider the differential weighting or feedback. There is a need to score or weight the different features.

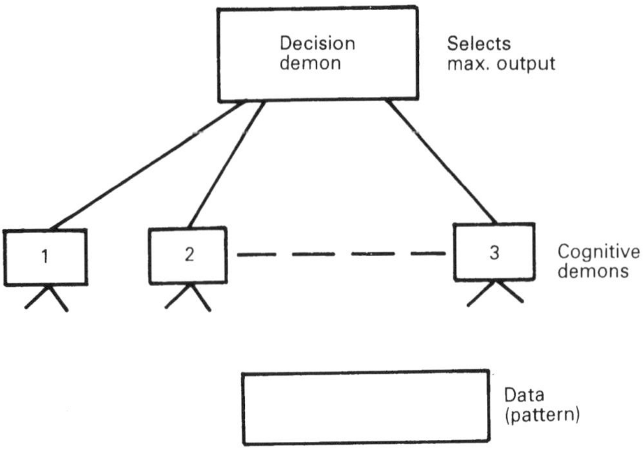

FIGURE 6 An idealised PANDEMONIUM as a classifying system.

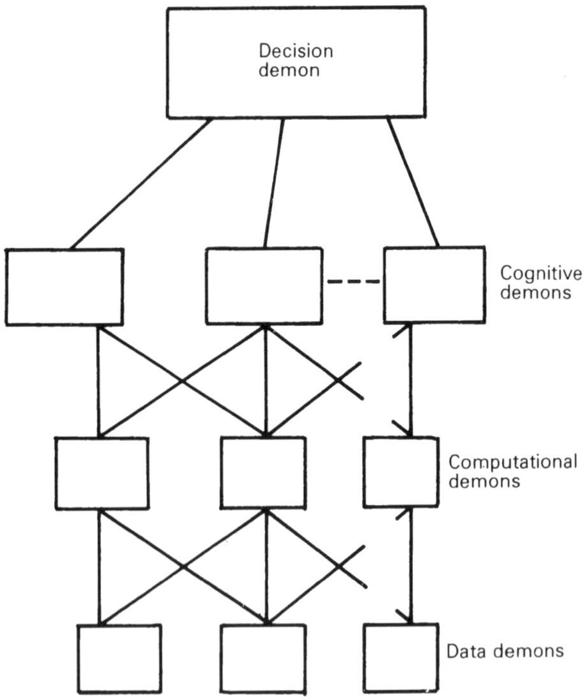

FIGURE 7 A realistic PANDEMONIUM extending to as many levels as are needed.

Given the output of a cognitive demon which has classified an input as:

$$d_i = \sum \lambda_j^i d_j$$

so that the set

$$\lambda = \lambda_1^1, \lambda_2^1, \ldots, \lambda_1^2, \ldots, \lambda_m^n$$

is a set of weights over all the demons. We now need to seek an optimum and this is (once more) a hill-climbing activity with all the attendant difficulties of dealing with local sub-optimal peaks and isolated optimal peaks.

We can, however, show an improvement in performance by changing our demons and sub-demons and "breeding" new ones. This all means that, like a heuristic modifying and heuristic generating system, PANDEMONIUM can be made potentially fully-adaptive. As a particular implementation of PANDEMONIUM Selfridge has developed a particular, or special purpose PANDEMONIUM for translating morse code into the printed word.

PANDEMONIUM provides an introduction to other linear processing feature detection systems. We next discuss that group of systems known as PERCEPTRONS.

PERCEPTRONS

PERCEPTRONS were the invention of Frank Rosenblatt (1962) and were very popular in the nineteen-fifties.

Inputs to a PERCEPTRON are provided on an ordinary, finite two-dimensional plane of discrete points, called R, where R stands for "retina", since Rosenblatt held the view that PERCEPTRONS were useful both as pattern classification devices (synthesis) and as models of a neurophysiological kind. They were though genotypic.

A figure (or picture) on R is given an assignment of binary values (0, 1) to all the points in R. Alternatively, we may think of the figure as an identified subset of "dark" (value = 1) points. By analogy with PANDEMONIUM we would require the data demons to report one or just two conditions about each point in the input; this is clearly the frequently used binary representation.

Computational demons in the PERCEPTRON model are called *predicates* since they function like the logical entities of the same name in the predicate calculus. A predicate P applied to a figure X inspects some or all of the points in R in order to discover whether the conditions of the predicate are met. The result is either P (X) = 1 (the predicate is "true" on X) or P (X) = 0 (the predicate is "false"). Predicates can test for conditions as simple as the presence of a 1 at a particular location in R, or as complicated as the presence of a particular type of figure in R (e.g. a circle). Any predicate which inspects less than the total number of points in R is called a *partial predicate.* Predicates can then be combined to give new predicates either by the normal laws of logic or in ordinary arithmetic. In the latter case we interpret 0 and 1 as numerical rather than logical quantities. A predicate P′ is said to be *linear in the set of predicates,* $P_i, i = 1, \ldots, n$, if P′ is true only when some weighted sum of the P_i exceeds some fixed quantity T, called the *threshold.* That is,

$$P' = \begin{cases} 1 \text{ iff} \sum_{i=1}^{n} a_i P_i > T, \\ 0 \text{ otherwise} \end{cases}$$

Note that the threshold is like one of Selfridge's special purpose PANDEMONIUMS. Now to the simple concept underlying PERCEPTRONS.

A PERCEPTRON is an example, as we have mentioned above, of what Rosenblatt calls a 'Genotypic model'. It is no longer supposed that the neurons or elements *and* topology of the nets are fully specified. Here we have a type of modelling that partially specifies the organisation of the net and offers probabilistic constraints which generate a whole class of models.

Rosenblatt's words are here worth quoting:

> "The genotypic approach, is concerned with the properties of systems which conform to designated laws of organization, rather than with the logical function realized by a particular system."

Let us now look at Rosenblatt's definition of a PERCEPTRON:

A PERCEPTRON is a network composed of stimulus-unit, association-unit and response-unit with a variable interaction matrix V which depends on the sequence of past activity states of the network.

A stimulus (S) and response (R) unit generate 'internal' and 'external' signals, respectively. 'Internal' means within the network and 'external' means within the environment. An association (A) unit receives signals and emits them.

Now a *Simple PERCEPTRON* is defined as satisfying the following five conditions:

1) There is only one R-unit with a connection from every A-unit.

2) The PERCEPTRON is series-coupled, with connections only from S-units to A-units, and from A-units to the R-unit.

3) The *values* of all sensory to A-unit connections are fixed.

4) The *transmission time* of every connection is either zero or equal to a fixed constant.

5) All signal generating functions of S, A and R-units are of the form $u_i{}^*(t) = f(x_i(t))$, where $x_i(t)$ is the algebraic sum of all input signals arriving simultaneously at the unit μ_i.

Now we must define 'transmission function', 'value' and 'interacting matrix'.

A *transmission function* of connections in a PERCEPTRON depends on two parameters, the transmission time of the connection τ_{ij} and the *value* of the connection U_{ij}. Variable values are called *memory functions.* The *interacting matrix* V for a PERCEPTRON is the matrix of coupling coefficient ij for pairs of units U_i and U_j. If U_i and U_j are unconnected then $U_{ij} = 0$. An interacting matrix is what has been sometimes called a 'structure matrix' in the field of logical (neural) nets.

A PERCEPTRON can be represented as a logical net, so that any of the logical or neural nets which have been described in this book would qualify for the name 'PERCEPTRON'. Rosenblatt has suggested other pictorial representations of PERCEPTRONS for different levels of precision. So far then, Rosenblatt has achieved only a new notation. Let us look at his first Experimental PERCEPTRON.

An "experimental system" can be called a simple PERCEPTRON coupled to a reinforcement/control system and in an environment. This again merely restates the simplest sort of cognitive situation.

From these beginnings, Rosenblatt builds up a Universal PERCEPTRON which can now be thought of as generalized logical nets, where the detailed topology is replaced by the general constraints previously mentioned.

A retinal set of S-units (sometimes called an R-set) can now be constructed so that "differential" stimulation from different shapes can be achieved. If we now project two distinguishable shapes X_1 and X_2 on to the retina we have set of A-units which simply fire or not according to whether the equivalent S-units fire, and step by step Rosenblatt constructs PERCEPTRONS or logical nets in an explicit manner. It seems to me, in passing, that Rosenblatt has indeed overstated the difference between

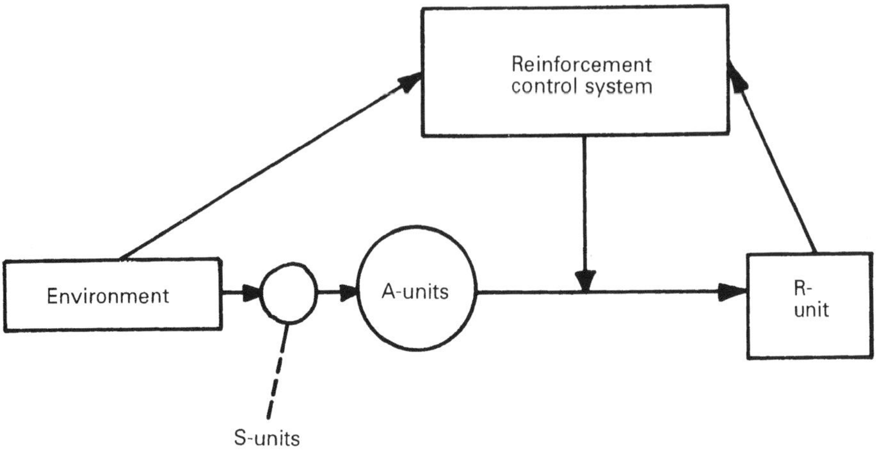

FIGURE 8 A simple PERCEPTRON

monotypic and genotypic systems and has obscured the fact that one can quite easily be made into the other.

As far as pattern recognition is concerned, Rosenblatt has been able to show that discrimination of shapes in an environment can always be carried out by the analysis of the statistical distributions of impulses arriving from suitably connected S-units. The whole picture built up is a great deal more complicated than this. The great value of Rosenblatt's work, however, stems from the fact that it supplies a means of transition from well-defined (monotypic) logical nets of the kind that can be drawn from such models as those of Uttley and Culbertson to the more statistical theories of Shimble (1955), Rapoport (1955) and others.

The fact is that the property of being "general purpose" as opposed to "special purpose" computers cut across the property of a completely specified topology. Osgood and Heyer's (1952) model for example is 'special purpose' with an incomplete topology, whereas it could be argued that the principles of classification is 'general purpose' even though it may be associated with a completely specified topology.

The classifying system with conditional probabilities, which is the Uttley model, differs from Rosenblatt's PERCEPTRONS, in that it is deterministic and classifies precisely as a basis for learning. Rosenblatt's system is, on the other hand, learning to classify, and does so on the basis of a statistical analysis of the input data.

This statistical analysis depends on the connectivity from S-units to

A-units and the reinforcing procedure, which in the course of time can bring about the discrimination between different shapes. Now to recapitulate in more general terms on the subject of PERCEPTRONS, consider the following.

A PERCEPTRON can be defined as any device which can compute all predicates that are linear in some specified set of partial predicates. Thus any change in the set of predicates gives us a new PERCEPTRON while the weights and threshold are adjustable parameters of a particular device. From the standpoint of pattern recognition we would like the basic predicates (feature detectors) to be "easy to compute". These notions can be formalised by specifying either the maximum *number* of points or the maximum *distance* between points that a predicate may inspect. Thus a PERCEPTRON for which none of the partial predicates looks at more than k points will be called a k-*order limited PERCEPTRON*, while a PERCEPTRON for which the points inspected by any partial predicate must all fall within a circle of specified diameter will be called a *diameter limited PERCEPTRON*.

This approach and definitions stem from the work of Minsky and Papert (1969). They were interested in identifying the theoretical limitations on the kinds of geometric figures which various types of simple PERCEPTRONS could classify. Minsky and Papert discredited much of the extensive work done on PERCEPTRONS that occurred during the 1960s, and they believed that many claims about the pattern recognition and learning capabilities of PERCEPTRONS were exaggerated. This is a criticism that is often justified by the over-enthusiastic workers in AI (Dreyfus, 1965, 1972).

Minsky and Papert showed that "diameter limited PERCEPTRONS" can function as template matching devices, and by partitioning R into regions we can arrange to detect an exact match of an input against a particular pattern in a particular position. Yet this was already achieved earlier by Culbertson. Furthermore certain limitations were observed even in this procedure. As an indication of the limitations of "diameter limited PERCEPTRONS", let us consider whether they can recognise the class of *connected* (without separated parts) figures. In fact Minsky and Papert offer a demonstration that diameter limited PERCEPTRONS cannot distinguish connectivity. But I shall not pursue such limitations, since the same sort of limitations can be found for all such pattern recognition devices, doubtless including the human eye and nervous system. A more detailed discussion of both PERCEPTRONS and PANDEMONIUM can be found in the literature referred to and also in Sampson (1976).

The Uhr-Vossler Model

Leonard Uhr and Charles Vossler (1961) developed a pattern-recognition program that generates, evaluates and adjusts its own operators, and in this is both PERCEPTRON-like in general and like PANDEMONIUM in particular. In the Uhr-Vossler system, a pattern is represented by a 20 by 20 binary matrix. If the pattern does not wholly fill up the matrix a rectangular mask is placed around the pattern so that only the pattern is showing and the blank marginal areas are eliminated from any subsequent processing. Then a set of 5 by 5 *operators* (feature detectors, diameter limited predicates) is applied to the pattern. These operators may contain any combination of 0's, 1's, and blanks. Each operator is translated across and down the pattern, one row or column at a time, so that the operator is eventually "centered" over every pattern cell. In each of the positions it takes up it determines whether the pattern of 0's and 1's in the test (unknown) patterm *matches* the binary entries in the operator.

In the working system blanks in the operator signify that the corresponding position in the pattern is irrelevant. Figure 7 shows an operator of the sort which might be used to detect upper left corners; also shown are two examples of pattern regions where the operator would match (Sampson, 1976). Note that cells outside the mask match if the operator is zero or blank at the corresponding position.

After all of the matches of a particular operator with the input pattern have been found, four parameters are computed: (1) the *total number* of matches, (2) the *average horizontal* position of the matches, (3) the *average vertical* position of the matches, and (4) the *average distance* of a match from the center of the mask. Each of these quantities is then scaled to a 3-bit value and stored for further computation.

The operators originate from four separate sources. In the first place, the experimenter can predetermine any number of operators which he thinks might be useful for the types of patterns being processed. A typical example of a preprogrammed operator is in Figure 7/1. Secondly, operators can be generated at random, subject to certain constraints such as a limitation on the total number of 1's. Thirdly, operators can be "extracted" from the input pattern itself. This can be done by selecting a random 5 by 5 subset of the pattern blanks inserted for some of the binary entries. This last step generalises the pattern sample and reduces the precision required in the matching. Fourthly, a new "combinatorial operator" can be produced by logical or arithmetic operations on corresponding measures of two existing operators. These combinatorial operators thus contribute a single value (instead of four) to the total description of the pattern. This brings the

$$\begin{bmatrix} b & b & b & b & b \\ b & 1 & 1 & 1 & b \\ b & 1 & 0 & b & b \\ b & 1 & b & 0 & b \\ b & b & b & b & b \end{bmatrix}$$

9/1

$$\begin{bmatrix} 1 & 1 & 0 & 0 & 0 \\ 1 & 1 & 1 & 1 & 1 \\ 0 & 1 & 0 & 0 & 0 \\ 0 & 1 & 0 & 0 & 0 \\ 1 & 1 & 0 & 0 & 0 \end{bmatrix}$$

9/2

$$\begin{array}{|cccc} \hline 1 & 1 & 1 & 1 \\ 1 & 0 & 0 & 0 \\ 1 & 1 & 0 & 1 \\ 0 & 0 & 0 & 0 \end{array}$$

9/3

FIGURE 9 Uhr-Vossler operator (9/1). Two pieces of the pattern with which it tries to match (9/2). The edge of the pattern (9/3). b denotes "blanks".

process to a close; it is a heuristic method. Uhr and Vossler typically used 48 regular operators and an unspecified number of combinatorial operators, each input pattern generated a description consisting of a vector of some 200 3-bit characteristics. In memory for each pattern class is stored a similar vector of characteristics, built up from experience of recent examples of the "pattern class". The input pattern is classified by computing a weighted average difference score against each pattern class vector and then selecting the class with the lowest score. It should be added that in the early stages the non-preprogrammed operators are generated as they are required.

Three types of "amplifiers" or weights are next involved in computing the "difference score". *Pattern amplifiers* consist of 3-bit weights particular to each characteristic of each pattern class. *General amplifiers* are 3-bit weights computed by averaging the pattern amplifiers across pattern classes. Finally there is an *average difference amplifier* for each pattern class. To compute a difference score the difference between the *pattern class characteristic* and the *input characteristic* is multiplied by the pattern amplifier and then by the general amplifier for that characteristic. The sum of these doubly weighted differences is then normalised through division by the sum of the products of the corresponding pattern and general amplifiers. Finally, this normalised weighted difference is multipled by the average difference amplifier for the pattern class to produce the difference score. This, in essence, is the Uhr-Vossler *learning scheme* at the computational stage, but the Uhr-Vossler system has to improve its performance (and not merely learn). So it must receive feedback about right and wrong classifications. Using this information, the program proceeds to modify pattern amplifiers for pattern classes "similar" to the correct one. This means noticing where the difference scores were close to (or even less than) the difference score which should have been smallest. The system therefore concentrates on reducing the tendency to conflate, or become confused by, similar patterns, which are nevertheless different. For a given similar pattern, each characteristic is compared with the corresponding characteristic in the correct pattern: a hexagon, for example, must have six corners and six "edges". If a decision based on this characteristic alone produced a correct classification, the corresponding pattern amplifiers are increased, thus giving more weight to this "discriminating" feature. If, on the other hand, the classification is incorrect, the amplifiers are decreased.

After the pattern amplifiers have been adjusted, the stored list of characteristics for the pattern class of the type just processed is updated to reflect a new experience with a pattern of that particular class. The general amplifiers are then in turn recomputed. Then the average difference amplifiers are modified by decreasing the one for the correct class in proportion to the number of similar classes, and by increasing the ones for all similar classes. Since characteristics which have been valuable in discriminating many patterns will have had their various pattern amplifiers augmented frequently, the associated general amplifier averages will be relatively large. This situation forms the basis for computing the relative success of each operator. When it becomes relatively unsuccessful any one operator is replaced by a new one. A new operator enters the stored pattern class vectors with characteristic values based on its application to the most recent example of each pattern type. All weights for the new operator are small at first, giving it a success count which is sufficient, but only just, to keep it available to show its use. It should be added that the success of the system with the recognition of hand printed letters was very high.

The Uhr-Vossler feature detection scheme for pattern classification introduced a number of important new ideas in the design of PERCEPTRON-like devices. Its learning algorithm demonstrated the importance of rewarding successful components of systems and this is wholly consistent with the Throndike law of effect.

The performance record of the Uhr-Vossler system still serves as a benchmark for those who would classify isolated and relatively simple patterns. Unfortunately, most "real world" vision tasks do not, of course, involve simple, isolated patterns. So we need to look at programs which attempt to work with somewhat more natural visual environments. This we shall do later.

The next system we look at is primarily for *Scene Analysis* and has been developed by Clowes.

Clowes' Picture Processing

As another example of an AI approach I will summarise Clowes' (1967) interesting work on *picture processing*, although it is in our terms mainly concerned with *scene analysis*. It is also related to Guzman's SEE in its *scene analysis* activity and we shall talk of SEE next.

Clowes recognises that ability to *interpret* and respond to the *significant* content of pictures is shared by a large proportion of organisms and some number of "machines". The machines are usually in practice digital computers. Suitably programmed they will classify simple shapes and printed letters and digits represented (by means of a television scanner) as a matrix of 1s and 0s. Such methods lack the flexibility of human perception and he asks what can be learned from a study of such 'machine perception' which could help us to understand human perception. This is clearly a question of simulation (as opposed to synthesis) in our terms. His answer is, and I would agree, that any model (however oversimplied) of perception may help to guide our research. This is a very large part of the justification for all AI work. The other main part lies in its practical applications in what can be called *automation*, in broad terms. Clowes proceeds with his picture interpretation process by setting up a linguistic grammar, within which the structure of sentences can be analysed and thus a descriptive process is added to that of classification. Reference is made by Clowes to the work of Ledley (1964) and Narasimhan (1964) which supply methods which are at least comparable, and are both worthy of note.

Clowes linguistic analysis is not addressed at linguistics as such but merely as a device for pictorial description. His example sentence is "the boy kicked the red ball" and this, in terms of his syntax, is read "The (T) boy (N) kicked (V) the (T) red (A) ball (N). Then, in his linguistic system, we find the right elements (e.g. T, N or NP, VP) linked by an operator + to be interpreted as "followed by" and this provides the contiguity in the symbol string. In the geometrical sense, this is the more general relationship 'next to'. Thus a simple pictorial property like 'Edge' (e.g., boundary between black and white regions of a picture) might be defined as "black area adjoining a white area". Specifically Clowes defines North Edge as 'white area above black area', which can be expressed in a computable form, granted the use of a suitable notation. In a pictorial notation the definition of 'North Edge' for a "picture" composed only of black or white elements might take the form illustrated in Figure 10. This asserts that the point arrowed will be said to have the property N EDGE if it and the points to the left and the right of it are black (i.e. *True*) and the three points denoted '0' are white (i.e. *False*). A Cartesian co-ordinate system is then introduced and this leads to a definition of a Boolean form as follows:—

0	0	0
1	1	1

FIGURE 10 A North Edge as defined in Clowes system.

$$\begin{aligned} \text{N EDGE}(x,y) = {} & \text{PICTURE}(x-1, y) \;\&\; \text{PICTURE}(x,y) \\ & \&\; \text{PICTURE}(x+1, y) \;\&{\sim}\text{PICTURE}(x-1, y+2) \\ & \&{\sim}\text{PICTURE}(x, y+2) \;\&{\sim}\text{PICTURE}(x+1, y+2) \quad (1) \end{aligned}$$

where (x,y) is the 'arrowed' point, a black point has the value *True* and a white point the value *False.* The assignment of a label (e.g., N EDGE) to a picture point involves a decision based upon the state of a number of neighbouring points. This notation is used in the actual picture analysis program in modified form for reasons of economy and ease of programming.

As a result of such an approach, Clowes derives the following "picture" of the number 2 (Figure 11).

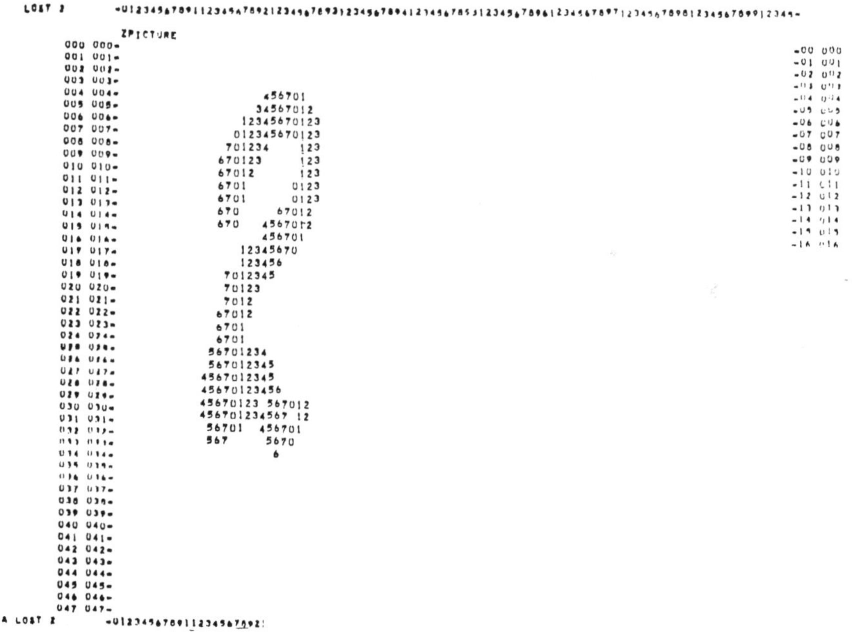

FIGURE 11 The internal representation of each "black" element is by a binary digit and for external (display) representation by an *Octal* system.

The program operates by applying each set of rules to the outcome of the previous set, starting with a picture stored in computer memory in terms of the linguistic grammar. The performance of the program is monitored by having it print out those portions of its memory which currently contain a picture after each set of rules has been applied. The "area" of memory is a matrix of 192 × 96 elements. As an example, Clowes gives Z(N)EDGE(048,48) is stored starting from location 48 (down), 48 (across). A feature of the linguistic grammer is that substitutions are always defined for pairs of *adjacent symbols*, nowhere do we find a rule which calls for the replacement of symbols *widely separated* in the string being analysed. In Clowes own words:—

> "In spite of this immediate phrase structure restriction it is still possible to reflect with a single label the structure of an extended utterance, because as we proceed with the analysis the string automatically shrinks by the very nature of the substitution operation. In the geometrical analysis we perform on a picture, the same immediate constituent limitation is imposed. If, however, we are able to label an extended property of a picture, e.g. a long line, with 'next to' concatenations, we need to draw together these local properties — hence this reduction in the size of the EDGE versions of the picture".

The parsing processing operation labels the main feature of this '2' (here shown as the Octal pictorial output in Figure 11) and for the purpose of recognition we can define each numeral as being some combination of features. For a '2' this definition will involve a curve, a diagonal and a horizontal; and the last group of rules contains such a definition. Comparable definitions for all the other numerals can be written, and all shapes can, in principle, be so classified.

Later Clowes (1969) followed up this same approach and applied the same sort of thinking to more general sets of shapes, which he likened to the "natural language program" BASEBALL (see chapter 7) at least in its data base structure. In other words the cataloging and storing of information about items and their relationships, using syntactical and semantic methods, is a powerful and effective means for the understanding of visual and (other) "pictures" in a manner similar to our understanding of purely verbal information. The link here is between knowledge by acquaintance and knowledge by description.

It should be added that a number of modifications and elaborations have since been made to the Clowes models, and there are whole families of such models now available (e.g. Coombs, 1969, Hilditch, 1969) and especially those by Guzman, Marr and others. Let us next look at some of their work and, in particular, Guzman's SEE.

Scene Analysis

Guzman's SEE (1968) is one of the best known examples of Scene Analysis (it is "bottom-up" rather than "top-down" in its processing), and comparable in some ways with the earlier models of Roberts (1965), even though Guzman does not depend on the same high powered computing and explicit model-making as does Roberts.

Let us now look at SEE in action. The input to SEE is a coded description of a line drawing representing a collection of convex polyhedral objects (cubes, wedges, pyramids, and so on). SEE uses information from the vertices (cf. Hebb's Cell Assembly theory) where lines meet in the drawing in order to identify the closed regions and the objects to which they belong. SEE contains no knowledge of the type of objects it may encounter and the program demonstrates effectively how far it is possible to proceed in *scene analysis* without an overall model. Its knowledge is of an operational kind rather than structural.

SEE is initially presented with a specially coded compact representation of a scene, and this is reminiscent of Clowes' models which it preceded. Such information is immediately transformed into an internal representation with which SEE works. The model contains (1) an unordered list of (numbered) regions and, for each region, counter-clockwise ordered lists of all neighbouring regions, all surrounding vertices, and alternating neighbours and vertices; (2) an unordered list of lettered vertices and, for each vertex, its type, position (x and y coordinates), and counter-clockwise ordered lists of connected vertices, impinging regions, and alternating regions and vertices; and (3) a designation of one or more regions as the background of the scene and not part of any object. The eight *types* (referred to under 2 above) of vertices with which SEE works are shown in Figure 10. The relative angles of the impinging lines can vary considerably. In order to assign the regions to objects, SEE looks for evidence which justifies linking regions together. These links may be "strong" or "weak". Some strong links that may often be inferred directly from the vertex type are shown as arcs connecting regions in the vertices of Figure 12. Other, more complex, strong links depend on configurations of vertices, such as the case of "matching T" vertices in which the stems are collinear and the tops of the T's face each other. Such a situation is considered good evidence that an object between the T's is occluding an edge of another object behind it. Weak links arise from fewer configurations than strong links.

Groups of one or more regions are called *nuclei*. Guzman's merging algorithm attempts to reduce the number of nuclei required to cover all (nonbackground) regions to one nucleus per object. Merging of nuclei pro-

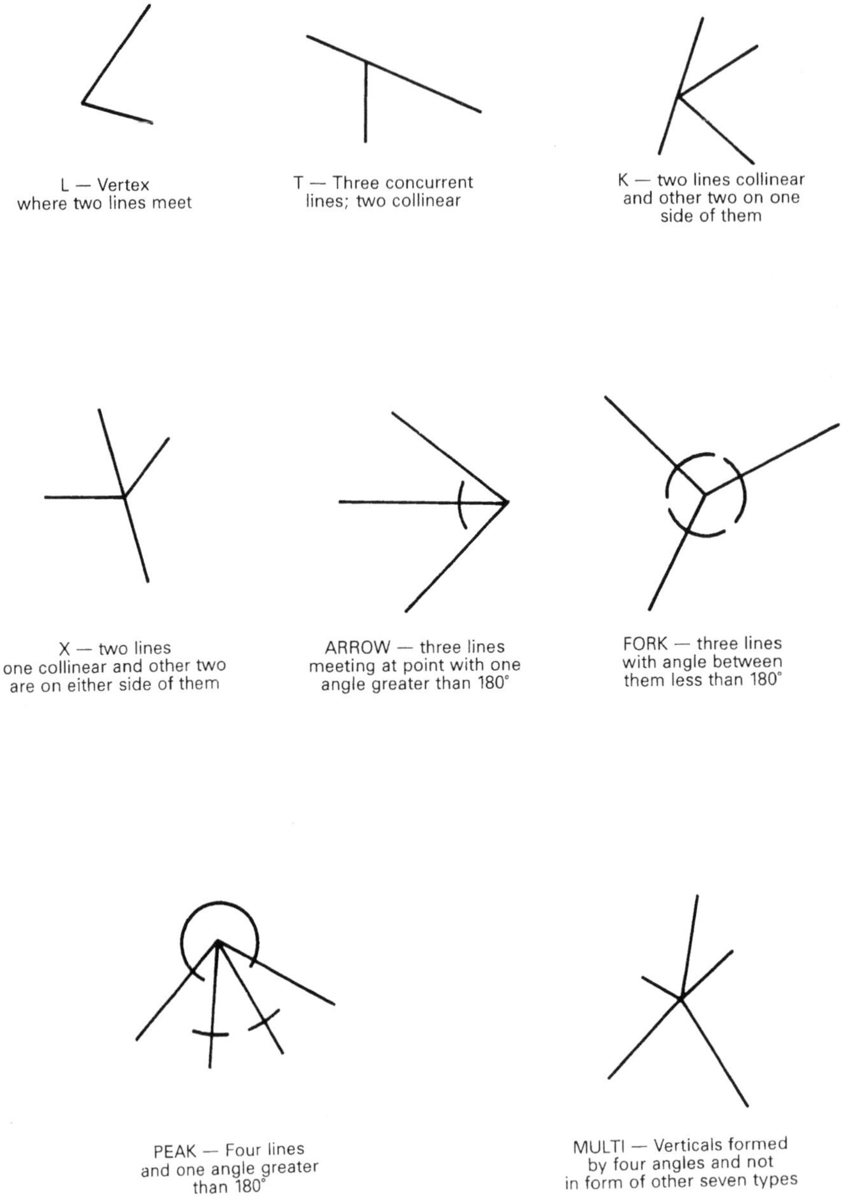

FIGURE 12 Vertex types used by SEE. "ARROW", "FORK", and "PEAK" produce the indicated strong links. (After Guzman)

ceeds in three steps: (1) any two nuclei connected by two or more strong links are merged into a single nucleus; (2) when (1) can no longer be applied, any pair of nuclei connected by one strong and one weak link are merged (and (1) is then reapplied if possible); (3) when (1) and (2) can no longer be applied any remaining nucleus consisting of a single region having only one strong link (and no weak ones) is merged with the nucleus to which it is linked. When these surprisingly simple rules have been applied to their fullest extent, SEE usually produces a correct list of objects and their component regions, even for quite complex inputs.

Figure 13 illustrates the linking and merging process for a simple example. The scene has 9 regions (number 1 is the background and will not be linked to any others) and 15 vertices. All the strong links shown in Figure 9 are of the sorts given in Figure 8 except for the matching T situation that links regions 5 and 8 through vertices H and J. There is also a weak ("leg") link between regions 8 and 9, which is based on the fact that lines KM and GD are parallel.

In Figure 14 merging step (1) has been applied to yield four nuclei. Merging step (2) then combines regions 8 and 9. Finally merging step (3) is applied to combine region 5 with the 8–9 nucleus. Note that the single remaining strong link satisfies no merge prerequisites. SEE can now report that the scene consists of three objects with regions 2–3–4, 6–7 and 5–8–9.

Although Guzman has shown similar correct analyses of scenes with nearly 50 regions, it should be kept in mind that his approach is limited to well-defined artificial "block world" scenes and would fail upon introduction of noise, shadows, textures and/or curved lines. This particular set of problems has since been considered by various writers (see Winston and Brown, 1979).

SEE is accompanied by a follow-up program called BACKGROUND and this uses geometrical knowledge to pick out the "background" of the scene. By such means (and they sometimes fail) an assumption that a body is convex can be overruled to make it seen as concave. So in Figure 15, X would be rightly seen as background & Y as foreground (even though the figure U 2D) since the *interpretation* of the 2D figure is 3D.

BACKGROUND analyses 2D linedrawings as 3D drawings correctly identified X as background but would be wrong to identify Y as background.

SEE is as we have seen "bottom-up" rather than "top-down" in operation, which means that local clues determine picture as-a-whole and not vice-versa.

Patrick Winston (1975) also developed such a scene understanding system. Winston's system accepts as its input a Guzman-type output, in

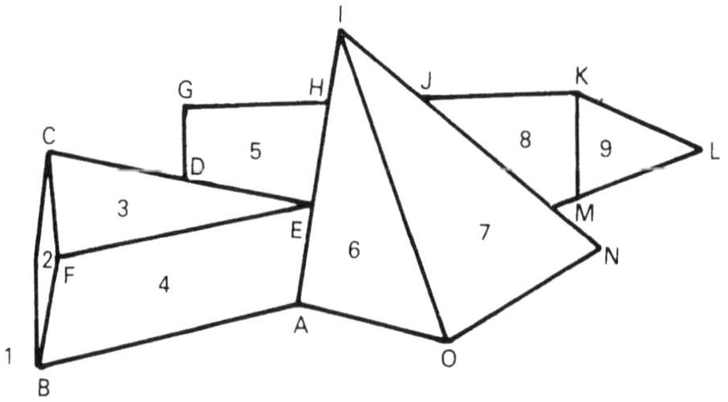

FIGURE 13 A simple scene. (After Guzman)

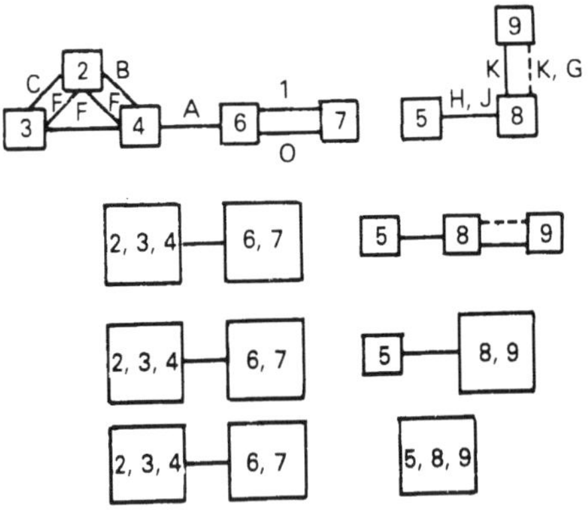

FIGURE 14 Links in scene; and the sequence of region-mergings done by SEE. (After Guzman)

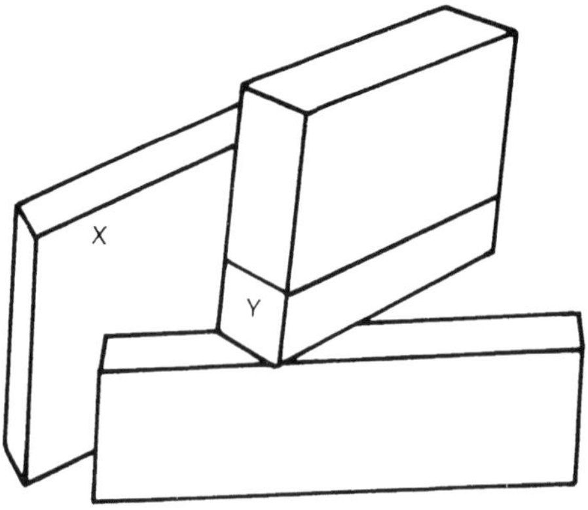

FIGURE 15

which the various component objects in the scene have been found. The Winston program recognises the various types of blocks, "bricks", "wedges", etc. Characteristics and relative positions of blocks (and groups of blocks) in a scene are described in terms of relations such as "has property of", "in front of", "one part is", "a kind of", etc. and his program represents a scene as a *description graph* of object nodes and relational connections. This *description graph* notation has a self-referential feature, allowing representation not only of simple scenes but also of relations and comparisons between scenes and even between description graphs themselves. Winston's system can be exemplified by the definition of the general concept of an "arch". The descriptive graph describing the "arch" model notes that the scene has three components (A,B,C) of which two (B and C) are a "kind of" brick and are "standing" with B to the "left of" C. Further, B and C "must not abut" each other and must both "support" A, which may itself be any "kind of" object. Similar networks can be used to describe other concepts, like "house", "table", and "tent".

The important thing about Winston's system is not so much the *representational graphs* themselves as the fact that the system can generate such powerful descriptions from such simple examples. The program *learns* best from a reasonably skilled trainer who can present a series of examples and counterexamples of the concept to be learned. Winston emphasises the importance of the "near miss" example. Apparent cases of the concept (which turn out to be fake) should differ *in only small ways* from true instances, so the system can easily identify the incorrect features and incorporate appropriate restrictions in the model. It should be noted here that Winston's program is largely a *learning program*, and this provides one of the bridges we are searching for between what we might call the different aspects of cognition; this indeed is a case of *perceptual learning.*

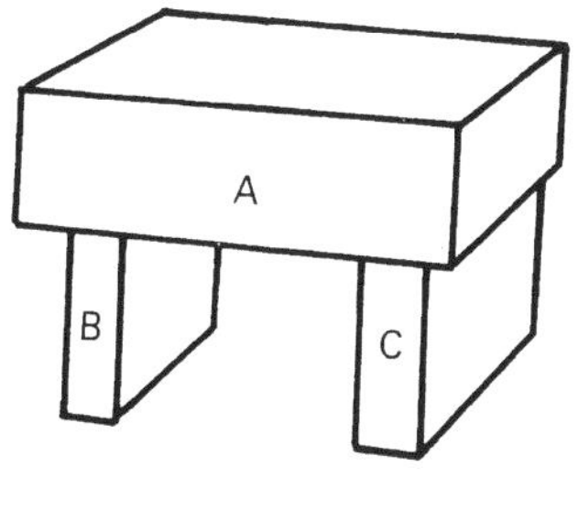

FIGURE 16 A Winston arch.

More on Scene Analysis

We are concentrating our entire discussion of perception on the visual system, and indeed many of our philosophical problems hinge on such cases as are involved in what we see (or say we see) and what we perceive, where the perception is what we 'see'. Herein lies the problem (Wittgenstein 1953, Price 1953) if we use 'see' as synonymous with 'perceive' then the interpretative step between sensation ("first impression") and the interpretation ("considered identification") is blurred. This blurred effect seems correct to Wittgenstein and wrong to Price, and indeed to me.

The whole process of visual identification or scene analysis (partially seeing, but mostly perceiving) has been given a great deal of attention recently (Winston and Brown, 1979), and a whole issue of *Artificial Intelligence* (Volume 17, numbers 1–3) was compiled by Brady (1981). Of the various problems considered there, was the visual interpretation of surface contours (Stevens) and here the problem is to computationally reconstruct a three-dimensional model from a two-dimensional figure or from line drawings. The latter is dealt with by Barrow and Tenenbaum.

Looked at from the AI viewpoint, we can now say a little more about AI approaches to vision (Winston and Brown, 1979) where the emphasis is the same, in essence, as the pattern recognition systems already described, but with slightly more emphasis on simulation (as opposed to synthesis) where the actual human visual methods are now the main target. This is indeed still primarily concerned with what is usually called *scene analysis.*

There are many aspects to work on perception and some such as stereopsis (Mayhew and Frisby, 1981), shadow graphing (Ikenchi and Horn, 1981) and the use of gradient and dual space (Draper, 1981) and we can only refer to these in passing.

Nishihara also deals with image analysis and visible-surface analysis viewed from a computational point of view and the search for algorithms to deal with the problem. If the algorithms exist and can be found they presumably leave an interpretation (heuristic step) to be made in some regard. But rather than talk generally I will look, if only briefly, at one or two concrete examples of such work.

Ullman (1979), writing in Winston and Brown, is more concerned than most with aspects of image processing and should therefore be mentioned first. He is concerned with the interesting and relevant problem of detecting light sources, and he is concerned with intensity and contrast in a limited visual world. The world is a computational world. Simple intensity and gradient comparisons seem to be at least necessary to the success of all such work, which is interestingly related to the now aged work on colour and shape constancy (and to some extent the Ames demonstrations) carried out by psychologists some years ago. The same origins and resemblances apply to Kent Stevens (1979) who follows up with another aspect of pattern recognition. He suggests that our impression of spatial objects being three-dimensional is as much due to an inference about spatial orientation as it is about size-distance, perspective and other factors.

Horn and Bachman (1979) also have interesting comments to make on aspects of pattern recognition. They regard alignment of images with surface models as vital. They see change of appearance as a function of the change of the sun's position as important and the alignment of images of parts of the scene with models of their surface make possible a distinction between real and synthesised images. They also make great play of *understanding* as a vital aspect of the processes involved.

Understanding the nature of an image then, implies a need to understand how light reflection depends on various combinations of surface material, surface orientation, and light-source position. This is in agreement with Ullman and Stevens, and of course makes us pause over the word 'understand'.

The following strategies are thought to be involved.

1) Automated generation of shaded relief maps.

2) The generation of low-level, obliquely-viewed images.

3) The generation of "special maps" that bring out particular terrain features.

4) The classification of "ground cover for crop prediction".

5) The matching of images to terrain data for satellite navigation.

6) The making of maps for automatic or semiautomatic change detection.

The roadmap for the theory development is shown in Figure 17. As shown, the progression involves a number of key representations: the reflectance map, the digital terrain map, the synthetic image, the multiple-sun synthetic image, the albedo image, and the change-detection image. Since understanding reflectance maps is a prerequisite to following Horn and Bachman's work, I will now describe what it entails.

The purpose of the reflectance map (Figure 18) is to make explicit the relationship among observed intensity, surface material, surface orientation, and light-source position.

All the points (x,y) in the space (Figure 18) correspond to surface orientations. For a given surface material and light-source position, a surface's orientation determines its reflected light intensity. By drawing lines through points representing orientations that have the same intensity, one has the isointensity lines shown.

The "line-of-sight" connecting the viewer with the surfaces viewed is taken to be on the z-axis, and x and y are actually the partial derivatives of the surface z (x, y) with respect to x and y. Thus the point (0,0) corresponds

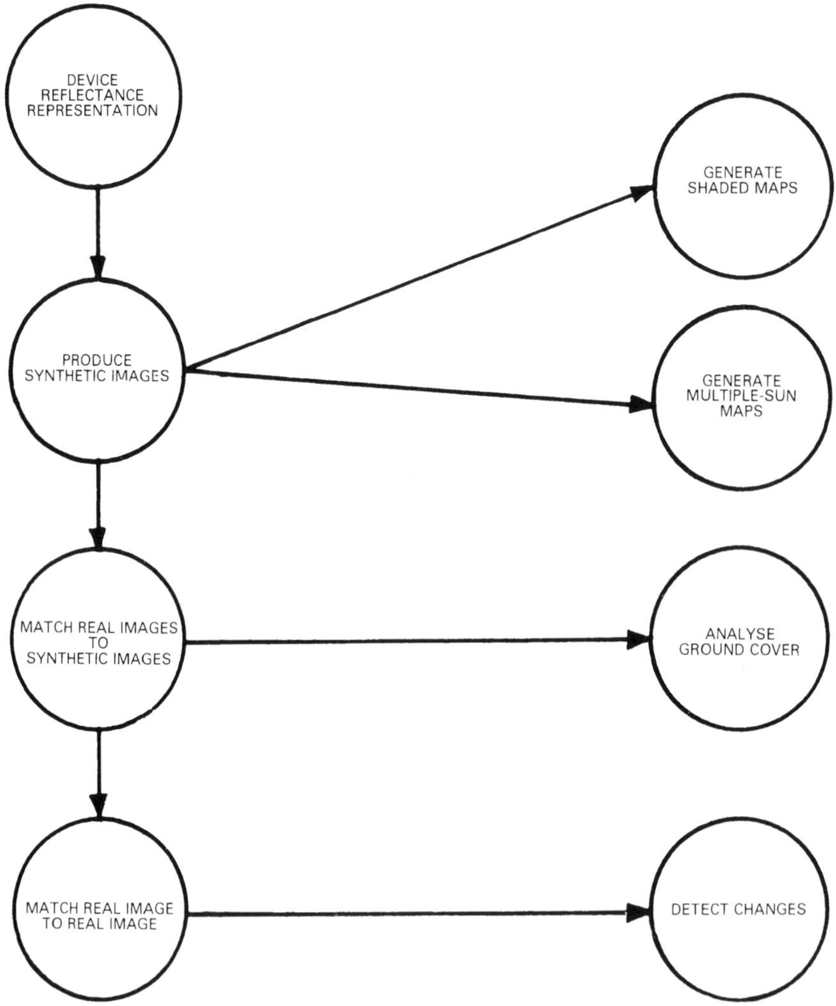

FIGURE 17 Roadmap for the development of an image formation and exploitation theory. Applications of the theory appear on the righthand boxes. (After Winston and Brown)

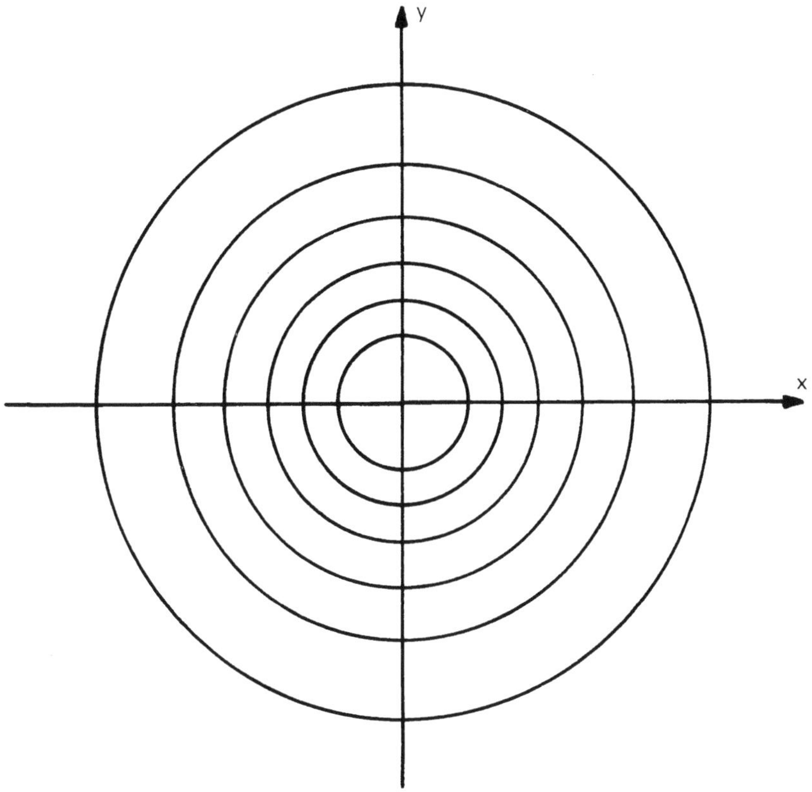

FIGURE 18 In a reflectance map each point is taken to represent some tilt of the viewed surface. For this particular reflective map, the circular contours of constant reflectance imply that the light source is behind the viewer and the viewed surface has normal reflectance properties. (After Winston and Brown)

to a surface whose *normal* points directly at the viewer. A point (p, 0) indicates a surface that is tilted by rotation about the y-axis only. The isointensity lines in the sample reflectance map are concentric circles because the surface material is assumed ordinary and the light source is assumed to be directly behind the viewer. These conditions assure that the amount of tilt, given by $x^2 + y^2$, is all that matters.

Using the same surface material but moving the light source off the z-axis gives the reflectance map shown in Figure 19. The point (0,0) no longer corresponds to the orientation of maximum intensity — the x and y of maximum intensity now specify the surface orientation for which the surface normal points directly to the light source.

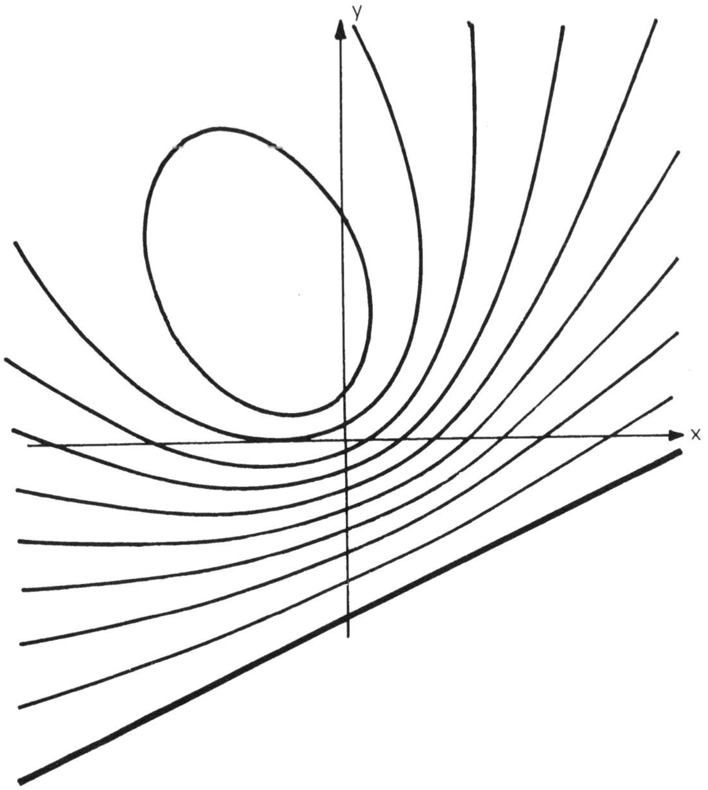

FIGURE 19 In this particular reflectance map, the contours of constant reflectance correspond to a normal surface material and a light source striking the viewed surface from the upper left. (After Winston and Brown)

When it becomes possible to predict intensities from material, orientation, and light-position information, it also becomes possible to produce synthetic high-altitude images, and these are immediately useful for producing shaded relief maps. An appropriate combination of ground cover and sun position can also be used to give the user the best possible feel for the mountains and hills that constitute the terrain. It should be noted that shaded relief maps need not conform to what might actually be observed. Horn (1979) has made images that correspond to terrain illuminated by three suns, one blue, one red, and one green. Such images give special insight into terrain properties at a glance. Slopes with exposure to the south, for example, are readily identified because of their red hue from the red, southern sun.

The main point made by Horn, however, is to make images that match photographs as closely as possible with a view to registering real aerial photographs with terrain models. Such a matching procedure is vital to the effort to improving the use of satellite images. When a "real" aerial photograph is registered with a synthetic one which is produced from a terrain model, some areas will refuse to provide a good match because the actual ground cover is not the one assumed in generating the synthetic image. These discrepancies suggest to Winston and Brown a solution to the classification problem. Since registration evidently does not absolutely require ground cover information, it seems sensible to use differences between two registered images to estimate surface reflectance. Then the ratio of real to synthetic intensity can be used in terrain classification, particularly if it is calculated for each of the special bands recorded in LANDSAT images.

An *albedo map* is defined (Horn, 1979) to be an image in which each point's intensity is the ratio of the intensity in the real image to the intensity in the synthetic image. In addition to use in classification, it seems likely that albedo maps will be useful in change detection. Change might be detected by subtracting one image from another. Unfortunately, again according to Winston and Brown, the changes in sun position from hour to hour and from day to day make this impossible by swamping changes caused by changes in the ground cover. Instead, Horn proposes to divide earlier and later real image intensities by the intensities predicted by the terrain model to give two registered albedo maps. Then, one albedo map is subtracted from the other, producing a change that will correspond to ground-cover differences occurring between the earlier and later recording times. For the use of human beings, the two albedo maps can be compiled in different colours and superimposed. The human analyst's eye is instantly drawn to places where changes have taken place because their hue will differ from the surrounding area. The notion of understanding is fundamental to this whole study and Waltz's study of line-drawing interpretations makes the idea of constraint propagation immensely popular. The idea is to catalogue all possible ways that junctions can be formed from various edge types, and then use the catalogue to analyse them as a jigsaw puzzler might. Locally, things fit together in only a few ways. The fit constraints, taken together, make for extreme global constraint that usually enables unique global conclusions about edge types.

Constraint propagation also features in the work of Woodham. It is combined there with Horn's notions about reflectance maps. In the course of his discussion, Woodham looks at the theory of reflectance constraints to provide solid, quantitative theory for the simultaneous use of multiple reflectance maps.

We now move on to a more general view of the perceptual problem due to Marr (1979, 1982). Understanding vision is clearly a central problem of AI and it has been attacked most frequently from two directions. First, there is the work of Marr (1979) that is essentially monotypic. Marr's main arguments will be summarised briefly. Marr believes that vision research must follow the following five steps:

1) A *competence* to be understood is observed and described precisely, normally by experimental use of human subjects.

2) *Representations* are selected (or invented) that facilitate explicit description of the products of processing.

3) The *competence* and the *representations* are combined into a precise computation problem. (This hints at a degree of formalisation).

4) Algorithms are used for solving the computational problem. (This is significant, if only in the light of heuristic methods).

5) Results are validated by some combination of computer implementation and psychophysical experimentation. (This statement has a ring of ambiguity which is worrying to the anti-AI lobby.)

David Marr's clearcut and stated aim is to provide an efficient symbolic description of the world in visual images, and the levels of representation are central to his theory. This is as much to facilitate computation as it is to provide information about the external world. The primal sketch (Figure 20) as he calls it being somewhat similar to other image processing systems (e.g. Clowes).

At the top level, observation of competences and definition of representations have led Marr to think in terms of the competences and representations suggested in Figure 20. Three levels of representation are shown, and the primal sketch makes explicit information about intensity changes, including the length, position, orientation and contrast of line fragments. The $2\frac{1}{2}$-D sketch makes explicit information about surface orientation. And the *generalised-cone* 3-D model makes explicit information about object shape. Marr's section provides details about these representations and describes some of the competences required to deal with them. The sections of Ullman and Stevens provide greater depth by way of close examination of particular competences and the algorithms that these competences engender. Part of the purpose of these studies springs from a desire to understand vision in humans and animals, and the other part has to do with making "machines" that *see* interims of both simulation and synthesis respectively. In the light of the desire to make machines that can

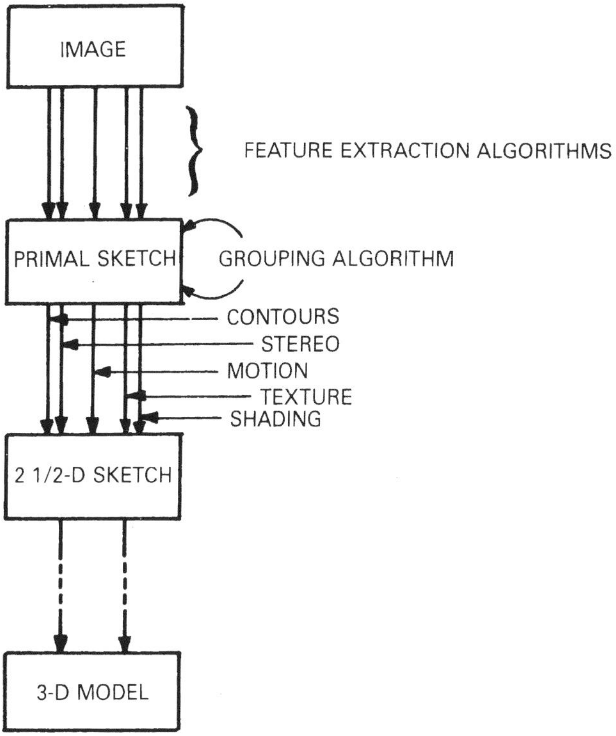

FIGURE 20 The model of vision proposed by Marr has three levels of representation, each of which makes appropriate information explicit. The first sketch makes explicit information about intensity changes, including the length, position, orientation, and contrast of line fragments; the $2\frac{1}{2}$-D sketch makes information about surface orientation explicit, and from that it proceeds uncertainly to the 3-D model. (After Marr)

see, it is natural to wonder if it would be sensible to copy neural mechanisms and use what is known about human physiology.

This does not mean that attention paid to human vision is relevant only to the goal of understanding the biological aspects of vision at some neural level. Indeed it seems certain that an understanding of the limits of biological vision cannot be ignored. Systems are needed whose power will derive from many subsystems. Consequently, it is very useful to know how strong each subsystem must be to do its part of the total job. Such information helps establish what subsystems must compute and whether various subsystems can be built to operate at reasonable speed. So much then, at the moment, for perception, except for a final physiological comment.

Some Neurophysiology

We will now say a few words on the possible physiological interpretation of the perceptual process.

We should note first (and interpret) the Pribram view of perception. He suggests a two-process coding mechanism of brain function. One represents a state and the other operations on that state. The state itself depends upon the slow potentials that are generated at the junctions between neurons. Recoding operations are performed by nerve impulses initiated by disturbances of the state which go on until a stable state recurs.

There are then three modification stages of the junctional microstructure. These three modifications are *enduring, temporary* and *evanascent* (to use Pribram's own terms) and they are basic to memory. This theory replaces classical neuron theory and up-grades the status of the neuron along the lines we have already mentioned in talking of the impracticality of a complete classification theory based on the old neuron theory.

One result of this is to talk of long term memory as a function of junctional structure which implies a growth process (cf. Hebb) involving new nerve fibres. The temporary changes depend upon decrementation and inhibition — the former leading to adaptation and habituation and implying extra sensitivity to novelty. The evanescent organization depends on each neural aggregate recoding its input. The picture at this level is more nearly that of the Sherringtonian or Pavlovian model, and as depicted in Pitts-McCulloch neural nets. It is natural for Pribram to interpret these activities within the compass of a TOTE-model (Miller, Galanter and Pribram, 1960).

In general terms, Luria (1973) has quite a lot of considerable relevance to say on this subject. He recognises the Hebb point that learning and having learned, perceiving and recognising (a re-perceiving activity) are different. As a result one expected short cuts to occur in the recognition process which could not be taken with an initial perception or initial learning.

This consideration alone might be thought to have some bearing on the problem of brain damage, and account for the fact that brain damage is less effective in reducing existing human abilities than in stopping the formation of new abilities. Like Hebb and others, he believes that no neural account of perception can be restricted to the occipital lobe, although the suggestions of Penfield and Rasmussen (1950) are accepted that area 17 is a primary visual area, with areas 18 and 19 as areas of visual elaboration. Luria says:

> An essential fact is that *spatial, organization is not a function of the occipital (visual) cortex itself,* and that the participation of the *inferior parietal* (or parieto-occipital) zones of the brain is essential for it to happen.

Hubel and Wiesel's work (1962, 1963) emphasises the specialist nature of neurons in the visual cortex and implies a type of organisation more in keeping with the visual theory of Osgood and Heyer (1952). Luria agrees that the perceptual processes closely interact with the non-perceptual activities such as hand movements. Lesions of the parieto-occipital areas directly impair spatial organisations if not visual synthesis.

It is in fact almost certain that the temporal-parietal areas, by virtue of their association with memory — both short term and long term — must be directly associated with perception. The ability to simultaneously synthesise a visual scene — as opposed to recognising a particular object — is something that requires parieto-occipital activity.

It is possible to compare the organisation of many AI systems with the organisation of the visual system, as revealed by microelectrode studies in the cat by Hubel and Wiesel (1962, 1965) as well as the frog (Lettvin, Maturana, McCulloch and Pitts 1959). The following two points of immediate resemblance should be noted:

1) Cells in the visual cortex only respond to local properties of the visual scene, e.g., edges, line segments. This mirrors the immediate constituent constraint imposed for economic reasons in picture grammar.

2) The visual scene is portrayed many times over in the cortex in terms of the different picture properties, each portrayal being 'laid-out' two-dimensionally and 'in register' with all other portrayals. This corresponds to the sets of arrays which are also preserved 'in register', in the computer.

It is understood that recognition is a special case of recall (and both special cases of perception), and is then the elicitation of the required response, which may be simple or complex (sequential or parallel) and may involve exploratory action by the system. Images are then the "internal" reconstruction of such whole or partial data. The fact of a pattern recognition system which can also set up new categories (perception over and above recognition) coupled to these other factors makes up our logical interpretation.

In behavioural terms there is little to add to this, except to extend the notion of imagery to imagination in the context of consciousness (and by implication the subconscious levels of processing). Such activities are "purposive" and are subject to emotive and other features which are often referred to as affective (or conative) aspects of behaviour. We do not mean in any sense, in talking this way, to separate the cognitive from the conative. They are inseparable aspects of the human being which are part of what makes the human being purposive and goal-seeking through feelings, needs and, in general, in terms of all levels of motivation.

At the neurophysiological level we can identify cortical areas, with relatively specialised control functions and accept their overlapping organisation, which doubtless represents the evolutionary fact of cross-associative storage arrangement (a computer data-base for the same purpose would be organised similarly). Thus, for perception, we proceed in stages from sensory recording at the retina to an Osgood-Heyer type of representation in area 17. This in turn is to be interpreted in the "perceptual elaboration areas" (Penfield and Rasmussen, 1950).

The structure of the system is conceptualised as a set of TOTE systems which in the context of a set of belief nets (George, 1973), which is the broad hierarchical structure of the occipital lobes. The two-state concept of Pribram fits with all these facts and has a great deal of supporting evidence which he himself quotes (1971).

This leaves many lacunae in any physiological model, since complex chemical features are almost certainly involved; the two hemispheres of the brain, which may be an evolutionary in its emergence, requires an explanation which may directly affect our perceptual notions (Luria 1973). Broadly speaking they are related to the complex interaction between perception, memory and language, and we must delay our interpretation until later.

So far so good. We see a probably working system at the neurophysiological level — even if more "special purpose sensory analysers" have to be identified, and we see many of the behavioural and logical constraints that make us think of perception (and pattern recognition) as an active participatory (transactional) system which is wholly embedded in the total system (both cognitive and conative).

Finally, we are reminded of the need to distinguish (and yet to relate to each other) the physiological and the conceptual models and levels of description. Like maps, or explanations, we need a sufficiency of detail in our descriptions to allow an explanation at many different levels of activity. This is what we are hoping to supply.

When we look at the perceptual process at the neurophysiological level, we again lean on Pribram's notions of feature analysis and the use of built-in detectors for elementary features such as lines and corners and the use of analysers for more complex transformations. In this he is in keeping with earlier views expressed by Sutherland (1959) on special analysing mechanisms in which both emphasise the "special purpose" nature of such aspects of perception, and very much in keeping with all that has been said about AI work.

Holography is an obvious addition to the list of special purpose analysers (Gabor, 1949, 1951; Longuet-Higgins, 1968a, 1968b). It is thus envisaged that the junctional patterns of neural activity can supply such holographic-like processes.

Another side of the Pribram view is to place emphasis on feelings which depend upon receptors in the central core of the brain stem. These feelings tend towards providing stop-go features at the motivational level.

The perceptual process is that of pattern recognition and, although this occurs at all levels, including the conceptual levels of human behaviour, we are considering it here now in the narrow context of *visual* pattern recognition. We are suggesting that the basic method by which this is possible is one of classification of information where that classification does not primarily take place at the actual retinal level. The classification is partial and hierarchical and takes place at the first stage, second stage, and perhaps at a third and fourth stage in the visual cortex. Complete classification must be replaced by adaptive classification, although it looks as if an argument can be made out for saying that the maximum flexibility occurs in the early years of the life of the organism and as time goes by the classifying system loses a great deal of its adaptivity. This is plausible on purely logical grounds, of course, since, as we have already said, as you fill up all the vacant spaces in a filing system or any other sort of classification system, so the number of spaces for new information diminishes, and this implies that the human nervous system finds it more difficult to reorganise combinations of stimuli than it does to organise them in the first instance. This once again reminds us of the Hebbian (1949) distinction between *learning* and *having learned.*

We should next ask ourselves where the "perceptual" (or sensory) theories (or models) of Marshall and Talbot (1942) or Osgood and Heyer (1952) fit into our general scheme of things. They are models which account well for some of the special features of visual effects such as the *figural after effect,* and do seem to fit immediately into the Pribramlike two-process theory.

The temporary neural changes which certainly include Figural aftereffects are dependent upon decrements and inhibitions and the evanescent changes on re-coding. These could well be interpreted in Osgood-Heyer terms. If this is so, a picture is gradually being built up of nervous function at various levels of description and detail, which shows a considerable measures of consistency, and are not inconsistent with AI models.

If then perception is thought of as the process of classifying and possibly re-classifying, and recognition is thought of as comparing an existing input with a previously stored input (which in practice will certainly involve an "attempt" on the part of human beings to remember the name of the object or objects) then the process of recall is involved in this latter stage. This is not to say, of course, that recall is concerned only with the remembering of names of physical objects; it is not. One can be told a name and asked to recall the face, as distinct from recognising the face when shown a set of photographs and asked to say who the person is. So recall can involve the complex matter of imagery. We here again turn to the Pribram view and accept that the original wave theory of nervous activity (Köhler 1958) replaced by the two mechanisms processes allows of a sensible interpretation of imagery in the central nervous system. So much for the time being.

Summary

The field of visual perception has been advanced enormously by the advent of AI modelling. One detects clearly many of the older psychological theories about constancies, distance-size, line drawings, ambiguous figures and the like, arising in a new computational form. This gives experimental psychology an effective modelling procedure which it previously lacked. The fact that AI models are synthetic is no barrier to them also being simulatory. When we have more information about how the human being (and his brain and nervous system) behave we shall be able to make the necessary comparison to ensure that some part (perhaps one) of the various synthetic models is the very match we are looking for.

In the meantime the increasingly sophisticated AI models are helping to find the very model of the human being we are looking for. In this respect we should regard such AI models as effective models on which scientific theories should be based. We shall be cumulatively summarising progress with each successive chapter of Book 2.

5

Learning, Problem Solving and Thinking

So far we have explicitly discussed 'perception,' the first of our cognitive terms under discussion. The treatment attempted was one of looking at the term carefully from a semantic viewpoint, and interpreting it as a philosophical and psychological term (mainly in terms of activity (acts) words and performance (process) words) and then seeing what models AI and neurophysiology supply.

"Learning" is a term that refers to a change in the state of a system such that adaptation has taken place and new "knowledge" has been acquired. We will assume that the change is normally both directed and motivated, although as we know learning is sometimes incidental (e.g. latent learning). In general, learning also depends upon memory in that "learning" leads to "having learned", and this implies memory. Certainly, if not retained, the new knowledge will be of little use to the organism (person).

Let us attempt now a definition of learning in terms of the Behavioural semiotic mentioned in Chapter 3. This will depend upon the notion of propositional attitudes, and therefore here on *beliefs*. *Learning* is the change of state of beliefs in some organism(s), X, as a result of some direct acquaintance with the environment E, or by description through language of that environment E.

The whole of the argument regarding learning by description is bound up with the use of beliefs in terms of meaning. As discussed previously we can summarise it here by saying simply that a meaningful statement that is believed to be true will lead to learning. If the statement is also in fact true then it will lead also to knowledge, if we think of knowledge as the totality of true beliefs held by a person. If the learning is explicitly directed towards some goal then it would be regarded as an aspect of problem-solving. This in turn may involve thinking and this now requires definition.

Thinking: the process of symbolising thoughts or events and the processing of those thoughts or events (symbolised or otherwise) by means of inference or, more simply, by association (which *is basic to* such inferences). This is in no way meant to encompass all that is, could be or should be, meant by the word 'thinking' in ordinary language, but will serve sufficiently our initial purpose. It goes without saying that *decision making*, *planning* and the like, are in the same stable as ("have a family resemblance with") learning and thinking, but we shall say no more about that for the time, since our purpose here is first to provide a link between chapter five and the central features (overlapping and hazily related as they are) of cognition.

We can now relate our cognitive account of learning and thinking to the use of signs by virtue of their association with communication by virtue of sense and reference for the utterer and the audience, and to this end we should first unpack the *processes* of learning and thinking. We suggest that *concepts* and their formation, as well as *hypotheses* and their formation, are important features of thinking. It cannot be overemphasised that we also regard rumination, thinking about (recalling and remembering events) and the like, as all being encompassed by thinking, but our present emphasis is to be placed on the manner in which concepts are the building bricks of hypotheses and of the processing of information involved in problem solving. 'Ideas' too is a term which we must carefully consider, and a comparison between concepts and ideas (Armstrong, 1973) could be our starting point.

We are already committed to the central notion of *propositional attitude*, and have concentrated on *beliefs as states* which have the same sort of internal complexity as propositions. We also continue to follow the Ramsay-Armstrong notion of the map which represents both the external world and our own conceptual world. It is indeed a conceptual map that allows us to think clearly about the external world. But we must look carefully at *ideas* at this point. The first temptation is to think of ideas as (embryonic) hypotheses, in which case the temptation is to think of concepts as being partially formed hypotheses, at which point we call them ideas. The belief-states (thoughts) involved may be separate, overlap or be identical. The ideas too regarding a concept (or concepts) may be varied and again be separate, overlap or be identical.

An example could help us here. If the concept is *cat* say, and I have an idea that cats are intelligent, and that I have seen a green cat, or one with a long bushy tail. Now if *cat, tail, bushiness,* etc. are the concepts, the propositions (in embryo) that I have as belief-states (thoughts) are capable of being made fully-fledged propositions, or even (given some measure of generality) hypothesis.

The having of a concept of *cat* is the capacity (or one might say 'disposition') to having any thought about cats. The distinction made by Armstrong between capacities and dispositions, being non-stimulus-dependent and stimulus-dependent respectively, is one we could readily accept. The same point arose earlier about belief as-a-state, as we shall normally conceive of it, and as a disposition, which we *could* conceive of it.

We shall make clear when and if we have any reason to move to dispositional language.

Our link to sign behaviour is straightforward and reflects the use of signs (types and tokens, natural and non-natural, lexical, indexical, iconic, symbolic etc.) as the representation of beliefs in the form of propositions. This is in essence a Peircean approach to the subject and as such merges the philosophical with the scientific. Let me now say a little more on the definitions and conceptual apparatus with which we shall be concerned.

Our Conceptual Apparatus

We next hope to provide a consistent terminology for the use of names. We will say that a name 'X' denotes X, e.g. 'Atlanta' denotes Atlanta. We will say that a name 'X' connotes the properties of X, e.g. "Atlanta is a large city", "Atlanta is a state capital", etc, where the totality of true statements which are predicable of Atlanta, are its *connotation.* When referred to a proper name like 'Atlanta', the use of a connotation is not really relevant, since we should not say "what does 'Atlanta' mean?", but "what does Atlanta denote or refer to?" 'Atlanta' is a label for something. But as Wittgenstein (1953) has said that to name (e.g. the king in chess) is not to give it meaning. If we add a definition then this is a "brief generalised *connotation*", which in the case of the king explains its permitted moves and its central role as primary target in the game.

There is a sense in which 'Atlanta' (or any proper name) and all class words represent concepts, and these are part of the connotation of beliefs. If we say "what does 'large' mean?", we say that 'large' denotes the class of anything above a certain size"; this is clearly relative and therefore vague, until a yardstick or measure is added. " 'Large' connotes nothing other than what the word denotes".

We look next at a classical example such as 'The King of France'. This may denote nothing at some time t, although it has denoted something at other times and could again. If we ask "what does 'The King of France' mean?", we should say "the person who might at any time be monarch of France", or some other circumlocution which is more or less synonymous with 'The King of France', but would add that we are not giving so much a meaning as a definition or a denotation for an empty class (at least at time t) so we must add that when the denotation of a term is null, all we need to know is how the label (name, word) could be applied should the denotation be non-null. In other words we can make up what names we like and they can be labels of ideas, real or imaginary in the physical world, but their "meaning" occurs only in the context of a complete sentence. From the computer viewpoint again, we can think of a label as denoting, like a name on a map, while the connotation is the set of entailments or true statements about the place. But given only the latter such a distinction becomes unimportant.

Now we come to Sentences (complete statements) and these are meaningful if we say we know how, in principle, to test them for truth, whether or not the test can be actually carried out. Empirical (synthetic) statements may be in certain circumstances hypotheses; which are to be thought of as generalised beliefs. Logical analytic statements are testable only for consistency and their truth in L, where L is some "language" or axiomatic system (AS).

By an entailment, we shall mean the implications of the connotation of a statement or of a term, e.g. "being married" entails "having a wife" or "having a husband". A term here is sometimes a phrase and not a single word or name. By synonymity we shall mean terms that can be interchanged without changing the connotation (meaning) of the statement, and this is closely linked to definition, which is sufficient, for our purpose, to distinguish such matters as analytic and synthetic (Quine, 1953). We may now use definitions (more or less as synonyms, for shorthand purposes). So it should name XYZ as A, for example, where

$$A = \text{df. } XYZ$$

and where df. is shorthand for "by definition". In assessing whether an object is an "individual" we shall need conventions, since we might for example be unsure as to whether the bell on a bicycle is a part of the bicycle or not. This is similar to the concept of systems, sub-systems and so on. We might indeed have to change our views as to what composes an individual and what does not. However, while this is a point to remember; it is also one that can fairly easily be decided in any particular context.

We may, let us next say, think of induction in the computer context as indentifiable with the collecting in some form of conditional probabilities; we must now go beyond this to the more general interpretative statements which we know are also a vital part of induction. Look at some more examples:

"All cats are black" (1)

"All cats meet in Hereford in May" (2)

"All Irish people are born with two eyes and two ears" (3)

etc.

Our computer methods are adequate to this new purpose, since, if we use the semantic rules as follows:

Cats = a, black = b, Hereford = c,
May = n, Irish people = e, eyes = p, ears = r;

then we have sentence forms

a.b (4)

a.c.n (5)

e.p(2).r(2) (6)

etc.

These are trivial examples in over simple form (since they are subject to analysis by the predicate calculus), but serve to remind us that properties (and individuals) occur together in space or time as a basis for an induction. Our problem is now not only to develop methods for performing an inductive check, but also to develop methods for both expressing that induction in language, as well as interpreting other people's inductions in language. We must now look at the matter as a linguistic problem akin to that previously discussed by the present author (George, 1968). This takes us into the field of what we have called "non-sequential analysis".

Heuristic Methods

In discussions on thinking, we tend to consider the creative activity of deriving hypotheses or "seeing" appropriate deductive inferences that can be made in a problem-solving context. Whereas simple learning, like habit formation, can be thought of as occurring sequentially, we do not as frequently draw attention to the sequential processes in thinking or problem-solving. Perhaps the main reason for this is that whereas we may acquire the information as a temporally ordered process, the basis for such inductions as are made are usually independent of how the information is collected. Peirce (1931-5) said a great deal about this whole process in his writings and asked (unlike Popper who took it to be random process) how we were able to hit upon plausible hypotheses so effectively. The answer as in Reichenbach's (1938) "context of discovery" lies in insight based on accumulated collective experience. Such experience lying as much in description as in aquaintance.

A detailed study of what they called creative thinking by Newell, Shaw and Simon (1958) dealt with those aspects of problem-solving which required originality, as opposed to explanation, definition, remembering, etc., all of which come into the day-to-day problem-solver's activities. This latter being more the "context of justification" of Reichenbach.

The work of Newell, Shaw and Simon has great importance because they were able to show by heuristic programming techniques how short cuts in routes to goals (solutions) could be achieved by assumptions that facilitated the problem-solving process. We shall be returning to their work in Chapter 7 in the field of logic.

The manner of their approach is simple enough in principle, and we can illustrate the method which is called heuristic. If you wish to avoid the combinatorial explosion, as would occur for example if you considered every possible move in chess, you need hypotheses, or *ad hoc* rules and this is exactly what heuristics are.

Newell, Shaw and Simon also refer to stages in problem-solving involving incubation, illumination, etc, and these can all be simulated in some measure on the computer; all part of the discovery process. They also used solution generators, trial-and-error learning and then the formation of hypotheses, often involving working backwards from the solution (deducing subgoals from goals) where the problem was, for example, to find some proof, and they used verifying processes to justify their steps.

Some problem-solving research differs from that of Newell, Shaw and Simon in its use of heuristics. They were concerned with simulating principles for theorem-proving, and they use the human-like means of substitution, etc ... We are more concerned with the delineation (through language) of a problem for which appropriate heuristics have to be sought (hypothesis formation by induction) and/or adapted to the needs of the situation. Newell, Shaw and Simon simulated the operations of the human problem-solver in the program GPS, but Samuel (1963) on the other hand synthesised his heuristics by a set of polynomials and thus the parameters could be adjusted by experience from which appropriate heuristics were, in effect, selected. We shall say more about Samuel's CHECKERS (draughts) playing system a little later. Tonge (1963) used heuristics to solve aspects of the line balancing problem, and the adaptivity of the heuristics was essentially pre-planned; a somewhat similar procedure was followed by Burstall (1966). As distinct from these piecemeal efforts, we wish to see heuristics in use in all these ways, operating together, and heuristic generation to occur as appropriate to the solution of a problem.

From the computer viewpoint, heuristics are like sub-routines in a computer program, and they can be edited or strung together to form new heuristics, or what have been called *plans*, (Miller, Galanter and Pribram, 1960).

We must remember to distinguish between adaptive and non-adaptive heuristics. This in fact reflects a distinction that is similar to that between "taking a set of hypotheses" as opposed to testing and, if necessary, modifying those hypotheses as a result of circumstances; or indeed even setting out "new" hypotheses. Relatively fixed numerical heuristics are already commonplace in computing; they include all mathematical models, such as those used in fields such as Sales Estimation or Market Research. The ability to adapt heuristics implies the ability to construct new plans which in turn implies the ability to set up and re-organise sub routines in computer programs.

It is in these terms that we see problem-solving as a synthetic undertaking. Problem-solving is the ability to construct or reconstruct sub routines to solve problems and learn new sub routines by experience as circumstances demand; this is done especially by way of (verbal) description.

This synthetic approach would be of limited value were it not regarded as experimental; the whole purpose is to write and run such computer programs to discover the extent to which the programs do in fact synthesise, *perhaps* even simulate, the conditions in which we are interested, when trying to understand human behaviour.

We must be careful now to distinguish the proces of discovering an induction (e.g. by counting, constant conjunction, Bayesian processing) and the inductive statement itself (the inductive generalisation). The first is a type of curve-fitting or pattern-recognition operation and we must distinguish between the method by which we arrive at the "best fit", and the formula which we actually adopt as a result of the fitting. This is rather like our rough distinction between sequential analysis (collecting the data) and non-sequential analysis (formulating the heuristic). Now let us turn briefly to the problem of induction.

A Note on Induction

To make our underlying assumptions clearer, it should be said that we are assuming that inside the organism we have the apparatus of language, which is built up through experience, like other learned skills. We assume that language, as we grow up, is increasingly used to refer to our experiences of the external world, and operates together with certain "physiological" or "psychological" occurrences called "images", and following Wittgenstein (1922) we can come near to identifying language with thought, (we would not actually go quite so far, but nearly so, for all practical purposes).

Language is both a description of, and also part of, since it is self-referential, the internal conceptual model (schema); we have an internal model of the world about us and of ourselves, and we as humans are assumed to be aware of words and images often in complex associations. At this level the "mental processes" are to be thought of as fairly crude and to depend on associative principles. But underlying these molar "mental processes" are the molecular processes which make it possible. In talking this way of schemas, we have to be careful not to assume that this is exactly how human's operate since the notion of "internal models" (even maps) may be an analogy rather than in any sense, a reality.

The molecular processes are all assumed to be activities of the nervous system. We are certainly unaware of our neurons firing in their various complex patterns, but there is reason to believe that this is what is actually occurring. The effect of these complex firing patterns is to suggest a mechanism which worked as if it were a sophisticated mathematical process; it seems reasonable therefore to try to both synthesise and simulate it. We can here use these same mathematical processes for both operations; they have become, in effect, descriptions of a fraction of the nervous system. The nervous system at this stage could be called 'conceptual' rather than real, although this is a difference which can only be one of degree.

We shall not discuss deduction (Raphael, 1964; George, 1966; Darlington, 1960) and the various work in theorem-proving until Chapter 7, since the problem of deduction in all its forms (classical and otherwise) will be already sufficiently understood to enable anyone to grasp a large part of its relation to thinking; such an argument though hardly applies to induction. We now turn to relatively straight forward processes of learning and their modelling.

Learning Models

Learning then we shall think of as adaptive behaviour (change of beliefs) based upon perception and memory, and often involving "insight". The notion of learning models and systems is to be interpreted in the same broad fashion as we have associated with the whole range of cognitive activities. In other words, we cannot dissociate *learning* from perception, thinking, problem solving, language and logic: they are all interrelated and overlapping and are only wholly distinguished (unreally) at the level of language. This is especially true if we are thinking primarily of human learning, and this is reflected by the fact that the four main chapters of Book 2 of this book spill over into each other from time to time.

The problem of learning was thought by experimental psychologists to be absolutely basic to their work for many years and during the period of early battles between Behaviourists and Gestaltists, we had various emphases placed on stimulus-response behaviour, holism, instinctive behaviour patterns and other variables once thought to represent key issues in learning.

The Neo-behaviourist theorists of the earlier days were in many ways too close to the animal world of the Norwegian rat, and only Tolman, among them, might be said to have paved the way for a theory that might be used to account for *human* learning. Suffice it that cyberneticians, who were watching events with special interest, tended to argue on one hand that they themselves were concerned with machine learning and on the other that if they needed to acquire a psychological mantle then perhaps the Tolman "expectancy theory" might prove to be the best bet.

Another theory of learning was developed (George and Handlon, 1955, 1957) which was concerned primarily with human learning. This theory also took account of philosophical considerations and tried to supply an account of learning that lent itself to ready formalisation down to the level of automata, logic or even hardware models. We shall repeat here only the basic ideas involved, since it has already been discussed in some detail.

The George-Handlon theory was based on the notion of a *belief* (a disposition to respond in an *if - - - then...* manner). This is something like a Tolman type expectancy and much like what we normally mean by 'belief' in everyday terminology; it could also be regarded as a state, rather than a disposition (Armstrong, 1973) and sometimes will be. Such beliefs are acquired by the association of events which might be either of a stimulus-response or stimulus-stimulus, or even of a stimulus-response-stimulus kind. The making of beliefs is dependent upon appropriate primary or secondary motivation which acts as a selector function. Beliefs are stored as memories and are confirmed or otherwise by experience of a stimulus-response variety. Beliefs are also tested for internal consistency and some beliefs are dropped and others formed as a result. Beliefs are also translated into language and related to each other by logical considerations. Such a model of human learning we shall now try to translate into precise models - automata and the like.

In our pursuit of learning in terms of "machines" we need to say something more about heuristic and adaptive programs, since by such means we see the way to provide learning by machine means. We have already discussed heuristic and algorithmic methods so we shall proceed directly to our application. It must be remembered that adaptivity is a necessary (if not sufficient) condition for learning to take place.

One important point we must certainly make and that is with respect to the degree of adaptability of the heuristics used. Any rule of thumb, hypothesis, etc. could be applied rigidly, but in general we shall want to use heuristics (and write heuristic programs) which are adaptive and change as the relevant circumstances change. We can clearly have adaptive computer programs which are not heuristic and we can also have heuristic computer programs which are not adaptive. But before we discuss existing heuristic computer programs, let us briefly discuss adaptive programs, and before we discuss adaptive programs, we should make one further point. This point is illustrated by scientific method.

We formulate an hypothesis H_1, or a series of hypotheses $H_1, H_2, \ldots, H_n$ and these can apply to some selected aspects of our environment. If *all* aspects of that part of our environment are completely predictable (and understood) we say we have learned 'all' about it. This means we need learn no more and our problem has changed from an inductive to a purely deductive one; i.e. $H_1, H_2, \ldots, H_n$ implies all we wish to ask about, and it does, as a result, supply all the answers we need deductively. By close analogy with the above we may say that a *complete* set of heuristics is the same as an algorithm. Normally, therefore, we expect to be using incomplete sets of, or even single, heuristics. We shall now move on to discuss adaptive programming.

Before doing so, let us remind ourselves that we are also asking ourselves what is happening in the nervous system while all these adaptive processes are taking place. We can guess that, in general, the whole of the brain is involved and that certain areas more than others (this especially applies in the form of cortical localisation) and that some activities are highly specialised (e.g. visual and other sensory activities have fairly specific input-output areas in the cortex). The question is what changes occur in the brain to match our changes in experience? Now, after that brief aside, let us return to adaptive programming.

Adaptive programs have been written for various purposes, and we shall examine briefly one such program; it is concerned with playing 'noughts-and-crosses' (OAX) (George 1962, 1967). We first assign the numbers 1-9 to the squares of the noughts-and-crosses board. This numbering seems to raise a problem. There are many convenient ways of carrying it out and the actual choice affects the statement of a won game. However, this is not important since, provided the computer is told which game is won and which is lost, it will still be able to learn to play the game regardless of the manner in which the board has been numbered.

The problem of numbering the board is, though, of some importance if we want to program the computer to learn *anything*, not merely to play one particular game. Every game is describable in terms of an array of "squares" which can be numbered, and we must be able to extend the notion of a *game* to cover what is usually regarded as learning. That is, the point of the game becomes simply to learn the nature of the environment, and indeed the game and the opponent(s) constitute the whole environment.

Whatever the game it is playing, if it is to be able to learn, the computer must be able to evaluate the final position in a game, as this gives confirmation or disconfirmation, in terms of which any organism is selectively reinforced. This is the basis of 'discouraging' moves that have led to a loss and 'encouraging' those that have led to a win; this is the central problem of reinforcement; it is known in psychology as Thorndike's Law of Effect.

In the game of OAX, the state of the board constitutes the whole of the environment of the computer. The computer's task is to learn the tactics that enable it to win, assuming that it is given direct instructions as to how to fill up the squares initially. It will then need to classify ways of carrying out this process of filling up the squares. To say that some ways are called 'winning' and others 'losing' implies the existence of concepts in the computer, and although this is, of course, the ultimate goal, it is better to state for the present that when the number 10 is punched at the end of a game, the moves of that game are discouraged; and when the number 11 is punched, the moves are encouraged. The number 12 represents a draw and, in general, will leave the 'tactical values' unchanged.

Each game of OAX consists of not more than nine moves. The registers of the computer must be used so that the order in which moves are made is recorded with the outcome. Associated with each such order there must be a value number (v_i; $i = 1, 2, \ldots$), representing the tactical values referred to above, which increase or decrease according to the outcome of the particular game. Taking this value number, we could add 1 for a win, subtract 1 for a loss, and leave it unchanged for a draw, or use any more sophisticated weighting that seems suitable. We do not need to take all the moves of a game together and give a value to that sequence; rather we shall want to break the game down into sub-sequences. For example, we could take three moves, starting with the opponent's move, followed by the computer's own move, followed in turn by the opponent's; or we could take five successive moves similarly alternating between the computer and its opponent. The strategy the computer adopts is simply to select those moves, from all the alternative possibilities, which have the highest value number.

If the aim is optimal learning, then the computer will record and use both its own and its opponent's moves. It is clearly necessary to keep a separate record of the complete set of moves making up a game, so that it will be possible to decide whether the moves were 'good' or 'bad'. In the generalised learning situation this is equivalent to (analogous to) saying that we cannot tell whether a hypothesis is good or bad (i.e. true or false) until we have tested it and seen the outcome. At that stage we are involved in adaptive heuristics.

Our adaptive program is intended to show that the computer can learn the tactical rules of the game after having been told the actual rules. The division between these is somewhat arbitrary, however, and it is important to note that the actual rules of the game can themselves be learned, provided the computer is able to watch the game being played, or has a sample of games fed into it for analysis into its component values; this implies the use of the computer as a sequential analyser of a stochastic kind.

For programming convenience and for purposes of illustration, the board will be numbered in the following way;

8	3	4
1	5	9
6	7	2

With this arrangement each row, column or diagonal adds up to 15. Now the game of OAX can be described as a game of playing in turn, the winner to be the first player to select three numbers that add up to 15. In terms of this numbering, the tactical rule is to check the board state to see whether two numbers have already been selected by one of the players, such that there exists a third number, not yet selected, which will collectively add up to 15. If so, then this number should now be selected either to win the game or to stop the opponent winning.

A new problem is now encountered. The times taken by the input and output of the computer will be very great as compared with the time taken up by computation, and a comparatively enormous delay will be involved in waiting for its human opponent to make his move. This problem is avoided by dividing the computer into two parts, which we will call A and

B, as was done by Oettinger (1952). A is programmed with all the rules and the tactics while B is given only the rules and has to learn the tactics by playing the game. In the illustrations which follow, A is the O player and B is the X player. Games and portions of games are described by strings of numbers, naming the squares of the board in the order in which they are filled. For example, 5/8/4 means that A begins by placing an O in the centre square of the board, then B places its X in the top left-hand corner, and then A places an O in the top right-hand corner. We next see a series of games played, assuming that originally randomly chosen tactical probabilities (values) were attached to the registers. Let us suppose that these are, after some time, as follows:

For fixed first move 5 for A, possible second moves for B are:

5/1/(7,8),
5/2/(0,0),
5/3/(3,4),
5/4/(3,11),
5/6/(7,32),
5/7/(13,29),
5/8/(40,52),
5/9/(26,40).

The last pair of numbers in each string is an ordered pair of random numbers constituting a probability. Thus p_{max} for the above table is (7,8) and therefore implies the use of move 1 by B if A moves in to 5. If, for the sake of illustration, we assume a fairly regular pattern of play by A, where L stands for lost by B and D for drawn, the following games may result:

5/8/4/9/6/L,
5/8/4/2/6/L,
5/8/4/6/1/9/3/7/D,
5/6/8/2/4/3/1/1/9/7/D,
5/8/4/2/6/L.

This table shows the independently-kept record of a series of five representative games. After this point, the game remains constant if played consistently. Exactly the same process occurs for A varying tactics, although it takes much longer to reach an equivalent stable state. We find that B can easily perform the operations described and quickly learns the tactics, after which it never loses unless A changes its tactics. But even then the time will come when, for all possible tactics by A, B will never lose a game, and this is so because the game has an algorithm which B can discover. At this point B is said to have acquired an *algorithm* for OAX.

B never, of course, finishes up with exactly the same statement of the tactics as had been provided for A. A plays on a purely deductive basis, while B behaves in accordance with the maximum values of the tables in store; the overt behaviour though becomes exactly the same, except for a possible difference in lead time prior to choice of move. Neither party can reasonably be said to show 'insight', since there is not yet any possibility of transferring the results to a new situation. For this transfer to become possible, the computer must retain the experience of playing OAX, and must be allowed to learn at least one other 'sufficiently similar' game. This point is related to one made in the first section of this chapter, where we said a 'complete' set of H's makes an algorithm. In our present program we need a *language* to formulate our H's to supply the algorithm as it was supplied to for the purposes of the above games. The computer must also be able to generalise its results.

An example of how such a generalisation may be achieved leads us to consider a game with an alternative assignment of numbers to the squares of the board, as follows:

1	2	3
8	9	4
7	6	5

with A continuing to make the first move and choose the centre square, the following games might occur:

9/1/2/3/6L,
9/1/2/4/6L,
9/1/2/5/6L,
9/1/2/7/6L.

On examination of these games, we can already see that the second move of B must be determined by the second move of A. Adopting, for convenience, a cyclic form of numbering, so that 11 is the number for example, a general principle can be stated. This is that all sequences of moves which follow the starting move of 9 should, from B's point of view, have the general form

$$9/m/n/(n + 4)$$

if they are not to be losing for B.

This principle, which can be extended to all moves of the game, is completely general and eventually states an algorithm (sequence). The computer is able to make this type of generalisation provided that it can recognise numerical differences and state such general mathematical forms, and these prerequisites must either be provided in the program or separately learned.

This latter problem is closely related to heuristic generation which involves the use of induction. This is also related to the generality of the methods used in 'numbering squares' and the like, and may include random features such as the throwing of dice or the dealing of cards. It is important to emphasise yet again that much (most) of what people learn is learned by description (other people telling them) and not through their own direct acquaintance with the environment. Hence the brain is much concerned with linguistic-event relationships.

It should be noted that in our example of OAX we have made clear the importance of natural language. It is *the formulation of the stochastic tables in linguistic terms that represents* the vital step from playing the game purely adaptively to playing it heuristically. OAX has an algorithm, but we could, by giving the computer a sub-set of the total set of rules have played it heuristically.

In the same way we can extend both heuristic and algorithmic programs to include the programming of natural language, logic and other cognitive activities such as concept formation, perception, pattern recognition, thinking and problem solving. All of these are "first cousin too" (indeed directly dependent upon) the process of learning. Inroads have been made in some measure on all these problems and we subsume this under learning, but cannot in a brief account follow up all the vast range of implications (George, 1979). All that we have said so far is a simple conceptual background for tackling the much more complex games we are dealing with today.

The point about language as opposed to tree-searching is sometimes raised, as if the first meant humanlike and the second meant machinelike (as opposed to humanlike). It is a distinction in some ways reminiscent of

Reichenbach's (1938) distinction between the context of discovery and the context of justification.

The rest of our experiment in OAX, where A (playing from the decision procedure) plays against B (playing from Markov tables which are the equivalent of decision trees), we already found that B quickly learned to play "perfectly" *but differently* and they can be made identical if B has a language in which to translate his tree-search. This is easily done (and we did it) by supplying the necessary language in which to describe the tables. This makes B identical to A, where A's rules are of the form "if you have first move, move into centre square". This translates from a table (or tree) which shows maximum success with such a first move, so all that is needed is to describe this fact. This is a fairly simple problem which is made more difficult if B has to learn the language rather than be provided with it, but this places the problem in a new "ball park"; we know such languages can be learned.

Back to Definitions

Before we continue our pilgrimage we should note that there are some complications involved in those definitions and concepts dealt with so far, when viewed through philosophical eyes. They mostly refer to purpose and to thinking. We shall try here not to delve too deeply into *purpose* or into the equivalent teleological explanations (George and Johnson, 1984) but we must notice certain features. The goal-seeking activities are made explicit, which excludes for our present purpose those cases where a *motivation* exists to satisfy some *need* (not necessarily known) which invites the organism to purposive behaviour without knowledge of what goal is required and even whether such a goal exists or not. Here we are thinking of the explicitly stated goal for problem solving (Rosenblueth, Wiener and Bigelow, 1943, 1950) although usually at a "higher level" than the roulette ball automatically homing on a number or a missile on a ship or aircraft. In other words it may be assumed that learning is taking place and the explicit goal may actually change in the process of goal-seeking. So we must be fully aware of the intensive restricting of such problem solving domains, which has very little loss of generality, since the missing cases can easily be added if necessary.

The more vital problem is that of 'thinking', since as we said earlier we have to try to decide whether to regard thinking as identical with language (Wittgenstein, 1953) and always conscious, as it would seem to be if always identified with language, or whether we allow it to be both non-linguistic and unconscious. We have made the decision (Armstrong, 1973) to adhere to beliefs as being sometimes non-linguistic and sometimes unconscious, and since we shall regard thinking — at least among other things — as the manipulations of and expression of beliefs in terms of actions, so that it would seem to follow that whereas much human thinking is both conscious and linguistic, it need not be either. It also follows that we shall regard animals as being capable of thinking (this implies holding beliefs) although we shall not think of such thinking as linguistic in form. This whole matter will clearly need to be borne in mind in our next chapter on language and logic, since there is considerable interaction involved in all these matters.

Conception Formation

Saul Amarel (1962) developed what he thought of as an automatic theory maker. He took the propositional calculus as his problem solving domain and treated such problems as a testing ground for machine hypothesis making. The machine works on a heuristic basis and procedures, by inductive means, routines which can be used to encourage further learning. The problem can be short circuited, in that a heuristic may be used to "guess at" an answer before the tree-searching operation is completed.

Concepts for Amarel are, as they are for us, classes or class names. What is needed is, essentially, to know to what class an object belongs and something about its denotation and connotation. Hypotheses are generated in terms of the language used and problems dealt with, and these in turn produce specific information for the machine. These can be used in dealing with problems and finding their solution (e.g. theorem statement and proof, or a game and its algorithm) or dealing with associated features of the environment. Given the possibility of a range of information, such problems are posed to the machine as having to provide an accurate representation of a particular class of events. This entails, according to Amarel, the need for an information processing routine. These routines are built up from previously stored information and can be used to provide various patterns of routines (or plans) to solve new problems. Plans here are to be thought of in much the same way as in Newell, Shaw and Simon (1959), Miller, Galanter and Pribram (1960) and Hunt and Hovland (1960). The problem method here is explicitly that of induction.

Two limitations, or points of importance, to be noted in Amarel's work are:

1) There is no attempt in Amarel's system to link it with natural language, and

2) The problem or relevancy has not been considered, since he assumes all the subsets of descriptive elements with respect to any class or set are automatically relevant.

These two issues are not of course to be read as criticisms, since Amarel's work seems to be wholly in tune with what has been done subsequently in AI. The next system is due to Manfred Kochen.

Kochen's Model

Kochen (1960) developed an algorithmic procedure, as opposed to a heuristic one for developing hypotheses to solve problems. He thinks of a problem situation which is defined by the need to complete some statement of class membership, say, and for this purpose presupposes the objects (represented by so-called "trit" words) and their classification have already been decided.

Kochen is concerned with a machine that can, for example, perceive a red square, a blue circle, a blue square, a green circle and a green square and on being told that they were positive or negative instances of a concept, can say what the relevant concept is. To the above set of coloured squares and circles, if the answers to the problem of relevancy has been Yes-No-Yes-No-Yes, the relevant concept would be square. If the answers had been No-Yes-Yes-No-No, the relevant concept would be blue. This sort of operation is sometimes called concept learning, but the closeness of concept learning to hypothesis formation is here clear for all to see.

Although Kochen is providing an algorithm for the purpose, the inductive step of a "guess" can be made on limited evidence, as it indeed must in situations where the evidence is unlimited. This last case will arise often where the problem posed is in nature itself rather than in the form of a person asking a question.

Kochen has written most elaborate programs with complicated criteria of performance. The goals involved are more or less the same as with Amarel, although in the first phase the emphasis is on synthesis and not simulations.

The differences between Kochen's work and the ideas presented in this monograph are not great. However, the exclusion of natural language and the fact that a solution to any problem is known to be available among a finite set of possible solutions are two differences. Similarities exist in relation to consistency of information stored and the emergence of new hypotheses as the result of sufficient inconsistency.

A major difference in principle is that we hope to have a self-modifying and more adaptive processing procedure than Kochen, whose solution methods are fixed.

Hunt and Hovland (1960) have also produced an information processing model which is equivalent to that of Amorel (1962) in some respects as well as Kochen (1960) in some other respects. It rests on the assumption that

> ... a useful model of concept learning can be built by programming a procedure for constructing a decision tree.

Hunt and Hovland themselves feel that their work is especially consistent with that of Feigenbaum and Feldman (1963)p and banerji (1962).

Again we would note the following two points:

1) There is no natural language base included in the system.

2) There is no emphasis on the generating of new heuristics, or of the closely allied process of heuristic modification.

These programs go one step beyond the earlier OAX programs, but serve my purpose in showing the development of AI approach. We now turn from concept formation which is a platform for problem solving, as it were, to problem solving itself.

Problem Solving

In game-playing we have accepted the need for heuristics under the threat of the combinatorial explosion, and the obvious inadequacy of brute force in problem solving, the GPS program was the precursor of a group of problem solving programs such as GRAPH TRAVERSER (which we will return to later in the context of logic, partly because of its sequential nature), and also including ABSTRIPS and BUILD. These problem solvers are essentially means-ends analysers and are therefore very much goal-seeking or purposive in their operation.

ABSTRIPS was developed by Sacerdoti (1979) from STRIPS which was a plan-producing system which produced ordered sequences of actions and sub-actions, and stored and generalised on its plans as a result of experience. ABSTRIPS improved on STRIPS in being able to abstract in a hierarchial manner which allowed it to separate the important features at each level of planning ranging from the detailed to the most abstract. At the general level a plan is conceived and then subject to scrutiny at levels of increasing detail so that assumptions about path AB being available (and optimal if available) may be modified on the discovery that it is not available and thus AC used instead.

A more powerful system than ABSTRIPS, which is limited in its power to face complex interactive conditions, is BUILD (Fahlman, 1974). It is a system that must learn from observation in a non-interactive way, since it does not have actual bricks to manipulate, so cannot directly experiment with the environment. This is a serious limitation compared with a human being who can, of course, try experiments, even on a trial-and-error basis. Nevertheless, based on an extensive knowledge of mechanics has important, even vital, advantages.

The plans formulated by BUILD start with a list of blocks out of place and the list considers first those that are simplest to put in place. At the more complicated situations BUILD may have to give a great deal of thought to which blocks to move first without destroying the edifice. It has the capacity to foresee what will happen if it moves C to R, or D to M, say, in that it may have repercussions for J, K and L. Thus a false start can be retreated from and a new start made. It may also, as indeed many a human being, fail in the end and give up the task, which may indeed be insoluble. The degree of sophistication now reached by such AI programs, mostly in the last decade, is very considerable, but we must leave the matter at this point and return explicitly to problem solving in terms of game playing.

Game Playing

We have already said something about game playing, and such programs have long been a favourite for research in AI. This is so because they are well-defined, clearly require "intelligence" and range from simple (OAX) to complex (chess). It should be noticed that not all games have been of equal interest to workers in artificial intelligence. Most programs play *two-person zero-sum games.* Thus the computer usually interacts with one other player, who is the opponent. Some work though has been carried out on games of more than two persons, like bridge and poker. There is no loss of generality in the restriction to two-person zero-sum games however, as there are a large variety of such games. Computers, as we have seen, have been programmed to play OAX, sometimes in three dimensions, Ludo, Halma, Blackjack and Backgammon. Recently in this last game a computer program (Berliner, 1980) beat the world backgammon champion. Especially popular, both because of their challenging complexity and the relative ease of storing positions within the computer, have been board games, like go, draughts (checkers) and chess.

Central to most computer game-playing is the notion of a game tree. A tree is an abstract structure consisting of nodes and branches. Each node except the top one, called the root, is connected by a branch to exactly one node below it. If the root node is called level O, the nodes just below it are level 1, and so on, then the successors of a node at level n are the level n + 1 nodes connected to it by branches. A node without successors, which may occur at any level is called a terminal node. Each node in a game tree corresponds to one possible state of affairs (board state etc.) in the game, so for OAX we have Figure 1.

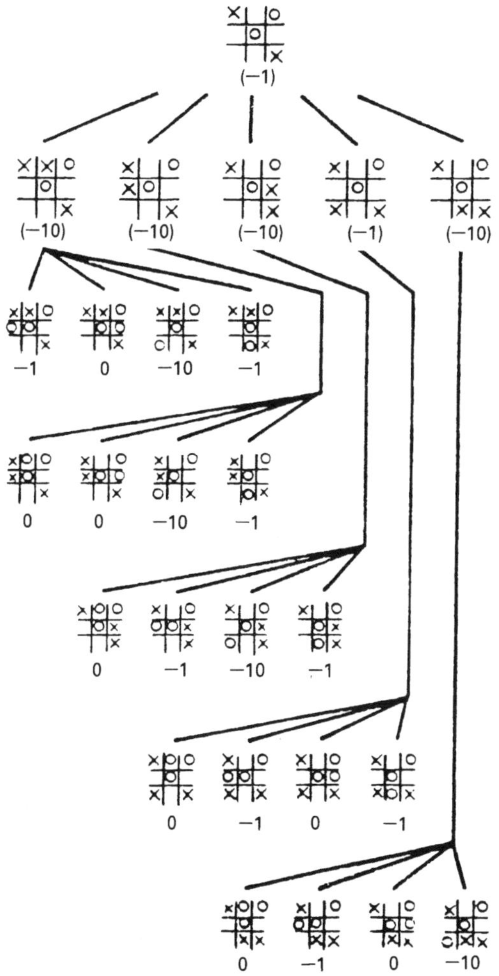

FIGURE 1 The choice of a move in noughts-and-crosses arrived at by applying the *static evaluation function* (or scoring polynormal) at depth two. This represents the process of looking two moves ahead without further exploration of the tree. (After Andrew)

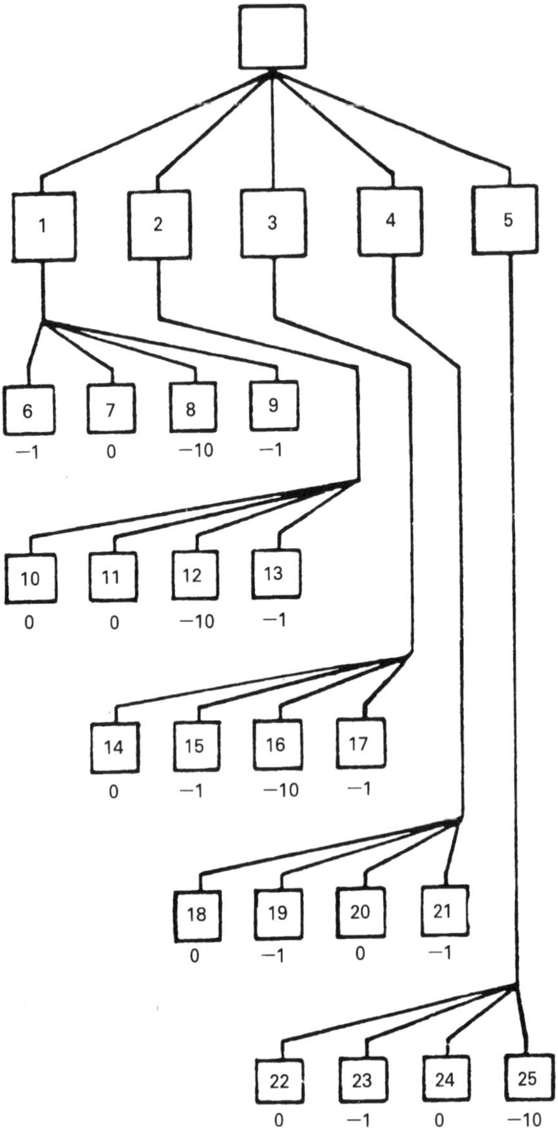

FIGURE 2 The tree of Figure 1 with the nodes numbered in order of generation in a depth-first search. (After Andrew)

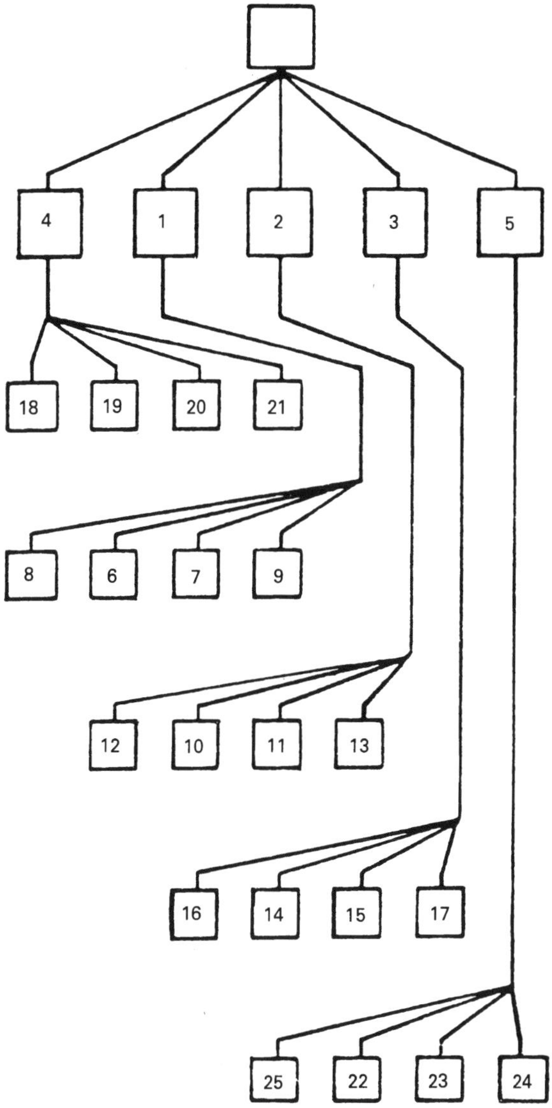

FIGURE 3 The same tree with the nodes rearranged to derive maximum benefit from the *alpha-beta technique*, as Figures 1 and 2. (After Andrew)

Now to return to our general description of such trees. Each branch corresponds to a (legal) move by one of the players. In draughts or chess the root node is the configuration of pieces on the board before either player has moved. There are 20 level 1 nodes corresponding to White's possible opening moves in chess, and 400 level 2 nodes since Black has 20 possible moves for each of White's first moves. A particular board state is represented at as many different nodes in the tree as there are distinct move sequences leading to it. So the tree is a "model" or "map" of the game, in our terms. The impossibility of playing chess algorithmically leads to the use of implicit game trees, stored as a set of heuristics or strategics allowing the production of all successors of a given node. The game playing program can then make explicit handleable portions of the tree in order to decide its next move. A mode of approach called Testrologic has been developed for this purpose as mentioned in Chapter 3, and we shall describe such methods again later. When implicit tree fragments are to be produced we require not only a generation procedure but also termination criteria which tell us when we have generated enough nodes. A frequently adopted termination criterion is that of the number of levels or depth to which the tree is to be generated. Another example of when tree expansion must terminate is at the end of the game. Among a variety of potential generation procedures the two usually employed are breadth-first and depth-first generation.

Breadth-first generation produces all successors of nodes, at the current level usually in a fixed order, such as left-to-right for each node before expanding the tree in depth. Depth first generation produces, a designated successor of the root, (extreme left or right) then the designated successor of that successor, and so on, until a termination criterion is satisfied. When termination occurs the procedure "backs up" to the next higher node which has not had *all* its successors yet generated. It then generates the next successor, and again carries on until termination. Figure 1 shows a small tree with the breadth-first node generation sequence in numerical order and the depth-first sequence in alphabetical order.

The generation procedures and termination criteria are the first two important components of an effective search procedure for game trees, but we also need some way of comparing nodes in order to choose positions which are favourable to solution finding. This is done by use of an *evaluating function.* These kinds of functions usually compute some weighted combination of features like piece advantage (e.g. one piece extra and a castle as opposed to a knight), potential captures, and mobility. This can be a complex matter because of its contextual nature. In general, there is no known procedure for producing an optimal evaluation function, although in many cases it can be found. Most game playing programs use so called

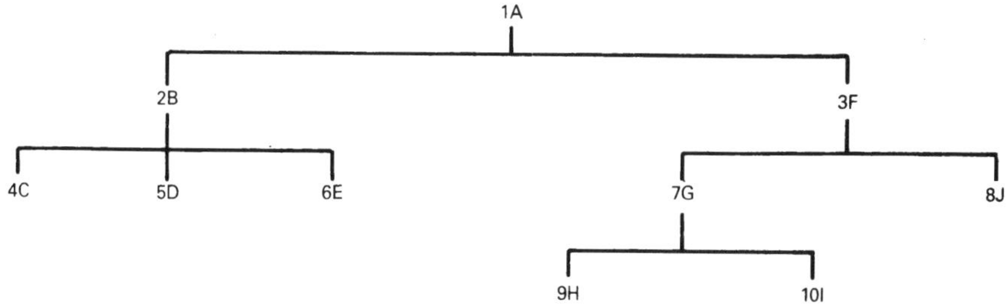

FIGURE 4 Breadth-first shown by (numbers) and depth-first shown by (numbers) and depth-first shown by letters as generation sequences. (After Samson)

backing up procedures, these compute the value of the current position on the basis of values of nodes further down the tree, such look-ahead procedures have great power and the most common example is the *minimax* backing up procedure.

Viewed from the standpoint of the player called MAX, say, for whom high values are advantageous, this procedure assumes that MIN, MAX's opponent, who seeks low values, will select alternatives which minimise MAX's possible gains, and vice-versa. Correspondingly, MAX will choose moves which maximise his own gains.

In what follows I have used an example due to Sampson (1976). Figure 5 shows a simple hypothetical explicit game tree which has been generated to a depth of three levels, when node letters show the depth-first sequence. The bottom level nodes have all been assigned values shown in parentheses after node letters. Values for the intervening nodes, which are shown in parentheses next to node letters, have been filled in by the *minimax* backing up procedure. Thus in going from level 3 back to level 2 and from level 1 back to level 0, where it is assumed that MAX will always choose the alternative giving the largest value. But in backing up from level 2 to level 1 MIN will attempt to minimise MAX's gain. The result of the backing up indicates that MAX should now move to the node S, assuring him a value of at least 10 three levels later. When combined with a depth first generation procedure, the *minimax* method yields a search procedure sometimes known as the depth-first minimax procedure.

The generation procedure, termination criteria, evaluation function, and backing up procedure from the bulk of the search procedure. The most important additional step is that of alpha-beta pruning; in what follows I have drawn directly on the work of Sampson (1976). To introduce this procedure, consider what happens on evaluation of node J in Figure 2. We

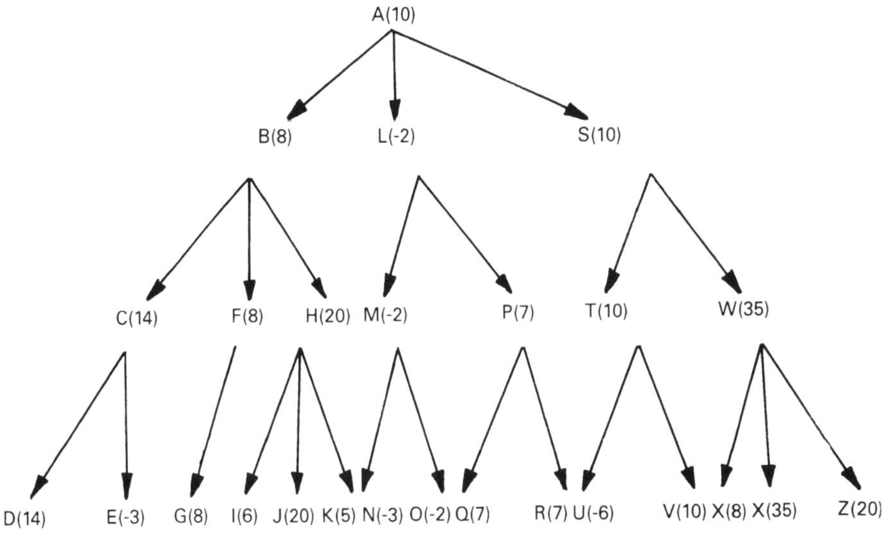

FIGURE 5 Fragment of a game tree showing minimax backing up.

know MIN will choose the smallest value from C,F and H if he has to move from B. And we know F has value 8. When we find a value of 20 for J we know H will have at least this value backed up, since we back up maxima for MAX's move. Therefore we need not look at node K. If its value is smaller than 20 it will not affect H; if it is larger, H will be an even more unlikely choice for MIN. So we can rule H out of consideration once we find the value of J to be greater than 8. The quantity 8 is the value of beta.

When backing up maximal values, beta is the smallest such maximum yet encountered among the descendents of a given node at the next higher leve. When a lower level node (like J) allows us to rule out further consideration of a higher level node (like H), we say that a beta cutoff has been encountered. Another beta cutoff occurs in Figure 5 at noe Y, when the value of 35 exceeds the beta value of 10.

Alpha is defined analogously to beta, as the largest minimum yet encountered in a subtree when backing up minima for MIN's move. Clearly MAX will not move so as to achieve a smaller backed up value. One alpha cutoff occurs in Figure 5. When alpha is 8 (based on B) the M value of −2 indicates that it is pointless to evaluate further successors of L, since it will be at least that small and thus never chosen by MAX. Although the savings from the use of the alpha-beta procedure are slight in this example, they can become very great in the case where each node may have dozens of successors. The number of alpha and beta cutoffs found in searching a tree can be increased by exloring the best moves first, and this leads to a modification to alpha-beta pruning called *plausibility ordering.* Here the first level nodes are rearranged so that the depth first search examines the most promising positions first. In order to rank the first order nodes in rough order of plausibility. This depends on applying the evaluation function at that level, without any backing up of values. In general, a shallow search may be carried out, with values backed up from some fraction of the depth used for the actual minimax values. This is a characteristic type of heuristic tree search and one that was used in both CRIB and RAFFLES, programs (Expert Systems) which we shall be discussing briefly later. It should be said that when comparing breadth-first and depth-first search, it is fairly evident from purely common sense considerations that the depth-first makes less demand on memory. On the other hand the depth-first search depends upon the use of termination criteria, so that too far is not gone on the wrong branch. This allows a combination of depth-first and breadth-first. This was made clear in our discussion above.

Samuel's Checker Playing System

I will examine next a checker (draughts) playing program which was first described in 1959 and then revised in 1967. Samuel has emphasised that he was using the game of checkers to explore general problems of effective machine learning. He employed a standard depth first minimax search procedure. His termination criteria were fairly complicated. At first, the entire group tree is explored to a depth of three levels. Further subtrees are then generated if either of the three following conditions are met

1) The next move is a jump,

2) The last move was a jump, or/an exchange is possible. Under restrictive conditions, and

3) Expansion of the tree can take place to a maximum depth of 20 levels.

Then Samuel's evaluation function was brought into operation. It was a linear combination of weighted numerical scoring parameters. Some 40 such plausible parameters were available, for use. Typical parameters measured features like piece advantage, centre control, exposure, mobility, and so on. At any particular time the program would be using some 15 or so of the available parameters, and these parameters could have their weight adjusted as a result of experience. As in our earlier OAX program, the fact that the game had been won or lost was explicitly noted.

Samuel's program and three types of learning schemes. The first is called book learning. In this method the program works through recorded games (the equivalent of a human being reading a book of old games) representing expert play, evaluating all possible moves from each position, and so on. During this reading, information is tabulated for each weighted parameter, providing experience to the program. The value of C which is a correlation function showing a re-weighting varying from +1 (complete correlation and an ideal move) to −1 (complete negative correlation thus a move to be avoided) for a given parameter can be used to adjust the weight of that parameter in a direction which will cause it to make a better contribution to the evaluation function.

The second learning scheme is called rote learning. In this method the program stores familiar board states together with their evaluation. This evaluation procedure can then either speed up the search (since the minimaxing need not be repeated) or extend the depth of the search. The first of three additional procedures was a means of storing board states for fast retrieval, and this was achieved by ordering states according to their relative frequency of occurrence and grouping them together by total number of pieces, presence or absence of Queens, etc. The second procedure eliminated redundancies in store positions through symmetry considerations. Finally there was a familiar promotion and relegation features (cf. league football) for getting rid of less useful procedures and board states, and acquiring better ones. This was achieved by the same sort of success-failure ratio as was used in the OAX program.

Samuel's third, and most important, contribution in his CHECKERS program, was a method of generalisation learning, and this, again as in the OAX program could make generalisations during ordinary play or by playing "in its mind's eye" as it were for both himself and his opponent. As a result of all this useless (or less useful) moves are eventually dropped and replaced by better ones. The principal changes that appeared in Samuel's later version of CHECKERS were in the areas of the search procedures and the evaluation functions. To replace simple depth-first minimax search Samuel introduced the alpha-beta technique combined with plausibility ordering based on shallow search. He also included the method of forward pruning and modified his termination criteria so that less plausible paths terminated more quickly. With respect to the evaluation function, it was realised that parameters interact. To deal with this he replaced the simple linear combination of weighted values by multilevel signature tables. We can follow Sampson (1975) and give a simple example of *signature tables.*

Suppose we have just three binary parameters which can sum to a net evaluation of 0,1,2, or 3. If the parameters are not independent then the three possible ways in which a sum of 2 may be obtained could reflect very different situations. We can take such interactions into account by constructing a table of all possible values of the function for each binary combination from 000 through 111. We can thus assign different evaluations to 110, 101, and 011, despite the fact that they all sum to 2. But as we increase the number of parameters it quickly becomes impractical to take all interactions into account. With just 8 10-valued parameters our table requires 100 million entries.

Samuel took the obvious step of reducing this evaluation by accepting an arbitrary partial set of what he called *signature* types and this led to six tables with 135 entries each, and used other reduction devices which we shall not discuss here, but merely say that it ignored the higher order interactions and all sorts of variations on this theme are possible, but it is essentially the same method as was used by Chapman (1959) to reduce a complete classification system to a handleable partial one.

Chess Playing Systems

A number of programs have been written for chess playing. Among the first were those written by Alan Turing, but because these very first ones were non-adaptive, the chess playing program played much like Turing himself played and since Turing's chess was fairly poor, so was the program's.

Next came some programs due to Claude Shannon (1950). He laid the basic plan for most subsequent chess programs and was the first to suggest many of the general principles of game playing we have already discussed. Among Shannon's ideas were evaluation by linear combination of weighted features, learning by modification of the weights, the *minimax* back up procedure, and tapered forward *pruning*. He also suggested that evaluations be made only for those available moves which would not "significantly" change the evaluation. As a result any exchange of pieces, should be followed through to completion before an evaluation was made. Shannon's plan was then to use different algorithms be employed for the opening, middle, and end games and then suggested that a chess program should be a simulation of the good chess player (cf. Clarkson 1963). Many of these ideas are directly comparable to those of Samuel's Checkers program.

Newell, Shaw and Simon's chess playing programs came next and their investigations came close to their interests in the simulation of human thought processes in LT and GPS. (see Chapter 6) and move generation is based on an ordered list of goals produced at the outset of each move by a preliminary analysis routine. The evaluation of the move is more goal-orientated than merely tree-searching, but this difference is only, at most, one of emphasis.

One difficulty in the Newell-Shaw-Simon Chess program was that because it generated a new list of goals at each move it failed to capture the continuity of human strategic thinking. Despite this the goal-directed approach to game playing was an important contribution and one which figured significantly in heuristic scheduling programs (e.g. SCHEDORD and SCHEDULER (George, 1974)).

In more recent chess playing programs mini-maxing and alpha-beta pruning still featured. Mini-maxing is more or less algorithmic in nature and alpha-beta is more nearly heuristic and with the avoidance of "brute force" methods has become more popular. Thus we find that one of the playing programs, written by Greenblatt and called MAC HACK, applies a sophisticated evaluation function to a small subset of possible moves, while another called TECH and developed by Gillogly uses a rough and ready scoring function, based solely on material difference, but attempts to explore as many nodes as possible. Since these two programs play about the same standard of chess it would seem there is a trade off in computer chess, between "brute force" exploration and sensitive, selective evaluation, or between algorithms and heuristics.

In recent years the bulk of AI work has moved away from chess and game playing to other forms of problem solving but is worth noting the reasons for chess popularity with AI workers (Winston and Brown, 1979).

1) Chess is a game that has a relatively small number of rules,

2) The chess pieces have a rich and complex interaction,

3) Brute force is combinatorially explosive and probably computationally intractable for world-champion play,

4) Plausible move generators (and evaluation functions) can be implemented that are capable of ordering reasonable moves by some criteria of evaluation,

5) A program can analyse upcoming disasters and thus gain insight into the current position,

6) A program can use "qualitative" as well as quantitative descriptions of positions,

7) A program can know a lot about chess. For example, it can have a book of openings and know about how to win with minimal mating material.

The properties needed to play chess well and the program possibilities entailed seem to fit many other problems quite removed from the domestic games. Electronics is one example, and we shall now look briefly at some of these programs.

Steps Towards Expert Programs

In principle solving electronics problems like chess is simple; there are only a few basic components whose mathematical description is straightforward. Yet the combination of components and their complex interaction is such that traditional numerical (algorithmic) techniques are impossible to use on any except the simplest circuits. Stallman and Sussman's electronics Expert program, EL, is able to handle configurations of electronic components and, for the purpose, uses qualitative descriptions in the form of modes of operation which is somewhat reminiscent of Bridgeman's Operational definitions. EL makes assumptions, and then if a contradiction is found, analyses the nature of the contradition to correct the assumption. This is a wholly characteristic method that is used very frequently in AI, in theorem-proving (see Chapter 7) and the like.

The use of situation-action rules, or if-then rules (or production rules) has tended to replace the minimaxing and tree searching so closely associated with the earlier game-playing work. The situation part of problem solving is a list of things to *do.* If situation-action rules are used to work forward from assumed facts to derivable conclusions, a system is said to be *chaining forward.* Alternatively, if rules are used to work backward from hypotheses to arrive at a list of facts that would confirm such hypotheses, then a system is said to be *chaining backward.* The earliest Rule-based Expert programs, which led to problem-solving Expert systems, were based on system-action rules are those of Feigenbaum and his associates at Stanford (1971, 1974, 1976, 1979). Among the best known are MYCIN, which is a simulation of a medical diagnostician and perhaps best known of all was HEURISTIC DENDRAL which was concerned with mass spectrogram analysis and being part of an analysis of organic chemicals. This was followed by META-DENDRAL which grew out of DENDRAL for a variety of reasons. It involved the automatic acquisition of domain knowledge, and they were interested in scientific theory formation as well as the understanding the need to break through the bottleneck in the acquisition of domain knowledge in the building of what is referred to as applications — oriented intelligent agents. Then we have another program PUFF which receives measured data other information regarding patents; its roll too is medical diagnosis.

There are other programs involved in the set, but the usual situation — action rule applies and Feigenbaum (1979) usefully summarises the main features of such rule-based systems in terms of:

1) Generating and testing

2) Situation-action rules

3) Domain-specific knowledge

4) Flexibility in data-base modification

5) Line of reasoning — a central organising principle

6) Many knowledge sources

7) Explanation — the line of reasoning explained into a language-user's convenience.

We turn next to problem-solving expert systems of a special purpose kind. Our example is called MECHO (Bundy *et al.*, 1979) is a program for solving problems in mechanics by a technique of meta-linguistic inference and using control search in natural language programming, as well as analysis of Predicate calculus, aided by model formation and algebraic processing.

The program demands that a formal model of a mechanical kind be constructed from statements in English such as "two loosely jointed rods (length a and b) are at right angles to each other when a is struck at right angles etc.

MECHO's general structure is illustrated by Figure 6:

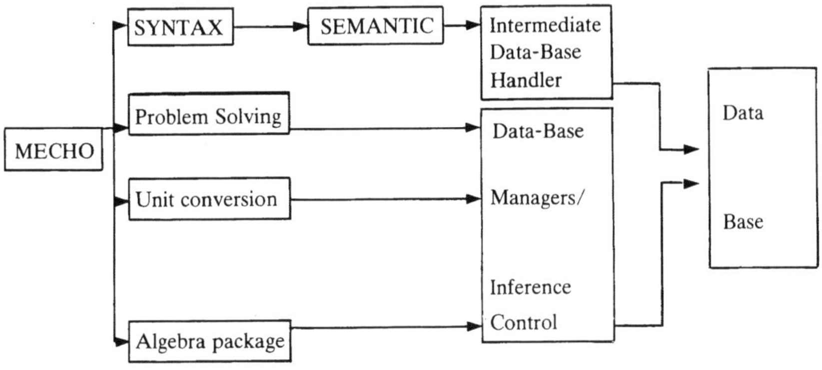

FIGURE 6 The program block structure of MECHO (after Bundy et al).

The English language description is translated into the predicate. The meaning is divulged after syntax-semantic analysis, where the syntax routing divides into clause and phrase syntax. Semantic analysis rules out unlikely syntactic choices.

For the problem "given two particles of mass b and c are connected by a light string passing over a smooth pulley, we need to find the acceleration of the particle of mass b". This leads to assertions as follows:

isa(period, period 1)
isa(particle, p1)
isa(particle, p2)
isa(String, s1)
isa(pulley, pull)
end (s1, end 1, right)
end (s1, end 2, left)
midp (s1, midpt 1)
fixed — Contact (end 1, p 1, period 1)
fixed — Contact (midpt 1, pull, period 1)
mass (p 1, mass 1, period 1)
mass (p 1, mass 2, period 1)
mass (s1, zero, period 1)
coeff (pull, zero)
accel (p 1, a 1, 270, period 1)
accel (p 2, a 2, 2, 90, period 1)
measure (mass 1, b)
measure (mass 2, c)
sought (a 1)
given (mass 1)
given (mass 2)

and then other schema can be cued to give any extra information needed.

The problem is then to decide what to do (e.g. solve equations) and combine input assertions with general facts and inference and rules to clarify goals.

This work is close to that of PROLOG (Pereira *et al.*, 1978) and is meta-linguistic as opposed to having a single (object) language in which to solve the problem. The influence of Weyrauch's (1979) FOL system and Davis and Buchanon's (1977) TEIRESIAS system are both evident and the general emphasis on the explicitness of flexibility of meta-linguistic systems. These have greater generality than one-level systems in controlling the use of knowledge.

Some Guides to Building Expert Systems

In building an expert problem solver, it is always necessary to decide the knowledge the program should have and how that knowledge should be expressed and in particular the following factors are listed:

1) Clusters of knowledge. By clustering facts together, a particular problem solver can say "apply this cluster" rather than having to know exactly which fact to use.

2) Levels of abstraction. In addition to reasoning with chunks, experts also need to reason about larger, more abstract chunks of information.

3) Qualitative analysis. Some kinds of abstraction involves qualitative knowledge, this is bound up with the need to make deductions at the highest levels of abstraction.

4) Meta-knowledge. In addition to being able to reason about the problem domain, we need to reason about the reasoning process; this was true especially of META-DENDRAL and MECHO.

Other Heuristic Expert Systems

The name expert systems has been coined relatively recently to operate retroactively, to depict various computer programs that have been designed in broad terms to *solve problems.* The term "solve problems" will be used in its broadest sense to include diagnosis, the formulation of plans, decision making and so on, and includes or may include any of those features already discussed such as tree-searching, mini-maxing, alpha-beta pruning, or the resolution principle (which we discuss in Chapter 7) and involves the setting up of assumptions and the search for contradiction. There is, even among this apparently diverse set of activities, a commonality that merits our attention. But in this section I shall be primarily concerned with those relatively simple expert systems that deal with corporate strategy, in its various forms, within the business field. With something like a problem solving capacity (including the variety of methods mentioned above) available and also artificial (near natural in the case of English) languages available for conversation (asking and answering questions at the very least) and the ability to draw inferences of every kind from classical logic to practical reasoning, we have the basic ingredients of an expert system.

There are already in existence whole sets of well known expert systems some of which we have already mentioned (Mitchie, 1979). Among the best known of which are DENDRAL, PROSPECTOR, MYCIN, MECHO and PUFF. But we shall be saying something later of these. I have myself been involved particularly in three such systems GOAL (a simple purposive logical system), (George, 1974) SCHEDULER, and CRIB, and am currently operating on expert systems which are particularly concerned with corporate strategy (George, 1982).

GOAL is a program for practical reasoning. A goal is specified by the end state and the method of reaching the end state is specified on a step-by-step basis. The only question is to the method of weighting the steps to make choice possible at each point. This can be done as a result of experience: A, is more often associated with B_1 than B_2, and the generalisation on this for a whole sequence A,B, . . ., N will produce a Markov net. Alternatively we may have *a priori* probabilities based on "design considerations" with respect to the complete (or part of the) "set up". Now to summarise very simply, the central features we start with:

$$A_1 \supset B_1, \text{ let us write this } A_1IB_1$$

and

$$A_1IB_1IC_1ID_1IG$$

then A_1IG
where G is the goal. So given choices

$$A_1IB_1OB_2OB_3OB_4IC_1OC_2I\ldots IG$$

where O is 'or' in the exclusive sense then it is the relative weighting which will determine the goal route taken. Since multiple choices

$$A_1IB_1OB_2OB_3OB_4$$

can always be reduced to binary choices we can have

$$(A_1IB_1OB_2)\ A\ (A_2IB_3OB_4)$$

where A is 'and', and the whole process can be put, as we shall see, into testrologic form. This in essence is GOAL; all it needs now is a process AB, . . . to control.

SCHEDULER was concerned with heuristic scheduling for a production line, and the problem here was to maximise ordered throughput and minimise cost (and waste). This starts with a priority ordering of contracts, so the most important client is dealt with first (or some such principle) and then follows the filling up of the schedule so that as far as possible no machine was not fully occupied and the machine's state change (which may be involved) was minimised.

This was done by use of both forward and backward scheduling over a period such as a week so that give m/amount of As(mA), n amount of Bs(nB), and so on, we could form a schedule in the light of available capacity, so that given rA capacity, where r = m/2 say, then we can load all As for the week, is sB and S = 2n, then we can load all B, subject in both cases that for C,D,... there is no change of state needed for rA and sB. We continue, ensuring maximum number of orders are completed each week, to "juggle" the schedule without necessarily achieving an optimal. If the program involved cutting materials (a Trim Loss program) then we should, of course, be concerned with minimising waste. So far we have dealt only with the forward schedule. The backward schedule is responsible for maximising completed jobs, and will work its method of compromise against the forward schedule and with the *delivery date*, and priorities in mind.

The SCHEDULER experience involved a great deal of time being spent on knowledge elicitation. The human being who scheduled in fact, was quizzed in detail about the way he did his job and he was watched doing it and eventually submitted virtually to psychoanalysis, in order to make explicit his *modus operandi.*

The next expert system to be mentioned is CRIB (Computer Retrieval Incidence Base) and this operated when faults were discovered on any machine, but rather especially on the computer. The symptoms were first reproduced if possible, intermittant faults presented a specially difficult problem since a reconstruction was made and then a hypothesis was formed on the information from the data base; this represented a model of the "patient" computer and sets of symptom-fault pairings, derived either experimentally or *a priori.* In general, experience took too long to gain — especially on modern computers — to provide an adequate base.

Heuristic methods were used to discover symptom-fault pairings and thus determined the route to be taken down the decision tree. This led to the location of the fault found, or a retreat and re-entry to the tree where the fault was not found. The "package" in the case of modular construction, was then replaced and sent for repair. CRIB works adaptively, so that the symptom-fault pairings can change their weightings as a result of accumulated experience on that particular "patient" machine (computer).

It goes without saying that this type of heuristic diagnostic program, can be used in medical diagnosis (e.g. PUFF). A more recent version of CRIB called RAFFLES (Addis, 1980) is also in existence, but the differences between CRIB and RAFFLES are not so great as to merit a discussion of RAFFLES within this relatively brief survey.

Let us now cast the net wider, since for any corporate plan there must be, apart from an assessment of the past and present, some forecast of the future state of the economy and the market place. This introduces a new uncertainty. But in spite of this additional uncertainty the only additional features required are in the form of additional hypotheses in the system.

There are a number of questions that must be asked about the methods to be used in this broader case. The use of testrologic (S. Foundos, 1980) has been of considerable help in the context of expert systems and has been used in studies of investment, acquisition and diversification, among many other disciplines. We shall outline the methods used and give a specific indication of the testrologic features with one part of the investment problem.

First of all then we proceed to state the problem in clearcut terms. What is our goal? What are we trying to achieve? In the case of investment let us say that it is maximising capital gains (as opposed say to maximising income), and let us think of the investment as being on the stock market (as opposed to the context of acquisition), and then let us say that the problem is to locate a field of activity (government stock, heavy industries, etc) in the future in such a manner as to yield large capital gains. This choice of fields is our first problem: in what kind of shares should we invest?

The first and most important problem (George, 1984) is the one involving forecasting the future of the demand in the economy, including especially the possibility of the occurrence of certain events, e.g. joining the EEC, a local war, or even a change in the law of any of the countries involved can wholly change the picture. There are a number of things which need to be considered and any decision will ultimately, as well as initially, be tested for its "sensitivity" to such changes. The probability of such events must also be considered. Let us assume that given this sort of information and the weighted forecasts for the relevant future, then we can infer which are the likely fields for investment. They may be spread over quite a few (the optimal may vary with the size of investment) different shares.

The plain fact remains however that within the field of activity, the important decision as to which share should be selected. We repeat roughly the same process now of conjoining the past, present and future. We set up hypotheses, draw inferences (by "practical or classical reasonings") and derive consequences which can be tested for sensitivity, or where more than one set of outcomes is derived, for comparison.

The processes can all be done in a variety of ways, but to be definite, and also to illustrate a method under current use, the hypothesis used will be embodied in the programming of the testrolog. Here the programming involves three important steps:

1) The wording and ordering of questions.
2) The nature of the questions.
3) The relative weighting of the answers.

In a sense, the programming is heuristic and the resultant program is algorithmic, in much the same way as a computer language (probabilistic say) would translate into machine code (deterministic).

A Testrologic Approach

To refresh the reader's mind about our earlier comment on testrologic let us here repeat the basic process. A decision tree of the conventional kind is most usually drawn as follows:

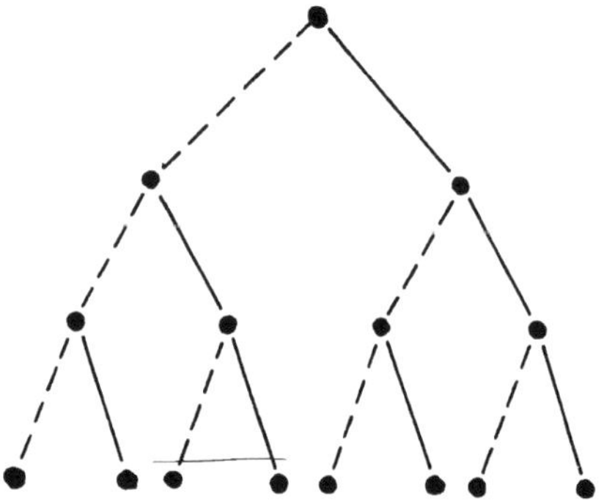

FIGURE 7 A conventional decision table drawn as a tree.

where ... represents Yes and ___ represents No, and the choice points are binary. A search of this sort of tree can be constituted in breadth or depth or, as is usual, some combination of the two. This sort of tree can also be put in tabulation. We find that trees with 2^n branches for large n are unwieldly and when the effective outcomes are substantially less than n, we can merge branches as follows:

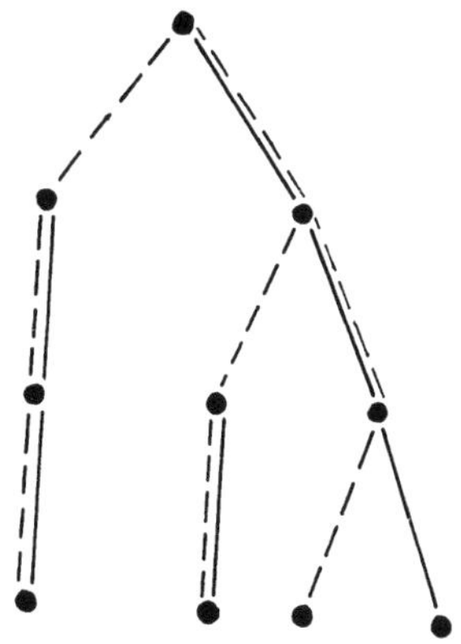

FIGURE 8 A testrolog type tree.

So for n = 3, we have 4 rather than 8 nodes, at the 3rd level and so the streamlining can be continued where --- means "either Y or N and we do not care which" and this most often means the question is not applicable. So for the set of Questions Q_1, Q_2, Q_3 above we might have:

Q_1 = Are you going to take a holiday this year?

Q_2 = Are you going abroad for your holiday?

Q_3 = Are you going to USA?

It is obvious that an answer of N to Q_1 eliminates any need to answer Q_2, which only applies to those who say Y to Q_1.

The use of testrologic in our Expert program will become apparent later, but in the meantime we can say that wherever practical logic (e.g. GOAL) can be used testrologic can be used as an alternative.

Apart from the use of logic whether "classical" or not to formulate hypotheses (mainly induction) and to derive their consequences (mainly deduction) in a goal-seeking situation, we must also add that all such systems can be made *adaptive* and the adaption can be built into the expert program. We should add finally that language is also available, so that the whole process can be described — questions answers and asked by both the expert program and the user. The use of natural language such as English would seem ideal for this purpose, but the complexity of translation from "free-idiom" English ultimately to a "machine code" is too complex and costly to make it worthwhile. As a result a form of conventionalised English is used and there are a number of such languages in the process of being built up. The originals included NAMER, BASEBALL, SIR, SAD

SAM (see Chapter 6) and now we have SHDLR and LIP and others (also see Chapter 6), which show increasing flexibility. The advantage of using language is obvious even though it may be a sort of "Pidgin" English. It at least allows the expert system to play its important role most easily as a specialist-reminder. The *spoken word* is also being researched and the spoken word is the subject of much current development involving a great dependence on phonology.

It should also be said that the scope and potential of expert programs is quite enormous and whereas they can obviously be used as "helpmates" it should be absolutely clear that they can also be used to carry through the whole process of decision making from beginning to end. They have already been used for many problems at many different levels, often very difficult problems.

Let us look at investment analysis (Clarkson, 1963) and more recent methods outlined by me (George, 1984)

We shall, as a beginning, use attributes;

Sales
Earnings
Cash Flow/Share
Profit Margin
Working Capital
P/E Ratio
Dividend Payout Ratio
Dividends per Share
Dividend Yield
Prices

and normally have records over the past ten years, so we have the average and then increase (or decrease) for each of nine comparitive years:

$$Y = \frac{x_i - x_{i+1}}{x_{i+1}}$$

where $i = 1 \ldots 9$, and x_i are the attributes, and average rate of change is given by Y. We can from this data calculate average rate of growth, etc for each company and compare each company with the average company in the relevant group.

The important point then arises as to the relative importance of our attributes, so that our hypotheses is that they have taken this or that order. We can then decide what attributes are crucial, what combination of attributes must necessarily be of sufficiently high standard, and in general how

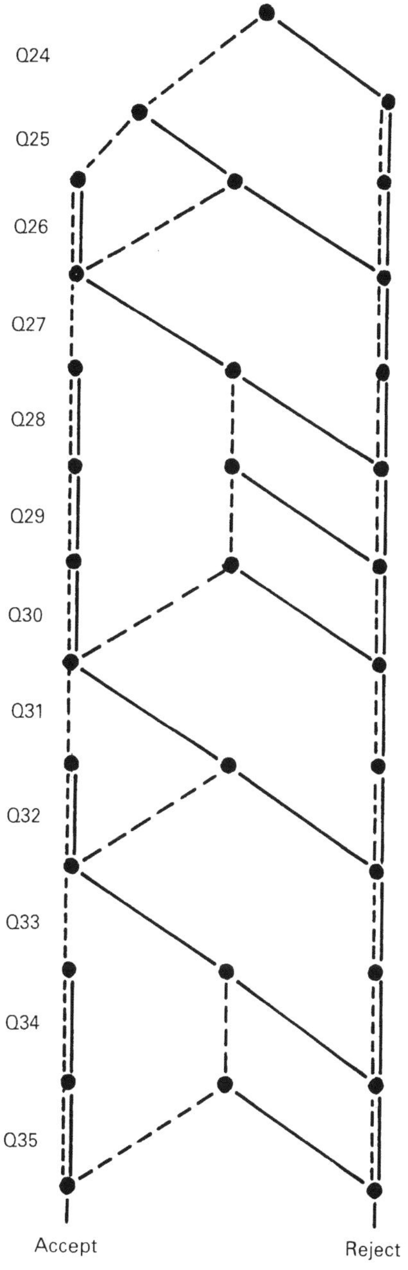

FIGURE 9 A Testrolog Tree for questions 24 to 35.

each company considered compares with the rest. The sort of questions to be asked are:

Q_1 = Are company's sales increasing?
Q_2 = Are company's sales average greater than industry's GTAI average?
Q_3 = Are company's earnings increasing?
Q_4 = Are company's earnings average GTAI?
Q_5 = Is company's cash flow/share increasing?
Q_6 = Is company's cash flow/share GTAI?
Q_7 = Are company's profit margins increasing?
Q_8 = Are company's profit margins GTAI?
Q_9 = Is working capital increasing?
Q_{10} = Is working capital GTAI?

and perhaps more. These then should be repeated for the same attributes as *forecasted.* Initially, and here we show the testrolog version, we have, when all else is decided and we have a list of "probables", the final decision to take. GTAI means "Greater Than Average for the Industry".

There are 23 questions in our version of the Clarkson System prior to this last stage, as they involve twenty questions as above (the ten repeated) plus three others on P/E and dividends; there could of course have been others, but these were hypothesesed to be sufficient.

The last stage is as follows:

Q24 Is mean growth past price >/20 per cent?
Q25 Is mean growth past earnings/share $>/K_1$?
Q26 Is mean growth past sales $>/K_2$?
Q27 Is F (growth earnings/share) 1 year $>/K_3$?
Q28 Is F (growth in sales) next year $>/K_4$?
Q29 Is mean growth in past cash flow/share $>K_5$?
Q30 Is mean growth in profit margins $>K_6$?
Q31 Is $y > K_7$?
Q32 Is P/E* < P?E by 10 per cent?
Q33 Is forecast dividend >/0?
Q34 Is forecast dividend = 0?
Q35 Is price >/10 per cent below average?

We need to choose levels for $K_1 - K_7$ to act as tests.

And now the relevant testrolog program:

Such methods are extremely powerful, whether testrolog is used or not, and we expect that the future holds enormous potential for such genuinely expert systems.

We shall be returning to a discussion of knowledge based and expert systems in Chapter 8, where we consider two particular examples in some detail.

In Summary

We have, in this chapter, built up progressively from simple to relatively complex systems. Some few years ago a large institution offered a prize to anyone who could write a computer program which *learned to play OAX* in the apparent belief that such a thing was impossible (not that they believed a computer could not be programmed to play the game, but that it could not be programmed to *learn to play* it).

Since then we have progressed through all sorts of domestic game-playing from draughts (checkers) up to chess and have developed heuristic methods so that today no one would question the possibility of a computer being programmed to learn to play chess and play it better, eventually, than any human player. All this has helped to clarify our psychological theories regarding learning and thinking, and sharpened our awareness of the need for greater semantic precision in our usage. It has also led on to more practical applications.

We now look at any and every problem — well defined or not — and think in terms of optimisation as well as explicit solutions. Expert systems have now been widely accepted as methods that can be used to tackle any problem whatever; anything a human being can do, at least at the cognitive level, a computer can do, or so we now believe.

As this work has been progressing, we have seen great progress in the use and understanding of logic (Chapter 7), and a broadening of our view of classical logic to probabilities, fuzziness and practical reasoning (e.g. logic of satisfactoriness) over and above the classical systems of deduction and induction. This has very much highlighted methods of computer theorem-proving (Chapter 7), we have also seen the use of decision tables, first cousin to decision trees, game trees and semantic nets, and also testro-logic. The power of testrolog trees is very considerable, and all such methods are capable of use within the compass of an expert system. That mathematics, probability theory and statistical methods, indeed any part of mathematics, can also be so used goes without saying.

Modern AI work has inevitably thrown up tactical and technical problems, and here one thinks of the *methods* of tree-searching, alpha-beta pruning, chaining — both forward and back — and the use of situation-action rules; these are all matters which we have briefly tried to illustrate. But my purpose in this monograph is to deal more with the general conclusions rather than the details. The vital question is as to whether we are making real progress in AI, and the second is whether we are making a form of progress that will help our psychological and physiological model — and theory-making and this is more problematic, and any conclusion, however tentative, I shall leave until the end of the book.

Thinking, of course, has inevitably involved language (Chapter 6) and we see clearly the interrelationship of all our cognitive activities. In the human being such interrelatedness undoubtedly also involves every aspect of conation, but the absence of conative aspects to problem-solving programs in no way inhibits the belief that progress is being made in our understanding of human cognition.

So much then for the great strides which are being made, especially in the field of AI. We will in the next chapter turn our attention to the closely related subject of language, as viewed primarily in AI.

6

Language

In this chapter I intend to deal with language, and now concentrate mainly on it from the AI viewpoint, since the issues raised by philosophers and semanticians are so complex that they have been the subject of a whole host of studies from various points of view. We can think of it, historically, from Ogden and Richards to Peirce, Wittgenstein and Russell, and on to Searle, Schiffer, Martin, Grice and a large number of others.

Even if we do not adopt the Wittgenstein view that thinking is wholly linguistic, we should still have to admit that the bulk of *human* thinking is closely integrated with language, and therefore if AI is to be successful in its ultimate task of integrating their sets of "cognitive" programs, then certainly the findings of the last chapter should be closely integrated with this. This implies also that both should also be integrated with Chapter 4 on perception and Chapter 7 on logic.

We have already made some sort of statement about our own linguistic conventions, but let it be said again that we think of words as denoting and connoting, and this distinction could be conflated by saying all words denote concepts. But clearly we also have proper names to consider and this is best seen in terms of denoting logically proper names are also acceptable and the special status of 'I' is noted, but discussions about its status come outside the scope of this book.

We shall assume all the while that part of the ultimate integration of AI programs will lead to the possibility of a pragmatic view of language in terms of a "machine" response (overt or covert) to human statements, where the whole statement is the unit of meaning. This would apply in the same way to human-machine, human-human or machine-machine "conversation".

We ought next to mention syntax, since although one's discussions of meaning might be couched primarily in pragmatic, or semantic terms, some minimum assumptions about syntax (if only the concept of "well formed formulae" are always made. In fact, more than this is involved, as we shall see, in many of the natural language programs. So some brief notes on syntax are essential. Let me start by quoting G.A. Miller (1956):

The syntactic structure of a sentence imposes groupings that govern the interactions between the meanings of the words in that sentence.

This emphasises the fact that syntactic structures help to determine meaning, and that, for example, the meaning of particular terms is contextually determined, at least in part. Should our language be completely formalised, then presumably the syntactical consideration could be wholly separated from the semantic ones (Carnap, 1937, 1942, 1943). Let us now look briefly at some forms of syntactic analysis.

The simplest type of syntactical analysis breaks sentences down into subject and predicate, where the subject is made up of the subject word or phrase (term) and its enlargement in the form of adjectives or adjectival phrases which refer to the subject (this all refers, of course, to Indo-European type languages). The predicate is more complicated, having possibly a direct, as well as an indirect object, or no object at all, but some predicative phrase, as well as a verb. The objects, if any, and verbs, can be enlarged upon in precisely the same way as the subject. Sentences can, of course, have sub-sentences coming in the above categories and this makes for complications.

Grammar can be conceived of then as a set of rules (incomplete in natural language) which express relations between the different parts of a sentence. Indo-European languages such as English are subject-predicate languages, so that a sentence S_1 "Harry kicked the ball" divides immediately, as we mentioned above, into the subject 'Harry' and the predicate 'kicked the ball'.

We can write:

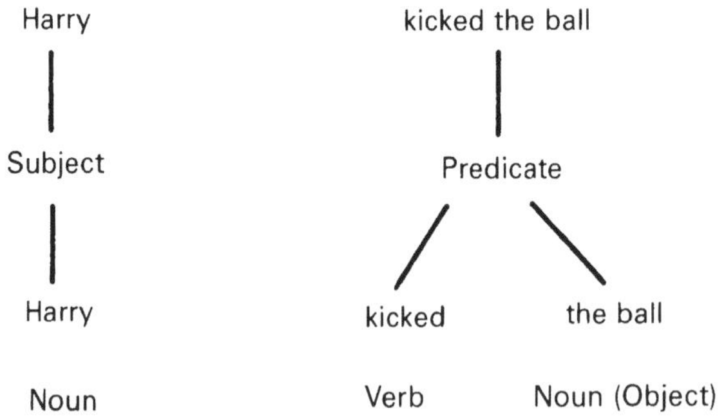

FIGURE 1

The word 'the' in front of ball is the definite article which is a member of the class of indexical symbols, and deals with 'the', 'a', 'this', etc. We shall use N, V, NP, VP, A, Adj, Ap, Adj P, P, PP, etc. for 'noun', 'verb', 'noun phrase', 'verb phrase', 'adverb', 'adjective', 'adverb(ial) phrase', 'adjectival phrase', 'pronoun' and 'personal pronoun', and add other abbreviations if we need them.

We must consider a more complicated sentence such as S_2, where S_2 = 'the small brown dog fiercely chased the small boy away from his home". We can represent this as in Figure 2.

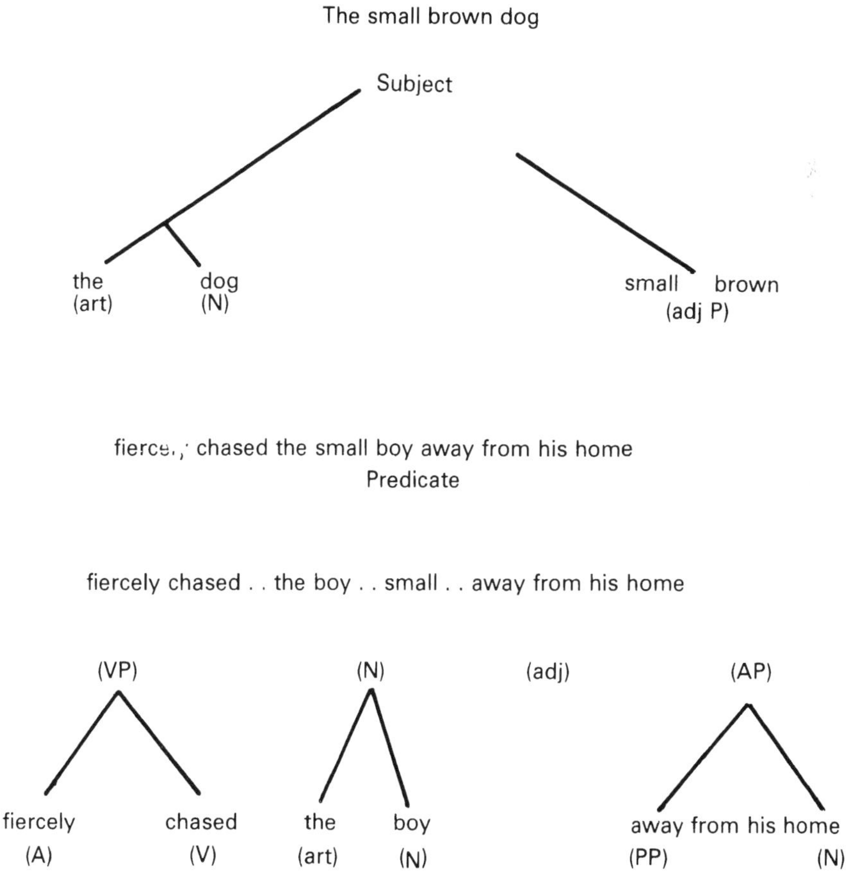

FIGURE 2

Alternatively, we could draw our representation as follows:

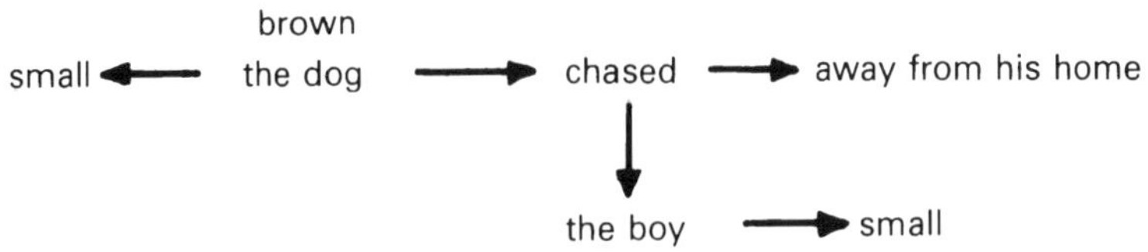

FIGURE 3

It goes without saying that all sentences with the same syntactic structure can be represented by exactly the same structured "graph".

Looked at from the point of view of semantics and pragmatics, one of the most important features of any sentence, if it occurs at all, is the interrogative word, and this is usually a pronoun (P.); this can be used to introduce a dependent element. So, for example, the links between the adjectives 'brown' and 'small' can be related to 'dog' by the interrogative phrase "What kind of - - -".

It is clearly possible to redraw Figure 3 or Figure 4 and write in the interrogative words for each link.

Next we look at *dependency grammars.* The work of Hays (1962) has emphasised the particular use of what is called dependency grammars. These are hierarchical syntactical structures which have dependency relations among themselves. For example, the sentence S_5 = "the dog chases the boy and girl in the field" can lead to a whole range of search nodes and trees, one of which appears in Figure 4

The syntactical class of the words determines the rules which apply to each sentence, subject to so-called agreement rules which determine some part of the syntactical dependencies. Such dependency grammars are necessarily open to error and thus explicitly employ *heuristics* such as:

1) Closest linkages are given preference, in general over more distant linkages. This means that the most frequently occurring links are always considered first.

2) Always consider the independent words first. Ambiguous nouns, therefore, always become subjects or objects in a sentence rather than modifiers such as adverbs, adjectives, etc.

3) Semantic analysis is always applied in the form of a test for statistical homogeneity to see if continuity of meaning is being established.

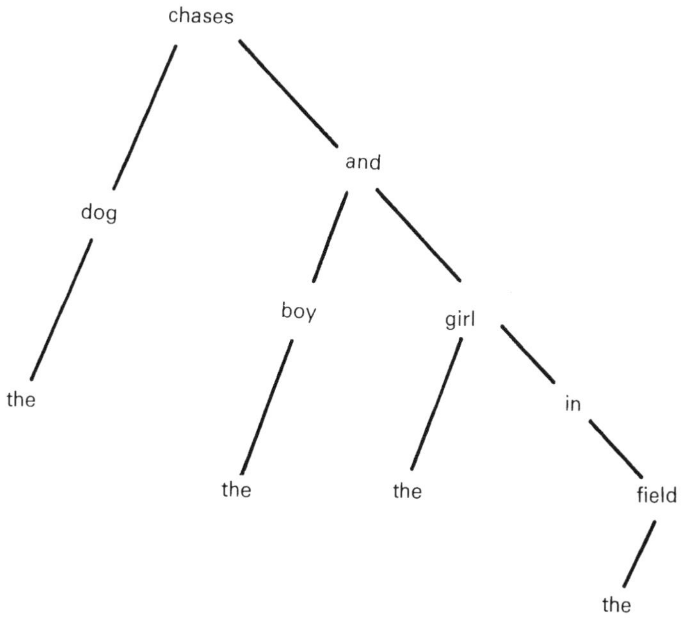

FIGURE 4

Chomsky's (1957) name is especially associated with context-free phrase-structure grammars, and his work has been especially important in the field. These forms of syntactical analysis are often called *immediate constituent grammars.*

The immediate constituent grammar is a grammar whereby the sentence, such as S_6 = "the dog chased the girl" is placed in non-overlapping parentheses:

(((the dog) (chased (the girl)))

Where braces { } are used for the sentence, square brackets [ ] for the VP and ( ) for the NP we get:

((the dog) [chased (the girl)]

The phrase-structure diagram for this sentence is as follows:—

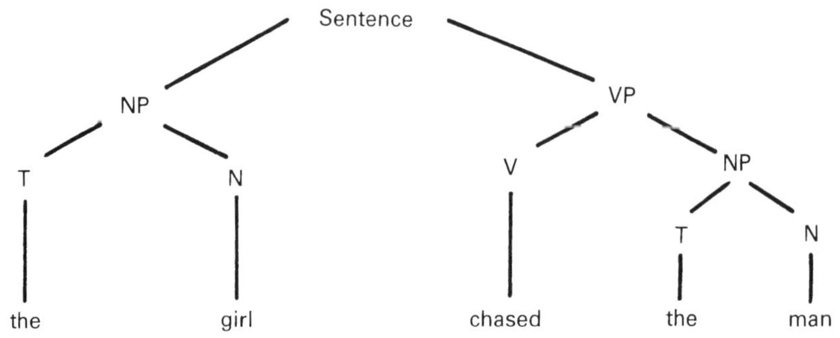

FIGURE 5

It should be noted that the nodal points of this graph are the syntactic classes and not the words themselves as in the case of dependency grammars.

The last form of syntactical analysis we shall mention is called *transformational grammars.*

There are grammars where transformation rules (sometimes called re-write rules) are used to identify the syntactical structure of the sentences. A typical re-write rule is of the form:

$$ZXW \rightarrow ZYW$$

where Z and W ar the context of X and where Y is a string of symbols. If we add the additional constraint that

$$Y = f(Z, W)$$

for some function f, then we say the sentence is context sensitive (as opposed to context free).

Consider the simplest example (Figure 6) such as S_7 = "he walks" where the structure is :

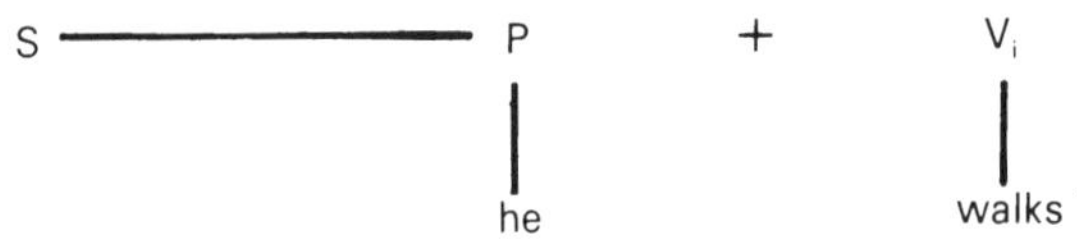

FIGURE 6

and where it will be remembered that P means pronoun and where V_i means intransitive verb. Then if we re-write this we can derive two structures (single and plural) giving "they run" as well as "she runs". The point about such transformations is to ensure that the range of possible transformations is utilised, and then the original sentence identified.

Phase structure grammars through such transformation rules transform, for example, a sentence in the active voice to a sentence in the passive voice. Then a comparison can be made with a sort of template, called here a kernel sentence, which again is used with the motive of identifying the sentence type.

Stockwell (1965) has given a clear account of phrase structure grammars, and he describes the processes of a transformation as that of converting one sentence type into another.

$$S_8 \rightarrow S_9$$

where we mean → to be interpreted as "converts into" and where, for example:

S_8 = "The man laughed at me"

and

S_9 = "I was laughed at by the man"

The source of such kernel sentences — the template referred to above — are the order set of context-restricted phrase structure rules suggested by Chomsky (1953, 1955, 1956, 1961). The kernel sentences range from simple forms like S_8 above through other types such as S_{10}, S_{11} and S_{12} which are exemplified as follows:

S_{10} = They gave John a gift
S_{11} = They annexed the whole of the property
S_{12} = The garden is green

Note that S_8 is of the form NP + aux + V_i + P; S_{10} has form NP + aux + V_i + NP + NP(adv); S_{11} is NP + aux − V_{tc} + prt + NP(adv); S_{12} is NP + aux + be + adj(adv). Here we have followed Chomsky and used *aux* for auxiliary, the suffices i, tc and S with V are *intransitive, transitive taking complement* and *sensation* respectively; prt means *particle.* It can be seen from the above that syntactic subdivision can be greatly extended beyond our original categories. Furthermore, there is no guarantee that the so-called kernel statements form an exhaustive base for all transformations; in fact, no one would seriously claim that they do. Such methods are obviously limited.

It seems certain that whatever the value of attempting a context free grammar for other purposes, pragmatic considerations suggest it is wholly untenable as a simulation of human conversation and therefore almost certainly undesirable as a syntactic base for computer-man conversation, for example. Enough has been said here to indicate a wide choice of forms of syntactical analysis. These should certainly be sufficient for any natural language program.

We accept the usefulness (even necessity) of syntax in the attempts to provide computer languages as approximations to natural languages. The use of phrase markers to subdivide a sentence into its components is now very familiar. As a further example, we give:

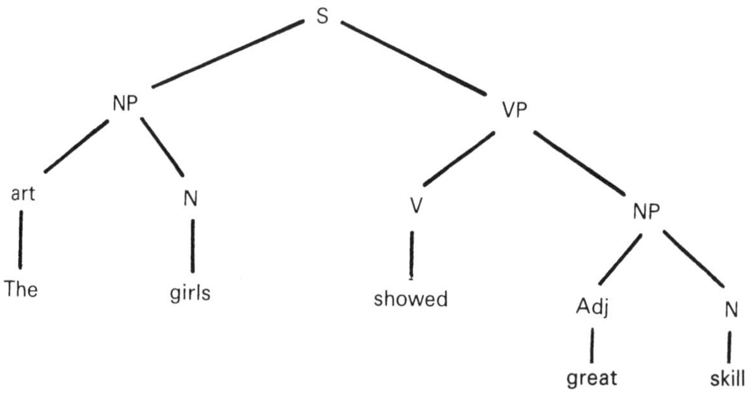

FIGURE 7

where the terminal string is the original sentence analysed. The technique, involving the scope of a word, can certainly resolve ambiguities, but the resolution depends upon being able to independently generate the phrase marker rather than let the intended meaning determine the phrase marker. Modern generative grammars have taken big steps in just this sort of direction. It goes without saying that the fast developing field of generative semantics and its relation to speech acts, while important in its own right takes us far beyond the compass of the present text.

We now proceed directly to the first of our computer languages which is NAMER. We shall say of NAMER only that it was a language in which shapes such as circles, squares and triangles were distinguished from each other and a name (label) then applied to each shape so distinguished. This meant that in a perceptual discrimination task, the computer could both carry out the discrimination and link it directly to a simple (ostensive) language. This is of interest both historically and as a reminder of the close relationship between perception and language.

Another early natural language system was ELIZA (Weizenbaum, 1960). ELIZA plays the role of a psychiatrist discussing the problems of its interlocuter. This situation lends itself well to the purpose and unlike Colby's PARRY (1964, 1975, 1976) (to be discussed next) was only concerned with the language aspect where unconnected remarks and sudden shifts of topic are not surprising. The program actually performs very little processing as such. Input sentences are matched against form classes and *key* content words are then extracted, and responses produced from groups of standard utterances, sometimes with keywords inserted by the person questioned (cf SYNTHEX). The following dialogue indicates ELIZA's conversational abilities:

Human: Men are all alike.
ELIZA: IN WHAT WAY?
Human: They're always bugging us about something or other.
ELIZA: CAN YOU THINK OF A SPECIFIC EXAMPLE?
Human: Well my boyfriend made me come here.
ELIZA: YOUR BOYFRIEND MADE YOU COME HERE?
Human: He says I'm depressed.
ELIZA: I AM SORRY TO HEAR YOU ARE DEPRESSED.
Human: It may be because of my father.
ELIZA: TELL ME MORE ABOUT YOUR FAMILY.
Human: Asdfghjkl.
ELIZA: WHO ELSE TAKES CARE OF YOU?
Human: My father.
ELIZA: ARE YOU CERTAIN OF THAT?

Simmons (1965) has divided natural language programs into major groups as follows:

1) list structural data-based systems;

2) graphic data-based systems;

3) text-based systems;

4) logical inference systems.

We shall discuss each of these types in turn and start with BASEBALL, a list-structural data-based system.

BASEBALL[1] is a program designed to simulate a part of natural language and designed in particular to answer questions of a factual kind, so that, if asked where the Boston Red Sox played baseball on July, 7 1961, then the program produced a specification list which uses the question to generate the details needed, e.g. Question: Where/Red/Sox/Date/ etc.

A dictionary is used to generate the specification list, and the program determines whether a question has been asked, and if so, to supply the content of the question, which cues the answer. The data is contained in a hierarchical fashion in store, e.g.

Months
June — July — August
Place 1 Place 2, etc.
Day 1 Day 2, etc.

and so on.

BASEBALL is written in 1PL—V, an information programming language that uses list structures. There are linguistic routines for *READ-IN* and for *DICTIONARY LOOK-UP*, and the program can add new words, as required, defined in terms of its existing vocabulary. The *CONTENT ANALYSIS* uses the dictionary and syntax to translate the question into a look-up procedure with respect to the baseball matter under discussion. The emphasis of BASEBALL is very much on meaning and understanding and very little on syntax.

The fundamental feature of BASEBALL is the specification list which is a canonical expression for the meaning of the question and it represents the information contained in the question in attribute — value pairs, e.g. Team = Dodgers, and the further details required regarding scores, dates etc. is generated in the same way by the specification list from the question.

SAD SAM is a program concerned with answering questions about data based in store. SAD SAM is an acronym which stands for Sentence Appraiser and Diagrammer and Semantic Analysing Machine (Lindsay, 1963). The program for SAD SAM was written in IPL V by Lindsay and divides naturally into two parts: (a) parsing and (b) semantics. The system is something like basic English and is concerned with family tree relationships (the data-base).

When a sentence is read into the computer, it is parsed, and we discover that someone is someone else's brother, father etc. This parsing system represents a separate program and provides an input to the semantic section which is a sentence whose parts are labelled respectively noun, verb, noun phrase, and the like, as well as a tree-structure showing the relationship among these grammatical features.

The semantic phase searches for subject-complement combinations which are associated with the verb "to be". Let us give an example: John's father, Bill, is Mary's father. "John's father" is the complement "Mary's father". "Bill" is analysed so that we find:

Bill (father) Mary
Bill (father) John

and these relations are added to the family tree, so we find:

Attribute	*Value*
Husband	Bill
Wife	Unknown
Offspring	John, Mary
Husband's parents	Unknown
Wife's parents etc.	Unknown

We now know that John and Mary are brother and sister. If we learn that Bill's wife is called Carole, then we also know the name of the mother of John and Mary.

The next type of natural system to be considered is of the *graphic data-based* kind. As an example of this, we shall take PLM (Picture Language Maker) (Rankin, 1961; Cohen, 1962; Sillars, 1963 and Kirsch, 1964). The input is composed of pictures and sentences. It translates both into logical form and assesses the truth of what is asserted. The relationship of PLM to the perceptual method of Clowes (Chapter 4) is very close in many ways, and it is natural to think of perception in such terms as graphic data-based systems.

PLM has three sub-systems: (1) a parser, (2) a formaliser, (3) a predicate evaluator.

The language is a part of English and the subject for discussion is three geometric figures. The parsing process substitutes symbols for words and continues to do so, until the top of the "parsing tree' is reached. The parsing produces a tree structure and the formaliser translates this into a formal sentence (the first order functional calculus) which involves the usual primitives as well as the usual quantifiers.

Singular predicates are as follows:

Cir(a) = a is a circle
Top(a) = a is at the top
Whi(a) = a is white

Binary predicates are as follows:

Smr(a, b) = a is smaller than b
Shp(a, b) = a is the same shape as b, and so on

The parsing produces the formalised sentence such as:

$$(AX_1)\ [CiR(X_1)\ (EX_2)\ [(Cir(X_2).Whi(X_2).(X_1{=}X_2)]]$$

So to the question "are all circles white?" and that is what is asserted above, the answer is "yes".

The information is scanned by SADIE which acts as input to the computer. The inputs are simple geometric figures. The problem of the input is the problem of various pattern recognition techniques being used to distinguish triangles from circles, and the like, much the same as in NAMER.

Text-based systems are best illustrated by the example of PROTOSYNTHEX (Simmons, Klein and McConlogue, 1964).

The attempt is to answer questions in English from an encyclopaedia. Protosynthex indexes the text, uses a synonym dictionary, an intersection logic and a simple information scoring function to extract from the text those sentences that most resemble the question being processed. The question and the text which has been retrieved are both parsed and compared. We then accept the sentences which match most closely and before final acceptance we analyse the semantic content of the sentences.

So-called VAPS numbers earmark the contents of the text in terms of volume, article, paragraph and sentence for the address of each occurrence of the indexed word. We now look up all the VAPS numbers and check the context. Look at the following example question:

Qi = "What animals live longer than men?"

VAPS words occur now such as:

Word	*Related Words*
animals	mammals, reptiles, fish
live	age
longer	older, ancient
men	person, people, woman

We now find where the greatest number of these words intersect. Those VAPS numbers with the highest score retrieve the associated texts.

Dependency-logic (Hays, 1962) is now used to parse further with the question of the text. We show a simple example:

Question: "What do worms eat?"

worms
  eat
    what

Answer: "Worms eat grass".

Second answer: "Worms eat their way through the ground"

The output would be: worms = worms; eat = eat; what = grass; what = their way; what = through the ground.

We need to score each of the words in phrases corresponding to "what". The system depends upon a "look-up" dictionary and supplies answers as a function of its experience.

Next, we have *logical inference systems* and one of the best known is SIR (Raphael, 1964). SIR stands for Semantic Information Retriever.

The input is made up of English statements. The model considers English words as objects having relations with other words (objects). The calculus of relations is the formalisation of the model and the program recognises fixed sentence formats and thus does not need syntax analysis. Information is structured hierarchially so "every girl is a person" implies that "girl" is a subset of "person" and "person" is a superset of "girl", and of course "boy", "child", etc.

Let us give an example of the input "every girl is a person". We make appeal to the relation SETR (Boy, Person)

Simiarly we get the following discourse:

Input Statement	*Formalisation*
Every girl is a person	SETR (Girl, Person)
Jacqueline is a girl	SETR (Jacqueline, Girl)
Any person has two hands	PARTRN (Hand, Person, 2)
A finger is a part of a hand	PARTR (Finger, Hand)

Question
How many fingers are on Jacqueline? PARTRNG (Finger, Jacqueline)

Computer Response
How many fingers per hand?

Input Statement
Every hand has five fingers PARTRN (Finger, Hand, 5)

Answer
The answer is 10.

All the question-answering systems have certain common features:

1) They all need large scale careful ordering of storage data.

2) All the systems require syntactical or semantic analysis, or both.

3) All the systems transpose the input into some sort of standard form, for matching or scoring purposes.

4) The text-based systems also include indexing methods.

The main difficulties are:

1) Ambiguity over meanings of words.

2) The enormous tree-searching problem in a realistic vocabulary.

3) The lack of sensory information accompanying the verbal inputs.

More recent languages such as SHRLDU, to be discussed shortly, go a long way to meeting these difficulties.

A further facility for formulating suitable (hopefully relevant) heuristics is now being worked on (George and Sarkar, 1981). The language LIP can be most effectively used in a list-processing form and where the vocabulary is itself adaptively stored.

BASEBALL (Green *et al.*, 1963) is another language we should mention. It was designed to answer questions of a factual kind. If asked where the Boston Red Sox played baseball on July 7, 1961, then the program produced a specification list which uses the question to generate the details needed, e.g. Question: Where Red Sox/Date/etc. A dictionary is used to generate the specification list and the program determines whether a question has been asked, and if so, to supply the content of the question, which cues the answer. The data is contained in a hierarchical fashion in store, e.g.

Months
June — July — August
Place 1 Place 2, etc.
Day 1 Day 2, etc.

and so on.

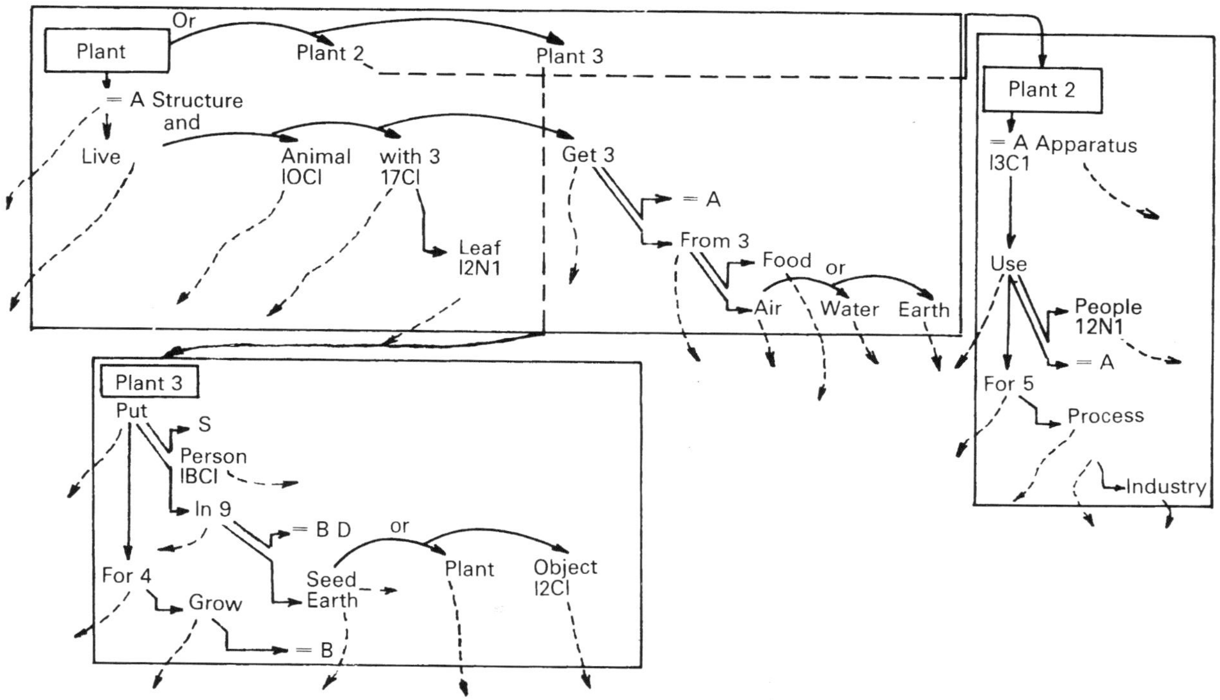

FIGURE 8 Three planes that represent three different meanings of "plant". Plant 1: A living structure which is not an animal, frequently with leaves, getting its food from air, water, earth. Plant 2: All apparatus used for any process in industry (cf. factory). Plant 3: Put (seed, plant, etc.) in earth, in order that it grows. (After Quillian)

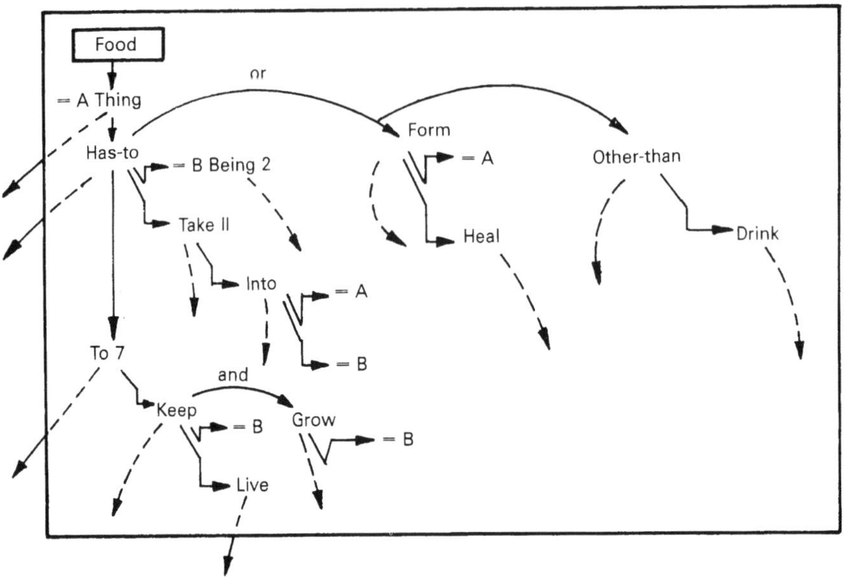

FIGURE 9 The plane represents "food". Food is that which living beings have to take in to keep living and for purposes of growth. Things forming meals, especially other than for drink.

Winograd and SHRDLU

In ELIZA there is very little by way of a data base and no "world" to discuss. ELIZA is entirely a responding verbaliser, whereas Winograd's SHRDLU has a rich vein of knowledge and a world of coloured blocks to both manipulate and describe. SHRDLU is in fact a robot that is represented in a computer program and evinces a great deal of understanding in its activities. Margaret Boden (1977) has made the point that the use of pronouns like 'it' and their processing are pointers to the depth of understanding possessed by a language, and Winograd's program is sophisticated in this respect in tracing various uses of 'it' and "understands" that 'it' can refer to actions as well as objects.

The following figure and the accompanying dialogue gives some of the flavour of the way the program works:

Gelb (1971) has developed a program called HAPPINESS which solves basic probability problems in English. The language analysis involves sentence transformation, what he calls keyword and semantic scanning and syntactic analysis based on a context-free grammar.

The keyword analysis uses heuristics and also recognises problem elements which contain semantic information. It is a system which is more general for example than STUDENT (Bobrow, 1964) and one which it would be easy to extend.

Among more recent attempts to provide conversational systems, we can list that of Ross Quillian (1968). He addressed himself to the problem of how semantic information is organised within a person's memory. As he puts it:

> What sort of representational format can permit the "meanings" of words to be stored, so that human-like use of these meanings is possible?

Quillian suggests a model which is composed of a mass of nodes interconnected by suitable associative links. A node is related to the concept underlying a word in two ways — it relates directly to other nodes which represent the meaning of the word (a node that does so is a *type node*) a second association is with the concepts type node (this is a *token node*). This represents, of course, a familiar distinction made by Peirce, Wittgenstein and others. The token nodes make it possible for a word's meaning to be built up from other word meanings. An example will help. We will consider the semantics of the word "plant" (Figure 8) and "food" (Figure 9).

To summarise Quillian's notion we say that a word's full concept is defined in the memory model to be all the nodes that can be reached by an exhaustive tracing process, originating at its initial, patriarchical type node, together with the total sum of relationships among these nodes specified by within-plane, token-to-token links.

Quillian's work is described in considerable detail in the literature and is the precursor of much work being currently done on semantic maps. We shall leave the reader at this point to explore the original literature on the subject and merely mention that vast linguistic data banks, composed of dictionaries and the like, are certain to be needed by any system aiming to reconstruct the full range of natural language.

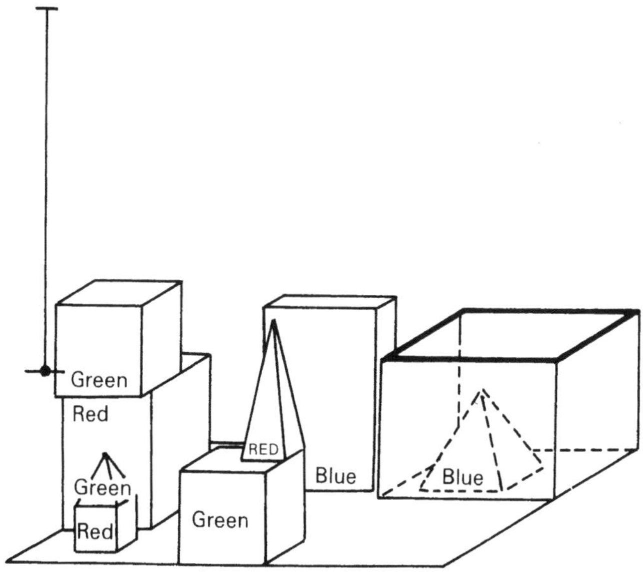

FIGURE 10 Winograd's block world. (After Winograd) (Prior to the green block on the red block, and the blue block being moved)

I DON'T UNDERSTAND WHICH PYRAMID YOU MEAN
find a block which is taller than the one you are holding and put it into the box.
BY "IT" I ASSUME YOU MEAN THE BLOCK WHICH IS TALLER THAN THE ONE I AM HOLDING.
OK.
what does the box contain?
THE BLUE PYRAMID AND THE BLUE BLOCK.
how many blocks are not in the box?
FOUR OF THEM.
is at least one of them narrower than the one which I told you to pick up?
YES, THE RED CUBE.
is it supported?
YES, BY THE TABLE.
can the table pick up blocks?
NO.
can a pyramid be supported by a block?
YES.
can a pyramid support a pyramid?
I DON'T KNOW.
stack up two pyramids.
I CAN'T.
(tries and fails)

will you please stack up both of the red blocks and either a green cube or a pyramid?
OK.
....
had you touched any pyramid before you put the green one on the little cube.
YES, THE GREEN ONE.
when did you pick it up?
WHILE I WAS STACKING UP THE RED CUBE, A LARGE RED BLOCK, AND A LARGE GREEN CUBE.
why?
TO GET RID OF IT.
why did you do that?
TO CLEAR OFF THE RED CUBE.
why did you clear off that cube?
TO PUT IT ON A LARGE GREEN CUBE.
why did you do that?
TO STACK UP THE RED CUBE, A LARGE RED BLOCK AND A LARGE GREEN CUBE.
why did you do that?
BECAUSE YOU ASKED ME TO.
how did you do it?
BY PUTTING A LARGE RED BLOCK ON THE TABLE; THEN LETTING GO OF IT; THEN PUTTING A LARGE GREEN CUBE ON IT; THEN LETTING GO OF THAT CUBE; THEN PUTTING THE RED CUBE ON THAT CUBE; THEN LETTING GO OF THAT CUBE.
how many objects did you touch while you were doing it?
FOUR OF THEM.
what did the red cube support before you started to clean it off?
THE GREEN PYRAMID.
there were five blocks to the left of the box then.
NO, ONLY FOUR OF THEM: THE RED CUBE, TWO LARGE GREEN CUBES, AND A RED BLOCK.
....

Winograd used a formal syntactical method which was the equivalent of the transition net shown in Figure 11, wherein sentence words and the like cause transitions from arc, and they are recursive. Such networks are said to be augmented because such transitions are usually dependent on the nature of the programs represented by the arcs. It is well known that such augmented transition networks have their own difficulties (Winston and Brown, 1979) and since Winograd's work there have been more "agile" ways of dealing with syntactical matters. We shall be returning to this matter briefly later. But to continue with Winograd's work let us look more generally at his plan of campaign.

Figure 12 shows a block diagram of the major components of SHRDLU, with arrows indicating interactions among the various components. SHRDLU is thus made up of several component programs.

MONITOR is a small program which invokes other routines to initiate

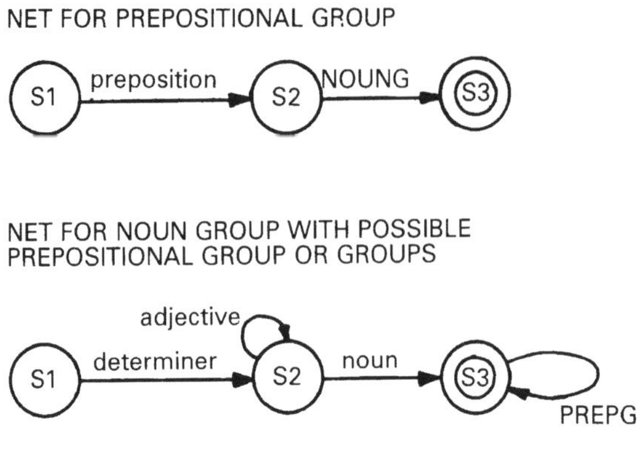

FIGURE 11 Transition nets describe grammatical constraints. In the first diagram, a simple transition network defines a noun group as a determiner, any number of adjectives, and a noun. The second diagram describes preposition groups, and the third shows a slightly generalised description of a noun group. (After Winograd)

and terminate processing of an input utterance. INPUT works with information in the DICTIONARY to carry out morphemic analysis on input sentences, and provides GRAMMAR with strings of words together with their definitions found in another part of the DICTIONARY. GRAMMAR coordinates the understanding process through its analysis of the basic units of English structure. The syntactic theory underlying Winograd's system is a systemic grammar, due to Halliday (1970). In the SEMANTICS block are routines which assist GRAMMAR in the interpretation of the input. PROGRAMMAR is a special language used to parse by means of interpreting grammars written as programs. PROGRAMMAR builds and maintains a parsing tree for an input sentence, while ANSWER converts the system's responses to reasonable English and keeps "an eye on" the context of the conversation. It being clear that in ordinary English, so much of semantics is contextually dependent.

Then we come to PLANNER which is a subset of a deductive language which is used throughout the analysis. Among other things, PLANNER deduces facts about the environment, which is of course the BLOCKS world. BLOCKS itself is a group of PLANNER theorems which embody the system's knowledge about its world and how in it goals may be achieved. Then DATA contains PLANNER assertions which describe the state of the BLOCKS world.

Let us return now to give a brief consideration to the systemic grammar of Halliday. His theory of syntax deals with three levels of syntactic units.

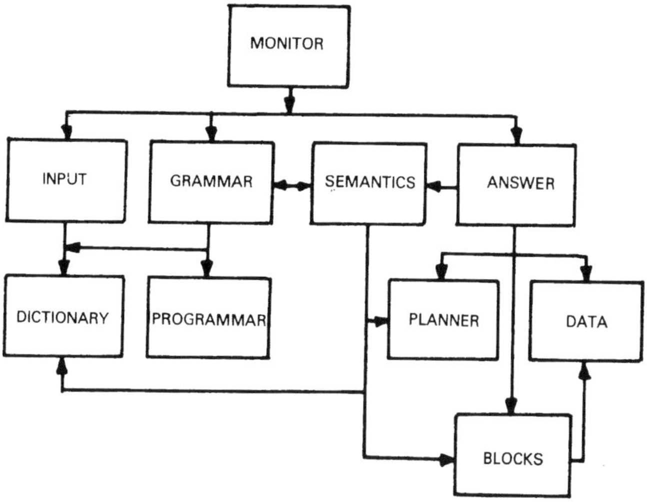

FIGURE 12 Block diagram of Winograd's system. (After Winograd)

The highest level or organisation is the *clause.* There are three kinds of major clause (imperative, declarative, and question) and an assortment of secondary clauses. Clauses consist of combinations of four types of *groups* (noun, verb, preposition, and adjective). A group is described by its component *words,* of which there are some eighteen different types such as *determiners, classifiers, nouns* etc. and by a variety of *features* denoting tense, number, and the role of the group in the sentence. This organisation leads in turn to systemic grammar parsing trees which are typically smaller, shallower, more highly branched, and composed of more complex nodes than parsing trees produced by generative-transformational grammars. Parsing is carried out by specialised routines which look for expected constituents of clauses or groups, guided by the syntactic features which have been discovered. This means that a fragment of a simplified noun-group program might seek a determiner, then an adjective, then a noun. The procedure could report failure at any point in the search, allowing backtracking to alternative parsing routines. This means that the syntactic knowledge of SHRDLU is thus mostly of a *procedural* sort, represented in the form of programs which are written in the special purpose language called PROGRAMMER.

Extensive use is also made of procedural representations for SHRDLU's knowledge base. The meaning of an input utterance is represented as a PLANNER program. Knowledge of what can be done in the environment is coded in the PLANNER theorem base, while descriptions of actual or hypothetical block configurations are kept in the PLANNER data base (the only nonprocedural part of SHRDLU's knowledge).

Thanks to ANSWER, as mentioned above, Winograd's system deals effectively with the problem of *context*. It handles context and other semantic problems through the use of another procedural device, the "semantic specialist" routines. These programs, of which there are about a dozen, are "experts" in analysing particular syntactic structures and the meanings of the words they contain, in order to construct PLANNER expressions for use in reasoning and question answering. The semantic routines interact with the syntactic analysis. Thus the noun group specialist might be invoked as soon as a noun group has been successfully parsed (or even during parsing). Systemic grammar is particularly suited to introduction of semantic considerations quite early in syntactic processing. Constant checking to see if what has been parsed so far makes sense can eliminate a good deal of wasted syntactic analysis in a language understanding system. It is here that the deductive language mentioned above comes in PLANNER (Hewitt, 1972) and it is limitations on PLANNER (for example over the ambiguous nature of negation) that creates some problems in the working of SHRDLU. One might, in passing, say that such limitations (and even greater ones) are often quite apparent in ordinary human beings' speech (use of language).

The limitations on SHRDLU are limitations of interpretation of conversation with respect to even the limited Blocks world. This stems largely from the attempt at precision which has entailed a large scale apparatus to do very little and thus gives the impression of the use of a steam-roller to crack walnuts. There are two principal answers to this sort of criticism and one is that one may expect a well grounded system such as SHRDLU to grow exponentially in its abilities, so that a conversation about a Blocks world could become quite quickly a conversation about any world at all. In saying this the enormous difficulties involved in human language are not being underplayed, but the second point is also important. This is to the effect (Wilks, 1976 and others have made the point) that much language in practice is more flexible, less precise, etc. than is the case for SHRDLU. This suggests a return to ELIZA (and later to PARRY) but immediately to the work of Roger Schank.

Schank and Natural Language

Roger Schank (1973) at Stanford has been working to develop a theory of human language understanding. It contrasts with SHRDLU in that it is more versatile and flexible, although it is less precise. This latter point is by intent since it was a criticism made of SHRDLU by Y. Wilks (1976) and others that logical precision was not a major characteristic of human conversation.

Schank's work is in the tradition of Quillian's approach which we have already looked at briefly. His basic premise is that people understand language by mapping utterances onto a *conceptual base*. This means that since a great variety of utterances may have essentially the same meaning, the mapping is many-to-one, and the relations between the components of conceptual representations and the English words in the corresponding sentences may be less than obvious. It follows that Schank is much more concerned with semantics than with syntax.

Concepts occur in three major types. A *nominal* like 'man' or 'tree', is a concept which can be thought of by itself, and which often invokes a 'picture' in the mind; they are obvious physical object words. Nominals are abbreviated by PP, for 'Picture Producer'. An *action* (abbreviated ACT), like 'act' or 'smile' are concepts which can be executed by (some) nominals. The third concept type is the *modifier*, which occurs in two forms that are similar to the syntactic categories of adjective and adverb. A 'Picture Aider' (PA), like 'big' or 'alive', specifies an attribute of a nominal. An 'Action Aider' (AA), like 'swiftly' or 'heavily', specifies an attribute of an action. Two or more concepts may be connected by a dependency relation. Schank specifies a set of about fifteen such relations in the form of *conceptual rules*. These rules are used to tie together all the concepts in some complete idea into a *conceptual dependency diagram*. Figures 13 and 14 show some of the more important conceptual rules and some very simple examples of conceptual dependency diagrams corresponding to sentences. In Figure 13, action concepts are not usually represented as any of the English words in the sentences. Schank prefers to fit all ACTs into roughly a dozen categories.

We cannot consider all the actions in detail, but some of the physical actions, like PROPEL, MOVE, GRASP, SPEAK, INGEST, and EXPEL, are fairly obvious. There are three transfer actions which appear quite often. PTRANS means to change the location of a physical object. ATRANS to transfer an abstract quality like control or ownership, and MTRANS to transfer conceptual information around in memory or consciousness. CONC means "to think about" (very roughly), while MBUILD refers to the reasonable combining thoughts. Now follow a list of relations, the notation user and an example:

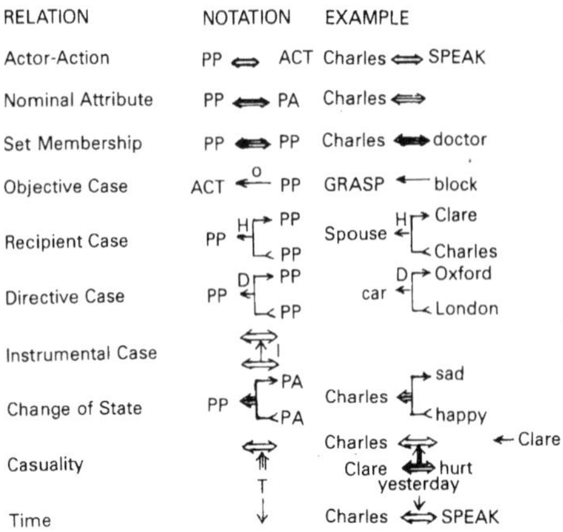

FIGURE 13 A sample of Schank's conceptual rules (Verbs may be tensed throughout). (After Schank)

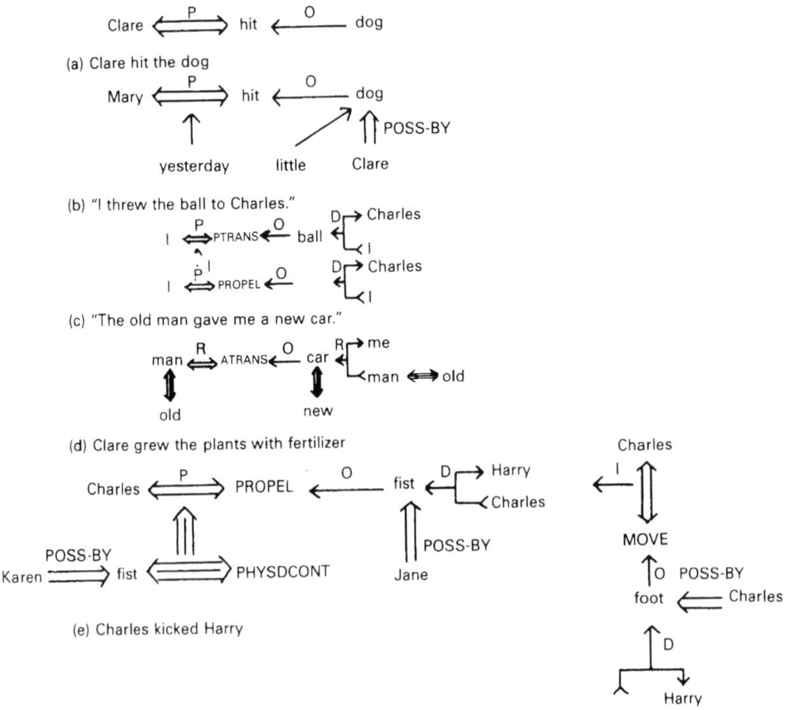

FIGURE 14 Examples of conceptual dependency diagrams. (After Schank)

Schank here uses very little syntax and this work contrasts with Winograd's, where the latter inserts semantic considerations to constraint what is really a syntactical approach.

PARRY

We now go full circle, through precision and "naturalness" in conversation to the use of language systems for simulation. Unlike ELIZA, PARRY was developed precisely to simulate, or model, paranoia. To some extent built up on the work of Tomkins & Messick (1963) who thought of a paranoid primarily in terms of being over vigilant in maximising insult detection and minimising personal humiliation. Thus PARRY scans every statement in this light and responds accordingly. Like ELIZA though, PARRY cannot claim, and this is the very acme of language, to *understand* (Wittgenstein, 1953). In the table that follows from Schank and Colby (1973), PARRY's rules for Malevolence and benevolence are shown and based upon this a most convincing set of interviews occur of a paranoid kind which could easily be mistaken for the real thing. It is of special interest because it is at least conative in a sense which distinguishes it from the earlier question-answering systems such as SIR, SYNTHEX and BASEBALL which are strictly "cognitive". We now look at PARRY's list of attributions of malevolence and benevolence:

(Other's Intention) ← (Malevolence) (Benevolence) (Neutral)

Malevolence-Detection Rules

1. (malevolence) ← (Mental harm) | (physical threat)
2. (mental harm) ← (humiliation) | (subjugation)
3. (physical threat) ← (direct attack) | (induced attack)
4. (humiliation) ← (explicit insult) | (implicit insult)
5. (subjugation) ← (constraint) | (coercive treatment)
6. (direct attack) ← CONCEPTUALIZATIONS ([you get electric shock], [are you afraid Mafia kill you?])
7. (induced attack) ← CONCEPTUALIZATIONS ([I tell Mafia you], [does Mafia know you are in hosptial?])
8. (explicit insult) ← CONCEPTUALIZATIONS ([you are hostile], [you are mentally ill?])
9. (implicit insult) ← CONCEPTUALIZATIONS ([tell me your sexlife], [are you sure?])
10. (constraint) ← CONCEPTUALIZATIONS ([you stay in hospital], [you belong on locked ward])
11. (coercive treatment) ← CONCEPTUALIZATIONS ([I hypnotize you], [you need tranquillizers])

Benevolence-Detection Rules

1. (benevolence) ← (positive attitude) | (positive story attitude)

2. (positive attitude) ← CONCEPTUALIZATIONS ([I want help you], [you understand me])
3. (positive story attitude) ← (story interest) | (story agreement)
4. (story interest) ← (topic comment) | (topic question)
5. (topic comment) ← CONCEPTUALIZATION ([bookies are not reliable])
6. (topic question) ← CONCEPTUALIZATION ([what did you do to bookie])
7. (story agreement) ← CONCEPTUALIZATIONS ([I believe you], [you are right])

Earlier we mentioned that Winograd's SHRDLU, using augmented transition nets (as do most natural language systems), is limited in its syntactical flexibility and Marcus (1979) offers a method that is in better keeping with actual linguistic structure.

Marcus argues the need for non-deterministic parsing is usually (left-to-right) deterministic in form. An example supplied by Marcus simply illustrates the point. Given sentence S, such that

S_1 = Have the students who missed the exam taken the makeup to-day

could be interpreted in either of the following ways:

[S[vpHave[$_s$ the students who ... taken the makeup today]]]

or

[S[AuxHave][np the students who ...][vp taken the exam today]]

Analysis of this situation leads Marcus to the conclusion that pattern-action rules in clusters properly constitute grammar which then allows the parsing to be data directed. Marcus' model differs from the "traditional" augmented transition nets in that back-up is replaced by look-ahead, and his production-like rules replace the statements of LISP which are not grammatically orientated.

Marcus develops a grammatical interpreter he calls PARSIFAL, and the grammatical rules themselves are written in PIDGIN and this is then translated into LISP. The result provides an exciting alternative to the transition net approach and we may expect to see further developments along these lines.

There are a number of related programs with respect to the ones so far but we shall mention only one which is of the type which is really a teaching system (Goldstein and Miller, 1976: Miller and Goldstein, 1979) and called SPADE. The idea is to teach elementary computer programming and does so by providing an environment which is embodied in SPADEE, a particular example of SPADE. Much of their work was involved with Paperts' LOGOTURTLE (1971) language for graphics programing.

An important ingredient of Goldstein's theory of intelligent computer coaches is a set of transformations that cut short formal proofs and precise arguments. These transformations delete portions of the proof on the basis of various constraints which are essentially context dependent. Examples of the transformations are as follows:

[PREMISE & SKILL => CONCLUSION]---> NIL
[PREMISE & SKILL => CONCLUSION]---> PREMISE
=> CONCLUSION
[PREMISE & SKILL => CONCLUSION]---> CONCLUSION
[C1 & C2] ---> CHOOSE (C1, C2)
[C1 or C2] ---> CHOOSE (C1, C2)

These transformations are intended to simplify the logical structure of an argument, so the main issue is when to apply a given rule.

To investigate this issue, Goldstein has constructed a Way world in which decisions are made in order to achieve the goal, which is to locate and destroy enemy ships, submarines and aeroplanes. The necessary evidence regarding location is obtained by "radar" and "sonar", and submarines and ships can be sensed when within one unit. The aeroplanes can be sensed within two units, and on the basis of a *single warning* the player knows there is a threat but not where the threat lies.

Goldstein used *genetic graphs* to represent the *evolutionary* relationship which are system developed. Analogy, generalisation, correction and refinement are all features of such a development. Figure 14 provides a sample genetic graph. The main point to be noticed is that the user's knowledge cannot be understood in a vacuum, it is dependent on the total knowledge context. In this case, the *task knowledge* is represented by a description of the program's capabilities.

The genetic graph model is built from an examination of the user's decisions in the light of the possibilities recognised by the program. Explanation and user modelling issues are dealt with and the domain of operation is essentially that of coaching novice programmers.

Language and the Brain

The complexities of language (at least of human language), some of which we have been looking at, have necessarily to be reflected in the workings of the brain, and our problem is to decide how. Luria has said:

Human speech, which is organized into a *phonemic system of language*, uses sounds of a special type and sharpness of hearing alone is not enough to distinguish between them . . .

This is in part because of the redundancy of language. One recognises the meaning of a word by virtue of the context in which it occurs. This means that a certain state of expectancy exists in the brain which makes it ready to interpret a particular word or set of words.

We accept a degree of functional localisation in the cerebral cortex and we would expect as a result to be able to identify some of the areas concerned with different facets of speech as well as their probable function. Whether we can go as far in localisation as Kleist (1934), for example, and identify area 22b as being concerned with the understanding of speech seems doubtful.

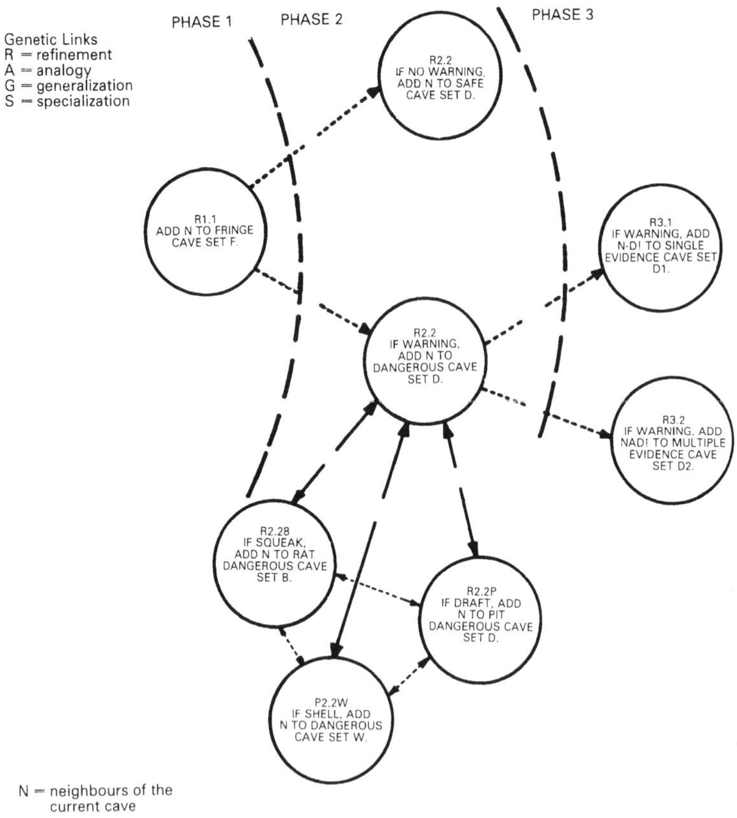

FIGURE 15 A portion of a genetic graph.

What does seem likely is that a process such as the following occurs in the brain. A word is spoken (we really mean here a sentence or a set of sentences) and it is recorded by the ear. If read it is recorded by the eye and then in each case involving the colliculi and the geniculate bodies, the stimulus pattern impinges on the cortex. In the first case the auditory cortex and in the second case the visual cortex. Then, in keeping with our notion of a hierarchy of classification systems, we would expect the auditory and visual elaboration areas (or perhaps both, and those parts concerned with language) to reconstruct the necessary image pattern — in logical terms these are the appropriate concepts.

In other words, events are stored in memory — mainly the temporo-parietal areas and reconstructed as required. Language is a form of internal representation of these remembered events which are interlocked with the "memory traces" of the events themselves.

The very fact that people can speak and write as well as listen and read, is a reminder that this representation has also a motor side to it that allows at least four types of aphasia to occur when faults occur in any of the four modalities. More important though, it seems to bear out the point that there is a sense in which there are two internal models of experience — both in the brain. One is concerned with representing events and the other with symbolising both the events and their representation. This is clearly a debatable matter and one which becomes doubtful if you accept the Wittgenstein identification of thinking and language. This in turn suggests that language and the "references" of language may somehow become "fused". But let us leave that aside for the while.

Clues to cerebral localisation are provided by a mass of evidence. But one again can quote from Luria:

> The last direct result of disturbance of phonemic hearing is *loss of the ability to write*, characteristic of patients with lesions of the left temporal lobe.

Such a defect results from loss of ability to analyse accoustic content since those same patients can write normally when *copying* the written word.

There seems to be a little doubt that damage to the posterior superior temporal cortex of the *dominant hemisphere* results in an impairment of *the use* of language. The more anterior lesion affects expression and the more posterior affects language more profoundly.

The main study of language-in-action from a neurophysiological point of view involves the general study of aphasia. The earliest classical work being associated with Broca's motor speech area in the posterior zones of the third dominant frontal gyrus, and Wernicke's sensory speech area in the posterior third of the superior left temporal gyrus.

Subsequent work, such as that in frontal leucotomy, shows that Broca's area can suffer considerable insult without demonstrating speech disorders in the person concerned.

A great deal of research of one kind or another has been carried out in the name of aphasia, so that lesions in the middle zones of the dominant temporal region appear to impair audio-verbal memory, lesions of superior zones of dominant temporal area cause sensory aphasia, lesions in the secondary zones of the temporal auditory cortex of the dominant hemisphere affect cerebral organization of speech and cause temporal aphasia (Luria, 1971).

Similarly logical-grammatical relationships are affected by lesions of temporo-parieto-occipital zones of dominant hemisphere. Optic aphasia is associated with the temporo-occipital zones of the dominant hemisphere and speech (and language generally, as we have said) is affected by lesions of the dominant temporal regions.

Patients who have articulatory disturbances usually have lesions of the posterior inferior frontal areas. Agraphia, where a patient cannot write but can talk and where there is a general deterioration of language ability and mentality, if often associated with such lesions in Broca's area.

Lesions of the posterior superior temporal cortex of the dominant hemisphere affects linguistic communication and when the lesion is more anterior then it is the *expressive* language that is most affected. Expressive speech with its internal representation is concerned with output and requires encoding into *phonemes* or *articulemes* (for pronounciation purposes). *Impressive* speech is concerned with decoding or input. This leaves *internal* speech which is the language in which information is stored and translated into and from expressive and impressive speech.

Figure 15 (Pribram 1971) shows something of the different kinds of aphasia.

The key problem of language in human beings which distinguishes it from the use of signs in higher primates is the extent to which the symbolic-sign representation within the brain intertwine to provide the complexities of language.

The complexities of language have been highlighted by an intensive study (Milliken and Darley, 1967) of language in its relation to cerebral dominance, temporal and parietal lobe functions and the like.

The general conclusions are consistent with what has been here so far and as far as cerebral dominance is concerned we can summarise some of the findings as follows:

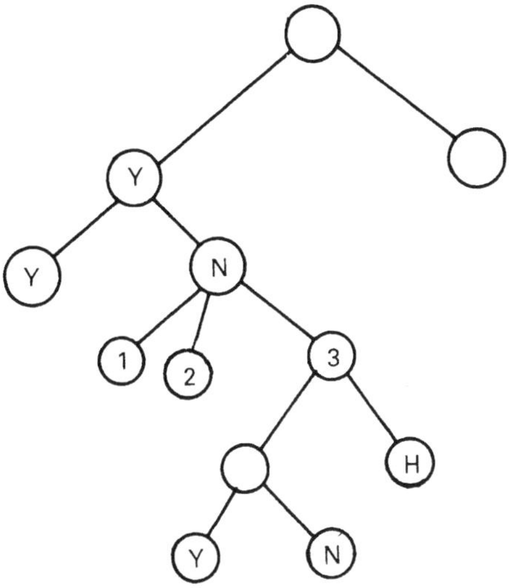

The linguistic dimensions which underly six different forms of aphasia. Two major linguistic axes are distinguished: one extending posterior-frontally in the brain which serves a decoding-encoding dimension: the other extending dorsolateral-mediobasally in the brain which serves a simultaneity (concurrence)-successivity (sequence) dimension. In addition two forms of language disturbance lying beyond the confines of cortex surrounding the Sylvian fissure were identified: frontal lesions result in the loss of verbal control over behavior and posterior parietal lesions result in semantic disturbance akin to the agnosias. (After Pribran)

1) There are certain functions for which only one of the hemispheres is responsible.

2) There are certain cerebral functions for which both of the hemispheres are responsible.

3) The linguistic abilities are primarily but not inclusively in the "left" hemisphere and it is this which makes it dominant.

4) 3., above, is supported by work on the *temporal* lobes which shows that visual memory, audition, auditory discrimination and other activities

"centred on" the temporal lobe which are greatly interfered with by non-dominant lesions, but are unaffected by dominant lesions.

5) It seems that the *parietal lobe* is concerned (omitting the anterior somesthetic portion) with the organising of verbal activities in the dominant hemispheres, although both hemispheres are involved.

6) It has been suggested that certain zones in temporo-occipital areas are concerned with categorisation (classification).

7) Both hemispheres (interacting) deal with most matters, with the linguistic emphasis on the dominant hemisphere.

8) The parietal linguistic organising activity suggests that they exercise control over more global mechanisms.

There is clearly still a vast amount to unravel with respect to language and the brain, but one seems emerging a picture in which the cerebral cortex is less a control centre and more an integrating centre acting in loops (usually feedback in character) with subcortical bodies such as the basal ganglia, thalamus and hypothalamus.

The concept-word relationship, and via short term memory (some disturbances here caused by parieto-temporal lesions) the "sentence"-hypothesis relationship are part of the integrated activity of the dominant parieto-temporal areas of both hemispheres interacting.

The ability to draw logical inferences depends upon associative principles, and we must remember the notion of Price's that logic is pre-linguistic and the example of GOAL (George, 1970) which showed that associative underpinnings of inferential behaviour. The association of the kind $A \rightarrow B$ and $B \rightarrow C$ implies $A \rightarrow C$ is then represented by the verbal equivalent, after which logic can proceed by the verbal description alone. Most certainly this is normally under frontal lobe control, but involves the parieto-temporal cortex and subcortical areas.

At this point we shall call a halt to our efforts with the clear understanding that we have a great deal more to learn about the relation of the central nervous system to language. But we are nevertheless in a position to formulate hypotheses and it is perhaps not too much to suggest that from the AI work which we have briefly reported (especially when the reader has the primary sources at hand), that a better model or map of the brain could be forthcoming, and perhaps one that is testable. One lesson that computational work has emphasised is that the function of the brain (however simple the principles may be) is extremely complex.

I believe however that a "mathematically-minded" neurophysiologist could provide a very exciting set of hypotheses.

7

Logic, Inference Making and Theorem-Proving

Logic

We shall not delay too long on the philosophical implications of logic. But it must be said that logic plays an obvious part in human information processing. We shall make the standard distinction between logical (analytic) and empirical (synthetic) propositions, and we shall not argue here about whether 'analytic' can be precisely distinguished from 'synthetic' (Quine, 1953), although we shall recognise what may be best regarded as a hazy boundary between them. Logical grammar, in Wittgenstein's sense, is the set of rules, which are not necessarily wholly explicit which determine our proper use of language, and this we shall bear in mind. The obvious philosophical problem is as to whether the rules are *sufficiently* explicit to permit the appropriateness of the appeal to the everyday, ordinary or proper use of language. The work of G.E. Moore is obviously relevant here, as is that of Ryle and Strawson.

The cybernetician has to be fully aware of the philosophical issues as in the case of all cognition, and especially in the case of language and logic. Generally speaking the problem is treated here in the same manner as in the last three chapters.

Much of logic is based on a simple associative procedure in behaviour terms and there are many psychological experiments (e.g. Tolman and Honzik, 1930), which illustrate how very simple inference making can be set up in behavioural situations which are clearly pre-linguistic. The big step then is taken to logic that emerges in language in forms such as the syllogism and the sorites and other forms that go back to Aristotle. Space forbids any discussion of these matters and we skip straight to a brief discussion of Boolean algebra.

Basic Issues in Logic

Boole assumed a great deal in his development of Boolean algebra, and he even went as far as thinking of it as the method of human thinking. We should clarify briefly some part of the point of what he actually did.

To start with he assumed the concept of class as being a basic one, and then he discussed operations on classes and relationships between classes. It was assumed that classes are well-defined and we can always precisely identify a class of objects and its boundaries, but in practice classes of objects usually have hazy boundaries, and we either decide arbitrarily on definite class boundaries, or accept what to-day is often called "fuzzy logic" based on classes of uncertain boundaries (this may take many forms).

George Boole's purpose in developing his algebra of logic was based on the belief that the laws of thought could be made precise and mathematical in form. Since those days, many arguments have taken place about the relationship between logic and thinking, it being clear that human thought does not always have the precision of an algebra. However, it has also been argued that such a logical system can represent idealised thinking, or rather idealised reasoning. The point here is that thinking and reasoning, of course, are not necessarily exactly the same thing.

It is of interest that although Boole may have overstated his case, there is some sign in the importance of Boolean algebra in computer design that systems that "think" may well operate from a more nearly Boolean basis than many have recently thought. The argument is reminiscent once more of Reichenbach's (1938) distinction between the logic of discovery and the logic of justification. The first seems to be a "leap in the dark" (a hypothesis, a guess, a discovery) and the second a carefully formal argument of justification. But it is by no means clear from this that the underlying mechanisms, which Quine and others hope one day to supply for explanatory purposes in meaning and thought, should not be very similar. The similarity could be rather the same as the similarity between inductive and deductive logic.

The main use of mathematical logic has been to provide a foundation for mathematics. For both linguistic analysis of arguments, and in order to provide a foundation for mathematical reasoning, the type of symbolic logic needed goes beyond an algebra of classes, and although this path will not be followed. It will be remembered though that some (Brouwer, 1913-14, Wittgenstein, 1956) have denied this logistic thesis.

In dealing with so-called 'idealised logic' (as opposed to the empirical logic of practical reasoning) we meet many problems, not least of which is the one of notation. Most people use the notation of *Principia Mathematica*, but we believe that for many purposes, Polish notation is more convenient. It has some obvious typographical advantages, and we will briefly indicate the manner in which it operates. Instead of writing the more usual: $\sim p$, $p \vee q$, $p . q$, $p \mid q$, we write Np, Opq, Apq, Ipq, so that the operator occurs at the beginning and has a scope commensurate with whether it is a unary, binary, ternary, etc., operator. This means that we can write:

$$(p \supset . p \supset q) \supset . p \supset q$$

as

IpIpqIIpq

Let us return though to consider symbolic logic in generalised terms.

Symbolic Logic

What is usually called symbolic logic, or mathematical logic, depends on the use of symbols in place of terms (symbolisation), and the development of axiomatic systems based upon these symbols which are used to examine logical arguments, the foundation of mathematics, and can also be used as empirically descriptive languages. Thus, as conceived here, they can be made into formal systems in a much stronger sense that could be constructed by the mere replacing of ordinary English terms by symbols. As a result, such axiomatic systems have complex properties which we shall want to examine.

Leibniz was one of the people who helped to set symbolic logic on its way when he devised the notion of an ideogram which was an attempt to improve on Aristotelian logic and release it in some measure from its "factual overlap" — the link between formal and factual. But it was not until the work of George Boole, and also to a lesser extent the work of de Morgan in the nineteenth century, two hundred years after Leibniz, that the first serious steps were taken in symbolic logic.

In setting the scene for symbolic logic, and in particular for theorem-proving, we should say that to formalise is to be seen as an essential procedure for many purposes. If we formalise something, we try to make it precise. Therefore if we try to formalise a term such as 'true' or 'meaning', then we try to say precisely what it means in every conceivable context. To do this we have to restrict its meaning in ordinary language, where terms are necessarily kept vague (have surplus meaning) so that they can have contextual meaning, and replace this context depended by a degree of precision, if we are to formalise successfully. We may doubt the usefulness (or in some cases possibility) of achieving a "universal" context, but we can at least go some way towards it; this is precisely what formalisation attempts to do.

Any imprecision that we have in our formalisation is always pushed into the meta-language of the language we are making precise. It is rather like a clearing in a wood; the wood is infinite and all we can do is to clear so much of the wood, and if we then want to clear more wood, we clear more wood and so on — there are always more trees left to be cleared. This is because the whole process of communication and understanding etc., is ultimately lodged within the people who are using the language in talking to each other. In symbolic logic we tend to talk of the lowest language as the object language, and we talk usually in terms of one level of meta-language which in this context is often called syntax language. Therefore the syntax language, which we can make as precise as we please refers to the object language which is intended to be wholly precise. In the case of such logical systems as the propositional calculus the object language itself will be devoid of meaning.

We shall not normally develop precise systems which are devoid of meaning without having some intended interpretation in mind. Thus we want to make a distinction between *models* and *theories*, or models and their interpretation (Braithwaite, 1953). We can take a map and it can be as abstract map, but it happens to be of the same shape and of the same dimensions as, say, Great Britain or Australia and then we shall say that the interpretation we intend to place on the map is that of Great Britain or Australia. The details of the maps and the interpretation placed on them will depend on the purpose for which the map is going to be used. If we are constructing a map for aerial use we shall emphasise different features of Great Britain or Australia than if we are providing a map for road or railway use, and we would use different projections for different purposes. The important thing to appreciate is that models and their associated interpretations are closely related to each other, rather like an object language is related to a meta-language. If we go from the interpretation to the model we say we are formalising the interpretation or theory; if on the other hand we are going from the model to the theory we say we are placing an interpretation on the model.

In mathematical logic, the interpretation we place on the axiomatic system that makes up the mathematical logic under consideration, and which is made up of a set of symbols in axiomatic form, will either be for the purpose of examining the foundations of mathematics, the purpose of interpreting and analysing ordinary language or for the purpose of describing empirical systems: for the latter two purposes, we shall call the systems a part of symbolic logic.

Having formulated the logical system, it is important to appreciate its general properties. Thus we are concerned to draw up an axiom set and rules of inference to derive the theorems from the axiom set. Then we look to see if the system is consistent, since we obviously do not want to be able to draw conclusions and the negation of those same conclusions within the same system (Rescher and Brandon, 1980). We also want to look for the property of completeness, so that we want to know that a formal of axiomatic treatment of Boolean algebra does in fact give a complete picture of the algebra of classes, it expresses all the properties we want to express, such as in the formalisation of a term and does not express those properties as valid statements in the calculus which are not what we intended. The axiom set must also be fertile in that it "breeds" a large number of theorems. There is also another property we look for in axiomatic systems and that is the search for an algorithm or decision procedure. The basic idea is that an algorithm or a decision procedure is a shorthand mechanical way of proving theorems and showing that a certain string of symbols is a theorem (or has or has not a certain property) within a system. If we have such an automatic procedure, which has sometimes been referred to as computable, then it greatly facilitates the system and makes it computable in the obvious sense of the work 'computable'.

Many axiomatic systems have decision procedures and many others do *not* have decision procedures, and we should also mention that in the building up of the foundations of mathematics, one of the primary questions which has been asked is whether the whole of mathematics has a decision procedure. Since the celebrated work of Gödel, Turing and Church we know the answer to this question to be "no". Our interest in this chapter is primarily in the use of logic by automata or robots (most often in practice in the form of computer programs). But in keeping with our belief that logic finds its roots in a simple associative processing, it is reasonable to have noticed the activity of maze-runners such as CEDRIC (George, 1979) which seem in their behaviour to be drawing simple inferences. This is in keeping with the evidence from psychological experiments cited earlier.

The next step though is to recognise the need for heuristic methods, as well as the use of algorithmic methods in this, as in all other fields of cognition. Let us now start to follow the pilgrimage towards the goal of theorem-proving, bearing in mind that it is not possible to give comprehensive coverage to all that has been done, all I can hope to dare is try to show the essence of what is involved. We shall, to this end, continue to bear in mind the distinction between the contexts of discovery and justification set up by Reichenbach (1938).

Early Programs

The names of Newell *et al.* (1963) are closely associated with the first heuristic programs, and we shall look briefly at some of their work, which relates to what we have called "higher cognitive activities", in this case logic and problem solving. It is clear, as we have frequently remarked, that we cannot and would not wish to wholly extricate logic from its context in use, both of a linguistic kind and in general problem solving.

The first program is called the Logic Theory Machine (LT) and it is concerned with theorem-proving in the propositional calculus (P). Wang (1960a, 1960b, 1960c, 1965) has shown that large tracts of *Principia Mathematica* could be reproduced by pattern-recognition methods which are essentially algorithmic, but Newell *et al.* were interested less in reproducing mathematics than in analysing human problem-solving methods (especially heuristic methods).

Theorems in P are produced by applications of the rules of inference to the axioms. Thus we use *substitution*, where for example substituting lpq for p in the following form

lplpq

gives us

lpqlllpqq.

We also use replacement which is simply a substitution by definition. So, for example,

lpq = df.ONpq

implies that lpq can be substituted for ONpq wherever it occurs. We also have the rule known as *modus ponens* which allows us to say of any well formed formulae A and B that if A is a theorem and if IAB is a theorem, then B is a theorem; A and B are variables in P's meta-language.

The executive routine of the programs uses these methods to try to prove theorems in P, much as a human being would. The executive routine uses also the transitivity of the material implication l to create sub-problems. Thus if the problem is lac, and lab is proved, then the new sub-problem is lbc, since if we can prove that then we can prove lac.

Newell *et al* generate a tree-structure of proofs for sub-problems and then they use a process called *matching*. This is essentially heuristic and looks for formulae whose main connectives and form are identical, so that the process of substitution is capable of being followed in order to produce the solution to a sub-problem. This is essentially a pattern-recognition process and short circuits the process of trial and error which would be followed by any sort of algorithmic process.

The second set of heuristic programs associated with Newell *et al.* is a human thought simulator called GPS (General Problem Solver). GPS deals with objects in the environment which can be transformed by operators. It can detect differences between objects and it organizes the information about the environment into goals. There are three types of operations: (1) transform object A into object B; (2) reduce difference D between object A and object B; and (3) apply operator Q to object A.

The basic method is to achieve goals by setting up sub-goals whose attainment lead to the goals. The methods used are then those of symbolic logic and the experimental method is to compare the protocols gathered from human problem-solvers with the *trace* of the program followed by GPS. The development of GPS depends upon continued experimentation by which the trace rules can be fitted more nearly to the protocols. But over and above this we see the need which is inherent in all this type of research for goal-orientated logic.

GPS, is, in a sense, in its infancy and is so because it is central to all other heuristic programs; it is central, in particular, to human (creative) problem-solving. The heuristics used are essentially those of pattern recognition and it is for this reason that we must think of pattern recognition as central to our conceptual problem.

It should be emphasised that in talking of pattern recognition we are talking of *conceptual* pattern recognition rather than *perceptual* pattern recognition. The latter is more usually associated with the function of the special senses, as was made clear in our earlier chapter on *perception*.

We should mention here the work of Nillson (1971) and Slagle (1971), who have described in detail tree-searching which draws attention to forward search, and a "breadth-first search" where we can think in terms of heuristic search procedures, some of which go broad and then deep and others which go deep and then broad. We have already touched on this.

Samuel (1963) has written heuristic programs for playing checkers (draughts) and we here briefly summarise what we said earlier. The game is played with a numbered board and is essentially similar to the adaptive program written for noughts-and-crosses. It involves, however, a 'look ahead' technique and a special scoring polynomial for assessing the play. The look ahead procedure is used to simulate all possible future board states for a few moves ahead.

The scoring polynomial considers 'piece advantage', although this is couched in terms which suggest that when the player is ahead on pieces, he will then try to exchange as many pieces as possible. The scoring polynomial also considers positional advantage which is couched in terms of considerations such as control of maximum number of (say central) squares and the like. It also weights Kings to pieces in a ratio of 3 to 2. An examination is made of moves from a 'minimax' point of view, and the look-ahead procedure can be varied in depth as a function of other conditions such as the last move being a 'jump' or the next move being a 'jump' etc.

Various programs were written and some involved the computer playing against itself. Learning takes place in these programs in various forms. Rote learning of look-ahead evaluations from previous games are stored and used when the same board position is encountered again. Generalisation was possible in certain programs where not only were the parameters of the evaluation polynomial adjusted in the light of experience, but certain parameters can be dropped and others brought in. The whole procedure followed by Samuel was, as in the case of LT and GPS, fairly complicated, and we are only able here to describe the essential features of the program (see Chapter 5).

One example of a practical application of heuristic programming is that of the trust investment process (Clarkson, 1963). This is again a problem in decision-making under conditions of uncertainty and involves list of industries and companies. From this list a search of selection process takes place with respect to a set of rules or criteria.

The rules involve the individual investor's own criteria. For example, it must be established whether he wants capital or income gain, etc., and any views he wants imposed on the selection procedure should be included. This information is conjoined with information about the general economy, information about industries and information about particular companies. From records held in store the current value, ten-year average value and recent changes in value can all be established.

The essence of the procedure is to create a portfolio of 'probables', and the process is both iterative and recursive. Its aim is to simulate the trust investor and this it already seems to do as well as most (human) trust investors. Thus the next step will be to try to show an improvement on any existing trust investment policy; there are many "more algorithmic" models in existence with which comparisons can be made.

There are certain obvious heuristics involved and one is that you do not buy a security if it is not held by other reputable institutions. This appears to inhibit any new security ever getting into the system but, of course, it is not necessarily rigorously applied in *every* case. Similarly, another heuristic is never to accept a loss, but this too cannot always operate. The remainder of the heuristics are all connected with sales, earnings, cash flow per share, profit margin, working capital, price earnings ratio, dividend payout ratio, dividends per share, dividend yield, prices, etc., and these are considered in terms of current state and average over past few years, with the emphasis on recent changes.

Such programs can be made adaptive and change to meet changing needs, but the principles involved are fairly straightforward.

Other heuristic programs have been written to deal with diversification expansion and acquisition and it is sufficient to say here that the principles used are essentially the same as are found in Clarkson's work. A slightly different form of heuristic program is one for 'balancing' an assembly line (Tonge 1963), but space forbids that we describe it here. A whole host of further heuristic programs are in the course of development at the time of writing, and these apply to every aspect of human activity; in a sense though they all involve inference making, even if one step removed from logic itself, certainly in the sense of theorem proving.

The Graph Transverser (GT) is the next type of learning system (to solve a "logical" problem) that we should mention. GT supplies automatic methods of search for solutions to problems of a certain kind. GT follows on GPS where a problem consists of a set of states, one or more of which is labelled goal, and this can collectively be thought of as a problem graph. A rule book says what moves can be made from one state to another and a solution in reaching the goal state, subject perhaps to certain constraints. We may, as with Burstall's network program (1970), start from a feasible solution or we may start in any given state.

State evaluation or operator evaluation represent the two main approaches to automatic problem solving, where the operators (as in GPS) are means of transforming states, and we evaluate them with respect to their effectiveness of producing 'good' sub-goals.

GT concentrates first on state evaluation, and then on operator evaluation, often over compound rather than elementary moves, and can integrate state and operator evaluation. GT will eventually be able to aggregate its previous experience and inductively derive general principles. Operator selection (or 'pruning' as Michie calls it) is a vital part of GT and several methods and applications have been developed to deal with the development of the nodes of the problem graph. The notion of penetrance is introduced as a measure of the efficiency of GT where penetrance is defined as

$$\frac{\text{Number of developed nodes on path,}}{\text{Total number of nodes developed.}}$$

Where penetrance is a 100 per cent then we have the highest efficiency since we have developed only those nodes (problem-configurations) that are necessary to reach the goal state (the arcs of the graphs are identified with the moves).

GT has been used characteristically on the eight-puzzle which has goal state:

$$\begin{pmatrix} 1 & 2 & 3 \\ 8 & 0 & 4 \\ 7 & 6 & 5 \end{pmatrix}$$

viewing the numbers as motor trucks which have to be circulated and parked, starting from some state other than the goal state. Heuristics are involved, under the name 'conditional-choice strategy', aided if necessary by random decisions at nodal points. We can now evaluate and order the operators in the light of final success or in the light of the operator's penetrance.

To write a problem-solving program for any particular problem requires the writing of input and output routines, the first of which transforms the external problem-state into its internal integer matrix representation, the second of which does the opposite. This is followed by a develop procedure which, when given a node, lists all immediate *descendents*, which are all the nodes which can be reached from it along a particular path, and this is followed by the *evaluation* procedure.

There are many applications of Graph Traverser and one we should mention here is that of Shen Lin's (1965) to the Travelling Salesman's problem. This is, in a sense, a typical transportion problem and Shen Lin supplied an algorithm (a conditional choice stategy) which was based essentially on the ability to take out a certain set of locations and change their order if necessary, and replace them in the complete 'tour' to see if the 'cost of the tour' can be reduced. All of Shen Lin's work can be put into GT terms and when this is done by representing a complete tour as a single state of the problem graph, an operator then corresponds to the extraction and replacement of a simple section of the tour (involving three 'cities' say, a so-called '3-cut'), and then, by partially developing the nodes of GT (thus leaving some developments for later as needed) it is possible to improve on the Shen Lin search technique.

Let us say here by way of summary that the on-going work on GT seems to hold out high hopes for development towards a general theory of 'automatic' problem-solving. At the same time it should be made clear that much of the work done by others on heuristic programming could, if needed, be re-stated in terms of GT.

The Generality of Learning

We should now mention the problem of the generality of our learning models. We tend to have "on-the-shelf" methods for limited aspects of learning and problem-solving, and when we look more closely at them we find they have a limited domain of application. This requires that we see how they can be adapted to real life situations. This in turn often requires that we move from the need to recognise algorithmic methods to the actual use of heuristic methods, where the heuristics used are approximations to the algorithms or an adaptation of the algorithms. We now move on to a brief statement of language and inductive logic and their importance in learning from the viewpoint of artificial intelligence.

So far we have discussed the use of heuristic programs for problem solving and the processing of either physical objects or data. We should now mention in a little more detail the close relationship that heuristic programming has to natural language, and each of those has to learning.

Natural language programming, as it is sometimes called (Simmons 1962), is concerned primarily with the organisation of information in store for question-answering purposes, and all this has already been discussed at length in the last chapter. But just to remind the reader let us say that the questions are asked in a natural language such as English, linked to the retrieval of data, or inference making, which also can include data retrieval. The beginnings of natural language programming go back only a relatively few years, when systems like NAMER, ORACLE, SIR and other language systems were developed. One of the most recent is LIP (Sarker and George, 1969; George, 1972a). LIP in its simpler form is merely a data retrieval system for questions asked in natural language, but in more complex form can deal with both inference making and detailed syntactical analysis. The end product is ultimately hoped to be something near the conversational piece envisaged by Turing (1951).

It is not our intention to discuss natural language programming further here, but merely to remind ourselves again of what was said in the last chapter, that it is often closely associated with heuristic programming and especially with logic, since so much of heuristic programming started from non-numerical foundations. It is natural too that, since heuristics are very much like hypotheses, these can be stated in natural language, and such hypotheses are representative of heuristics. It is obviously true that heuristics can also take a numerical form, but it is also true that most of the heuristics, certainly as used by human beings in ordinary day to day planning and problem solving activities, tend to be in the form of natural language statements. Furthermore, such planning and problem solving is a central ingredient of learning, or at least overlaps it in some considerable degree. Natural language progamming and heuristic programming is done heuristically, and logic is so often one of the principal ingredients.

The construction of natural language programming and its close relationship to heuristic programming makes one think of another aspect of heuristic programming which is also relevant, and that is heuristic generation. When we talk about heuristics being adaptive we mean that they can change as circumstances change. But the modification of heuristics. It is perhaps easiest to liken it to a function f(x) where changing the function from f to g, giving g(x), say, is heuristic generation.

Heuristic modification (simple learning) and heuristic generation (more complex learning) differ no doubt only in degree, but the degree to which they differ does seem to be important. The generation of heuristics is akin to the formulation (i.e. learning) of new concepts or the having of new ideas, and presumably plays a central part in human intelligence, and therefore is an important part of artificial intelligence.

Only a few programs have so far been written which deal with heuristic generation, but the attempt to do so (George, 1972) takes the following lines. Either heuristics can be generated from existing heuristics or they can be generated *ab initio*. The generation of heuristics from existing heuristics can be achieved by taking an existing heuristic and simply changing its detail. For example, rather than have a heuristic that says 'control the centre of the board', and here we are thinking of chess playing, we may, for the phrase 'centre of the board' read 'the left side of the board'. It might be, however improbable it may seem, that controlling the left side of the board is a very good tactic.

To some extent we see from this example that the generation of new heuristics from old is much more akin to heuristic modification than the generation of wholly new heuristics. The generation of wholly new heuristics implies the ability to computerise the inductive process. Given a set of particularities one has to formulate the generalisation which is appropriate to them.

One of the most important features of heuristic generation is that the logical methods used should be goal directed. In other words, logic, whether inductive or deductive, is normally a permissive discipline telling you what inferences *can* be made. In practical problem solving situations, the scientist and therefore the heuristic generator, must have his heuristic *goal directed* to achieve the desired end. As a result of this, a certain amount of attention has been given to the need for setting up empirical axiomatic or quasi-axiomatic systems: these are precisely learning models or, more correctly, models capable of learning. Although a certain amount has been done in the past to try to place empirical descriptions on an axiomatic basis (Carnap, 1958; Woodger, 1937, 1939; Reichenbach, 1947), most of this work was still not goal-oriented logic and this work will be closely related to heuristic programming, and therefore closely related to learning. Now let us proceed to theorem-proving as such.

Theorem-proving

In recent years work on theorem-proving has greatly intensified, and the early work of Newell, Shaw and Simon, and Hao Wang, has been greatly extended.

The Propositional calculus, the Predicate calculus, and the Functional calculus have been the principal systems on which theorem-proving has been based. One notable exception to this general trend lies in one of the early, but very excellent program by Gelerntner (1963) on theorem-proving in geometry. The methods used by Gelerntner are similar to those used by Newell, Shaw and Simon in LT, and the following flowchart shows the general principles on which it works. It is of interest to contrast again the work of Newell, Shaw and Simon with that of Wang and Gilmore (1959, 1960) where the difference of emphasis is that of heuristic methods and then use in the case of the former and an interest in theorem-proving *per se* in the case of the second. The second, as one might expect is more efficient, but the former of greater interest from the point of view of future methodological development.

In talking of logic theorem-proving we should certainly mention the work of Meltzer, (1974). He reminds us that the main single method has been syntactical, and recent work has depended especially upon Robinson's resolution logic. This is so because a proof procedure depends upon two things: Robinson's logic provides a framework for both tasks simultaneously by the use of a single rule of inference. We can take Meltzer's example to illustrate what is entailed. We want, let us suppose, to show the contradictions of the sets of literals in the four clause instances:

~M (a) or D [f (a), a] or ~N (a) (1)

~D [f (a), a] (2)

~M (a) or N (a) (3)

M (a) (4)

We can carry out the test by use of truth-tables, but we can do it more simply since (2) contains the negation of one of the literals in (1). This means we can infer the clause

$$\sim M(a) \text{ or } \sim N(a) \tag{5}$$

from (1) and (2). Similarly from (5) and (3) we can infer

$$\sim M(a) \tag{6}$$

(6) and (4) now yield an immediate contradiction. We can, by analogy, infer from (6) and (4) the so-called empty clause: this concludes the proof. There are a series of steps in the process. Any two clauses are examined to see if one contains a literal which is a negation of a literal in the other. For example, in the above argument (3) and (4) clearly contain ~ M(a) and M(a). If they do have this contradiction then, a new clause is formed which is the set of all the remaining literals. One merely writes the two clauses after eliminating the two complements and when the clause inferred is empty, the proof is complete.

Robinson's resolution logic avoids the need to generate the set of instances. It operates more generally using clauses with variables. In the above example, it takes as input the four general clauses. In the following, primes are used to indicate that the different clauses have different variables:

$$\sim M(x) \text{ or } D[f(x), x] \text{ or } N(x) \tag{7}$$

$$\sim D(x^1, y^1) \tag{8}$$

$$\sim M(x^{11}) \text{ or } N(x^{11}) \tag{9}$$

$$M(a) \tag{10}$$

You now look for literals that might be made complementary by applying an appropriate substitution to the variables. Thus in (7) and (8) if we substitute $x^1 = f(x), y^1 = x$, we can infer:

$$\sim M(x) \text{ or } \sim N(x) \tag{11}$$

Then in (11) and (9) we make the substitution $x^{11} = x$ giving

$$\sim M(x) \tag{12}$$

Now (12) and (10) with substitution x = a giving the empty clause and the proof.

The resolution procedure is permissive and says only what can be done. To convert this to a proof procedure, which says, what *shall* be done, constraints need to be added which we shall not describe here. There are, of course, other limitations on these methods such as its clumsiness in handling equality, but nevertheless such methods hold out hope for future development in logic theorem-proving. We have also similar hopes for what is perhaps an even more important task, the development of inductive logic.

Much work has been done on logic theorem-proving and we should draw attention to the work of Darlington (1969) on theorem-proving and information retrieval. He makes the point that an information retrieval system should be able to perform logical inferences as well as merely retrieve data. He goes on to say that such inference making is similar to that performed in logic theorem-proving and in question-answering programs.

Simmons and Bruce (1971) have worked on the relationship between a predicate calculus and a semantic net representation of discourse. They show that networks can be used to represent the syntactic trees of the semantic relationships holding between different words of a sentence. They present a method for converting a semantic network into predicate calculus formalism. A semantic network is defined as a system of unambiguous symbols interconnected by definable semantic relations. We will shortly define it more precisely. The value of using such semantic networks is that rules can be supplied to cover vague or partially defined concepts. They provide an example:

"The young man ate some meat."
"Did the young man eat some meat?"
"Yes."

Such a dialogue does not presume a precise understanding, for example, of the word 'some'. Such semantic nets allow the use of simple matching procedures and seems nearer to natural language form that the predicate calculus.

Kling (1971) has also developed the use of heuristics for problem solving, and the special interest in his work lies in the use of analogical thinking in a manner reminiscent of Bobrow (1966). His work is designed to speed the problem solving search and to this end he has designed a system called ZORBA which helps the generating of analogies. The system uses a simple logical theory and semantic rules. The analogies are not formal, but they can be handled within the context of a formal theory which can be conveniently dovetailed to individual needs, furthermore it not only supplies relevant analogies but suggests the manner in which such analogies could be used.

Next we should mention among our selection of contributors, the work of Koenig and Schultz (1972). They have made a mathematical analysis for a general logical discourse to enable the computer to communicate conveniently with a human being. The mathematical analysis is essentially set theoretic and deals in combinational mathematics in order to establish sets of primitives for what they call a "prerequisite graph" and a "sequence graph" for logical discourse. These represent methods for structuring logical discourse for the interaction between man and machine and is in some ways reminiscent of Amarel's work on the representation of problems and the effect this representation has on the simplicity with which such problems can be solved.

The bulk of theorem-proving is generally of two forms: heuristic, as with Newell, Shaw and Simon, or axiomatic-complete, as associated with J.A. Robinson. A third possible approach is by use of models, and as Meltzer (1968) has pointed out, Herbrand's theorem provides a link between the axiomatic-complete and the model approach.

Herbrand's theorem can be expressed in the form that, given a set of axioms of a theory expressed in the lower predicate calculus, these can, by certain transformations, be converted into clauses which are the disjunction of atomic predicates (negated or otherwise) over arguments which are either constants or universally quantified variables.

From Herbrand's theorem, theorem-proving programs show that the conjunction of the axioms with an alleged theorem lead to a contradiction. The approach is analogous to trying to show a wff is not a theorem by use of truth-tables. This use of a Herbrand domain turns out to be a very powerful tool in theorem-proving and is the basis for much current research.

Robinson's (1965, 1968) generalised resolution principle has, as already noted, also played a major part in this work. The principle is a single-inference principle which provides a complete formulator of the quantifier-free first-order predicate calculus with equality. The completeness theory of the generalised resolution principle uses the idea, as above, of trying of construct counter-examples to the theorems, which we wish to prove. To this end a detailed syntactic and semantic description are necessary and we then consider any proposition of the form "sentence Y follows from a set of sentences X" and Y follows from X if and only if the interpretations which (strongly) satisfy X, there is none which falsifies Y.

To see a tree of sentences is a proof to see that the proposition at each of its interior nodes is a theorem. This leads us directly to semantic trees, which we now define more precisely.

T is a *semantic tree* for P, if K is a set of atoms in the premises (X) or the conclusion (Y) of a ground proposition P. T is a tree of sentences (nodally connected) each one of which is a conjunction whose literals are all atoms (or complements of atoms) in K. All this is subject to the following four conditions being satisfied at each node N of T, where C is the conjunction of all the literals in all of the conjunctions at the nodes on the branch of T down to and including N and $C_1, \ldots, C_R$

1) There is no atom L in K such that C → L and C → ~ L

2) C → (C_1 V ... VCK)

3) There is no literal M in C_v, such that C → L and C → ~ L for each L in K

4) If N is a tip of T, then C → L or C → ~ L for each L in K.

X → Y means that X implies Y and X → Y is a ground proposition where "strongly" is omitted from the above definition of X → Y. Such methods have had a great impact on theorem-proving (Luckham, 1968, Kowalski and Hayes 1969).

More recently Pastre (1980) and others have worked on axiomatic theorem-proving within set theory and have made great strides in theorem-proving, while recognising some of the limitations of their work, especially in understanding more completely how mathematician's do their job (Remember Clarkson's (1953) simulation of the trust-investment officer) and the need for introducing learning and accumulated memory into the context of theorem-proving.

One example, of this more recent work must suffice. Murray (1982) has shown theorem-proving operating on quantifier-free formulae of the predicate calculus (non-normalized for truth-functions). He used a single inference rule NC-resolution which is shown complete.

NC-resolution is defined in terms of sets of wff U_jS and U_iS and the notion of polarity. Polarity is defined wth respect to A, B, and w as wffs. W is positive in A if (if and only if) at least one occurrence of w in A is positive (similarly for negative) and the polarity of the constituents of a wff as (1). If w is positive in A then w is negative in A and A → B (and vice-versa). (2) If w is positive in A then w is positive in (A v B), (A . B) and (B → A). (3) If w occurs in A, then w is positive and negative in A ↔ B. (↔ means "logical equivalence"). From such beginnings Murray shows a number of theorems, and we can here only outline one example.

Murray uses NC-resolution in terms of the factorial function (Fact) given by

$$\text{Fact}\ (01) \qquad (1)$$

$$(\text{Fact}\ (x + 1\, y)\,) \rightarrow (\text{Fact}\ x\ z).\ \text{Times}\ (x + 1\, z\, y)\,) \qquad (2)$$

A new predicate Fact * is now defined in terms of Fact, which is interpreted "if the factorial of x is y, the factorial of u is v". This is written Fact * (x y u v). This computes bottom-up, iteratively. Fact * is a wff and is:

$$(\text{Fact}\ *\ (x\ y\ u\ v)\,) \leftrightarrow (\text{Fact}\ (x\ y) \rightarrow \text{Fact}\ (u, v)\,) \qquad (3)$$

He next NC-resolves (1) and (3) by matching the positive atom Fact (01) with the atom F (x y)

He next takes

$$\text{Fact}\ (01)\ \{F/\text{Fact}\ (01)\}\ v\ (\text{Fact}^*\ (01\ u\ v)$$
$$\rightarrow (\text{Fact}\ (01) \rightarrow \text{Fact}\ (u\ v)\,)\ \{T/\text{Fact}\ (01)\}$$

which is reduced to

$$\text{Fact}\ (u\ v) \leftarrow \text{Fact}^*\ (01\ u\ v) \qquad (4)$$

We have a copy of (3) written for x′, y′, u′ and v′ and the four atoms involving Fact are unified the mg u {x/u, y/v, x/x′, y/y′, x/u′, y/v′} The matching atom is positive and negative (3) and its copy, but the two NC-resolvents are identical

$$\text{Fact}\ *\ (x\ y\ x\ y) \leftrightarrow (\text{Fact}\ (x\ y) \rightarrow \text{Fact}\ (x\ y)\,)$$
$$\{T/\text{Fact}\ (x\ y)\}\ v\ \text{Fact}^*\ (x\ y\ x\ y) \leftrightarrow (\text{Fact}\ (x\ y)$$
$$*\ \text{Fact}\ (x\ y)\,)\ \{F/\text{Fact}\ (x\ y)\}$$

which reduces to

$$\text{Fact}\ *\ (x\ y\ x\ y) \qquad (5)$$

He then derives the iterative part of the program by NC-resolving (2) and (3), and so on until he derives

$$\text{Fact}\ *\ (x + 1\ y\ u\ v) \leftarrow (\text{Times}\ (x + 1\ z\ y).\ \text{Fact}\ *\ (x\ z\ u\ v)\,) \qquad (6)$$

and then (4), (5) and (6) comprise what is called a Horn-clause logic program for computing the factorial function. The problem is a characteristic one, as is the method, which indeed requires a considerable knowledge and background familiarity with the work of theorem-proving. But the example at least gives some idea of the sort of processes involved.

It is not our intention to pursue this increasingly specialised field any further here, but return to a consideration of the work as viewed more globally.

More Generally

Now to widen once more the approach to logic (moving again into the broader context of problem solving), two further programs, one LOGO-turtles (Papert, 1973) and the second MYCROFT (Goldstein 1975) might reasonably be considered together as was done by Margaret Boden (1977). Indeed she also included HACKER (Sussmans 1975). The idea is that HACKER is, as its name suggests, a sort of general purpose problem solving device which learns from experience and does so by collecting particular experiences, classifying them and noting the mistakes to be avoided in future. It operates mainly in the world of Winograd's SHRDLU. The process is a logical compilation of the sort of order in which things are best done, so to put block A on block B, make sure B is available and has not already got a block on it and so on. The sophistication of HACKER is very considerable and it is essentially a learning-by-doing (acquaintance rather than description).

LOGO programs (or LOGO-turtles) are capable of carrying out live drawings of people and things which can be clearly representational. The task is equivalent to block building, and in either case the role of MYCROFT is to act as critic, or even rather like a tutor. This enables MYCROFT to look at HACKER or LOGO-turtles at work and point out errors (debugging in a sense) or possible sources of improvement. This means more than pointing to an error, it also means explaining why the error occurred and how it can be guarded against in future.

This particular approach, akin to the simulation of a tutor and pupil, has the obvious element of logic in it, and of course can, given the appropriate knowledge, actually look at any of the theorem-proving programs and suggest improvements in them.

Enough has now perhaps been said to give the flavour of the broader aspects of logic within the problem-solving context. For a detailed account of this sort of approach reference should be made to Margaret Boden's excellent book *Artificial Intelligence and Natural Man.*

Before we come to our summarising thoughts, a brief word on neurophysiology would seem appropriate.

A Note on Neurophysiology

If we think of inference-making behaviour and logic in neurophysiological terms, we quickly see the limitations on our knowledge of the brain's function. A great deal on one hand is known about language (Pribram 1971, Sommerhoff, 1974) and to the extent the logic occurs in language, then the speech centres will be involved. It is also known (Luria and Tsvetkova, 1967) that lesions of the frontal lobes disturb the processes of inference making. It has been suggested that posterior zones of the hemispheres are responsible for the operative conditions of problem solving and the details of inference making, while the integrative action of the frontal lobes is necessary to organising the inference making activities.

We now define 'concept' for one purpose here as a network of sign-significate inferences by which one goes beyond a set of observed criterial properties exhibited by an object or event to the class identity of the object or event in question, and thence to inferences about other unobserved properties of the object or event.

In neurophysiological terms, concepts occur in the secondary (elaboration areas) connected with the various senses, which means for example, areas 18 and 19 for vision; the more complex (higher level classifications) of complex concepts, are more centrally placed probably in the tertiary temporo-parietal areas. Korner (1959) has argued that *conceptual thinking* is typified, although not exhaustively illustrated, by the application and acceptance of ostensive rules. An ostensive rule is typified by a pointing operation accompanied by such a statement as "this and everything like this is green". This requires that bases for concepts be defined, and they may be defined in many ways rather as coordinates can be chosen in many different ways to define a space. The problem of interest that arises from Korner's work is that of the derivation of non-ostensive concepts and rules from either ostensive or non-ostensive bases.

The problems that Korner himself is most concerned with are those such as the derivation of mathematical or other such non-ostensive concepts, from ostensive or non-ostensive bases. This represents another challenge — how can, if at all, a computer program be written so as to perform these sorts of operation? It can be said straight away that this *may* turn out to involve no more than the ability to generalise, although this is a vital step and not easy to simulate over the same range as human beings operate. This is bound to remain one of the acid tests, since ultimately we must be able to simulate "original and creative" thinking, whatever that entails.

Korner himself was concerned with rules that can be applied to conceptual thinking and carefully distinguished this undertaking from the obviously empirical one of deciding how people actually use concepts. We are concerned to some extent with both problems and certainly with the logical one of prescribing rules and of course, even more at the moment, with the way these rules and processes are represented neurally.

Thinking, as we have made clear, will be (and will contain inference making as a principal ingredient) explicitly thought of as contiguous with problem solving and learning, but will in human beings depend a great deal more on the internal symbolic representation of what Sommerhoff (1974) calls externally derived experience. This is fair comment, but may also involve, as in the case of logic and confirmation for example, internal experience, in an obvious sense. It is also assumed here that the internal model refers to internal events as well as external ones; somewhere here indeed arises the question of consciousness.

It is clear that much of thinking is accompanied by images, and much is accompanied by visual images as well as linguistic symbols: these clearly go together.

Luria (1973) has said:

> ... the young child thinks in terms of visual forms of perception and memory or, in other words, he *thinks by recollecting.* At later stages ... abstract thinking with the aid of the functions of abstraction and generalization is so highly developed that even simple processes such as perception and memory are converted into complex forms of logical analyses and synthesis, and the person actually begins to *perceive or recollect by reflection.*

Later in more neurological terms Luria says:

> ... *the tertiary zones of the posterior cortical region play an essential role in the conversion of concrete perception into abstract thinking,* which always proceeds in the form of *internal* schemes.

By the tertiary zones we mean, of course, the overlapping areas between the occipital, temporal and post-central cortex and mostly in the inferior parietal region. The areas mainly involved are Brodman areas 5, 7, 39 and 40 of the superior and infererior parietal regions, area 21 of the temporal and areas 37 and 39 of the temporo-occipital region.

The primary areas of the general sensory (parietal) cortex are mainly composed of associative neurons in layers II and III and the secondary areas (1, 3, 5 and part of area 40) are superimposed on the primary areas.

The implication from much research work in these areas suggests that these are areas of increasingly high-level integration (higher level classification systems). Primary zones are highly specific in every case in the cortex and as we go to second and tertiary zones so their activity is increasingly less specific. One should note here that the primary cortical zones of each hemisphere are thought to have identical roles and only the higher level areas are specific to the relevant hemisphere.

Much of thinking is admittedly explicitly and obviously motivated. Indeed much (but we continue to argue not all) of thinking is identifiable with problem solving. In so far as this is so then the second stage is as much — or more — concerned with the "delaying of a response" (Korzybski's (1933) term) than with responding. What should happen now is an examination of the relevant data, which means a consideration of more perceptions and more beliefs of a conceptual kind, and this brings us to the performance if any is required. But what happens in the brain? Let us look at the effect of lesions on different cortical areas.

In the case of Koh's blocks (or equivalent tasks), the spatial synthesis is necessary to place the blocks in appropriate patterns is disturbed by lesions in the parieto-occipital zones of the dominant hemisphere. Serious lesions altogether destroy the ability to form the necessary patterns. According to Luria the use of spatial co-ordinates, providing a framework for such cases, greatly helps them towards a satisfactory solution.

Those people with lesions of the frontal areas are very different. It is now the necessary analytical capacity which has either deteriorated or vanished. As Luria has put it:

> ... they do not proceed by trial and error, they do *not work actively* in order to complete the test, and they do not *evaluate* their mistakes.

Such patients are helped by analytical aids which are necessary to answer initial questions such as "how many blocks are there?" etc.

A different type of symbolic thinking is embodied in arithmetical problems and linguistic or logical problems, and their solution is based on methods which overlap the discussion of the last chapter on language. These problems tend to require the retention of a good deal of information in STM, and we find that lesions of the left temporal region disturb the necessary audio-verbal memory and also disturb the intermediate speech components in the solution process. If the problem is presented in writing, the solution finding process is helped.

A more detailed analysis of recordings and lesions in the dorso-lateral pre-frontal granular cortex in monkeys suggest (Stamm and Rosen, 1973) that where tasks involve spatial cues and delays, firing of groups of cells with large receptor fields fire prior to any required movement on the part of the monkey. The implication that "delayed response" and therefore attention (and thinking) may be involved is clear-cut. This is perhaps primarily representative of STM.

The past partietal cortex with lesions shows *apraxia* for dressing and other such manipulative activities, while lesions in areas 5 and 7 lead to deficits in tactual perception and visual fixation, tracking and the like (Mountcastle, 1975). The detail of this sort of work is like trying to piece together an almost infinitely large jigsaw puzzle.

Pribram (1971, p. 369-370) has expressed his views on thinking in fairly general and fairly definite terms:

> My hypothesis is that *all* thinking has, in addition to sign and symbol manipulation, a holographic component.

The reason for this belief is the admitted excellence of holography as an associative mechanism. There is no reason to question the Pribram hypothesis, but there are reasons to seek confirming evidence.

Pribram also asks as to the difference between thought and interest. Interest he sees as an emotional-motivational arousal which projects on to the outside world. Thought on the other hand is concerned with the world within. That thought be of interest, and a matter of *interest* can produce it, is fairly evident. Let us then try to make some explicit interim statement on logical thinking and the brain. It is necessarily interim because of the link with language which has not yet been made explicit.

Our problem occurs on various levels and we have sufficiently indicated how the process of forming simple and complex concepts and then bringing them together into hypotheses and other more complicated associations take place. Logical thinking is the processing of these associations linked to experience via perception and internally by a processing of the conceptual model.

Clearly the motivational features will play a part hence so we expect the involvement of the limbic system and other cortical areas of motivational representation. We know the frontal, temporo-parietal and occipital cortex are all involved and we can identify primary, secondary (elaboration) and tertiary areas (secondary elaboration) with each of the senses and somesthesis.

We also know that in the temporo-partietal areas — aided doubtless by chemistry, slow potentials and holography — a cross-associational process takes place in the hierarchical classifications necessary to thinking, but when we come to the exact role played by the amygdaloid nucleus or area 7, say, we have to be much more tentative.

In Summary

Finally I would like to make some overall comments on the findings of this chapter and do so in relation to the three previous chapters.

We have clearly arrived at the point where highly sophisticated programs are being written in order to both simulate and synthesise human cognition. Thus we started with perception and saw how there were many ways in which pattern, shape and colour recognition was possible at the level of *primary recognition* (Price, 1953), and we might think of this as primarily a visual matter. Then we saw how complex events involving people and things in a temporal context could be recognised (*secondary recognition*). The point has perhaps been sufficiently made to the effect that these achievements can themselves be made by various methods and no one would pretend that we *know* (with any degree of certainty) how human vision and perception worked, only some of the ways it might, or could, work.

Perceptual learning, as always, serves as a reminder, that perception overlaps the processes involved in remembering and adaptation that are so necessary to learning. These in turn imply inference making, which at least at the primitive level is so similar to learning. Both have at least seem to have their common roots in an associative process.

The advent of logic, and the wealth of AI work on theorem proving, and the advent of natural language programs, points to the higher level type of cognitive activity, and goes a long way to justify Wittgenstein's belief that thinking (at least in human beings) is entirely a linguistic matter. To some extent though this is a semantic issue in which we have to decide how widely (or narrowly) to use the word 'thinking'.

There is a sense in which problem solving is the broad context in which all these activities take place. In an obvious sense, to understand what a speaker says, to draw a valid inference (in whatever context), or to correctly interpret something presented to the visual system remains a problem to be solved. Problem solving in turn involves learning and thinking in some measure, and two of the most important features involved whether for the human being or the computer ("machine") seem to be pattern recognition and heuristic methods.

In this present chapter on logic, inference making and theorem proving, I have only been able to summarise quite briefly what is, of course, a vast subject. Logical problems and inference making permeate philosophy and psychology, and are bound, as Quine has made abundantly clear (1975), eventually to be of major interest in neurophysiology. It is clear that AI, should be especially interested in what is such a fundamental feature of human thinking.

We can abstract from a behavioural context in which inference making takes place and think in terms of linguistic and symbolic logic, and such logical activities, including theorem proving can clearly be carried out on the computer. For a human being to do the same thing is difficult and requires, in the limit, a great deal of specialisation. We can guess that concept formation and the ability to formulate hypotheses is an essential part of what is entailed. Thus we have classes (or properties) and induction which is the formal result of concepts and hypotheses, and no doubt these are the result of extremely complicated classifications and cross-associations in the nervous tissue of the cerebral cortex. Even if we can guess too that something like a Milner-modified (Milner, 1957) Hebb Cell assembly (1949) is operating (Palm, 1982), we still have a lot to learn to synthesise such a system, and even more to claim it as a simulation of the human brain. This though is a long term aim of AI and no doubt will one day be fully realised. For myself, I can think of no reason why it should not be possible. There is no reason (and this is a fundamental belief of most people in the field) to doubt that a "machine" (computer program) or some such model of the full range of human behaviour should be possible, even if it takes a lot longer to achieve than I once thought it might.

This brings to an end our discussion of what is primarily the development of what could be called the AI part (perhaps the most important part) of cybernetics, or perhaps let us say that I have attempted to show the context (philosophical, logical, psychological, cybernetic and neurophysiological) in which AI operates. An awareness of this context seems essential in order to highlight and encourage the most exciting of all modern science — artificial (machine) intelligence.

8

Knowledge-based Systems

In this last chapter we take up again the increasingly important matter of Knowledge-based systems and Expert systems. We have already said something earlier about both; we can distinguish the two in terms of generality (Feigenbaum & McCorduck, 1983). Knowledge-based systems contain large amounts of varied knowledge which is brought to bear on a given task. Expert systems are knowledge-based systems which are generally more specialised and concentrate on simulating the expert in some field such as medicine, fault finding or geological studies. Knowledge-based systems and expert systems are two terms that are sometimes used interchangeably.

Expert systems usually explain their logic as well as use it; some can even explain why one path was rejected and another followed. Since expert systems function best where inference-making is maximal, we shall expect to be influenced by this in our choice of subjects for treating in this matter. Then, having made the choice, we have the problem of *Knowledge Elicitation* which means examining one or more experts in our chosen subject in great detail with a view almost to performing psycho-analysis upon him. We want him to make his expertise explicit; we may have to watch him at work and see the degree of match between what he says he does and what he actually does, even if he can describe it at all.

The expert system we hope to arrive at has the following basic structure:

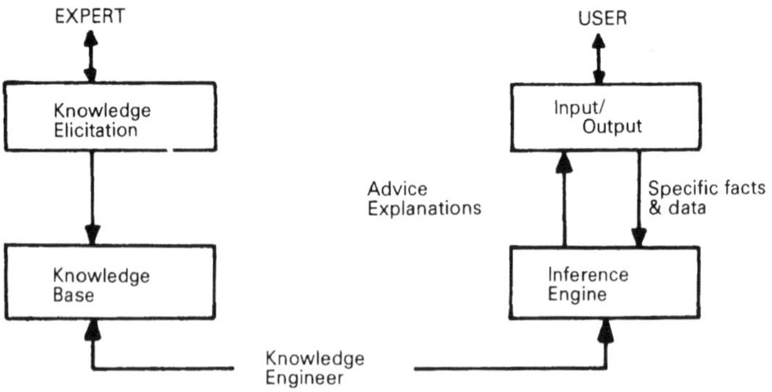

The two kinds of knowledge needed by an expert are the *facts* of the subject (the full "textbook" treatment of it) and the *heuristics* of the subject. This last, more difficult requirement, is that of good practice and judgement ("greenfingers") in the field. Your data base is the detail of the particular case you are dealing with; in medicine it is the patient's record sheet, while the knowledge base contains all the relevant knowledge of both the *factual* and *heuristic* type.

The knowledge elicitation state of constructing an expert system is carried out (excavated or "mined" out) by the knowledge engineers, who have, when the heuristic knowledge is made explicit, to formulate it appropriately for the computer.

The inference engine contains the reasoning and problem solving skills.

We will now illustrate the structure of expert systems by taking two examples: PROSPECTOR and INTERNIST 1. These are two that have been described with great clarity by Johnson and Keravnou (1984) and I have drawn directly on their work. First PROSPECTOR —

The application area of PROSPECTOR is Geology and its principal researchers are P. Hart and R. Duda of SRI International.

The function of PROSPECTOR is as an aid to geologists in evaluating mineral sites for potential ore deposits; this is clearly a matter of great importance in this day and age. PROSPECTOR (Gaschnig (1982), Duda et al (1979) and Reboh (1981)) accepts field observations from the user through an interactive dialogue and at the termination of the diagnostic process, produces a list of possible types of deposits present and their likelihood of actually being there; the most favourable drilling sites may then be located. The knowledge associated with a particular type of deposit is coded into a set of production rules, where uncertainties are inevitably associated with the rules. The 'inference network' resulting from the rule chainings (referred to as a *model*) is represented in the system as a *partitioned associative network.* Taxonomies of mineral types, rock types, physical forms and geological ages are also represented in the system's knowledge-base within the formalism of associative networks; this is the data store. Well authenticated facts appear as assertions within the inference networks. These are collected by interrogating the user. Initially *forward chaining* is used and then information volunteered and is taken from the user. After this initial stage the system switches to *backward chaining* and asks for information, but the user may still volunteer information and this may result in a new current goal hypothesis being chosen to investigate.

The hypothesis with the highest probability asserts the presence of some deposit class, this is selected as the goal. Every untried rule having the current hypothesis as a consequent, is scored according to how greatly it is thought to influence it, the highest scoring rule is selected and in this way a chain is linked.

PROSPECTOR with its static characteristics is atypical in allowing for taxonomies of concepts to be explicitly represented in its knowledge-base. The conceptual components of PROSPECTOR's knowledge-base are the taxonomies of concepts and the inference networks where each network models some class of deposits and are represented within the scheme of partitioned associative networks (Hendrix, 1979). The knowledge-base contains taxonomies of rock types, minerals, physical forms and geological ages.

The taxonomies are represented as hierarchical tree structures where the nodes are simple concepts of the domain connected by arcs indicating the element (e) and the subset (s) relationships between these concepts. Each node X in the hierarchical structure is said to be a restriction of its parent nodes or *of any node occurring on a chain of outgoing "e" and "s" arcs* from X. Similarly, X is a generalisation of any descendant node occurring on any chain of incoming "e" and "s" arcs to it.

For a more precise encoding of taxonomies, the standard set theoretic notions of set membership and set inclusion ("e" and "s" arcs respectively), are supplemented by the more restrictive notions of disjoint subsets (ds) and distinct elements (de). A "ds" arc from a node X to a node Z shows that X is a subset of Z and that X is disjoint from any other set Y with an outgoing "ds" arc to Z. Similarly, arcs labelled "de" indicate that each of two or more nodes denotes a different element of a set.

The rules coding the general knowledge associated with some class of deposit implicitly define an inference network of assertions, referred to as the model of the deposit class.

Each inference network (Figure 1) indicates how the observations (evidence) associated with the given deposit class, relate to intemediate geological hypotheses which eventually relate to the ultimate hypothesis, they assert the presence of the relevant deposit class. The assertions in the knowledge-base are represented in terms of places, and relations and arcs representing arguments. The associative network (inference) representation of a PROSPECTOR rule is represented in terms of a (rule-arc) plausible link, linking the space enclosing the network representation of the evidence statement to the partition enclosing the network representation of the hypothesis statement.

Different pieces of evidence can also be combined logically to form a single, compound piece of evidence. The simpler elements are combined by means of the logical connectives AND, OR and NOT. Rules can interconnect in various ways, such as through "chains" where the hypothesis for one rule is the evidence for another, through several pieces of evidence bearing on the same hypothesis, and through the same piece of evidence

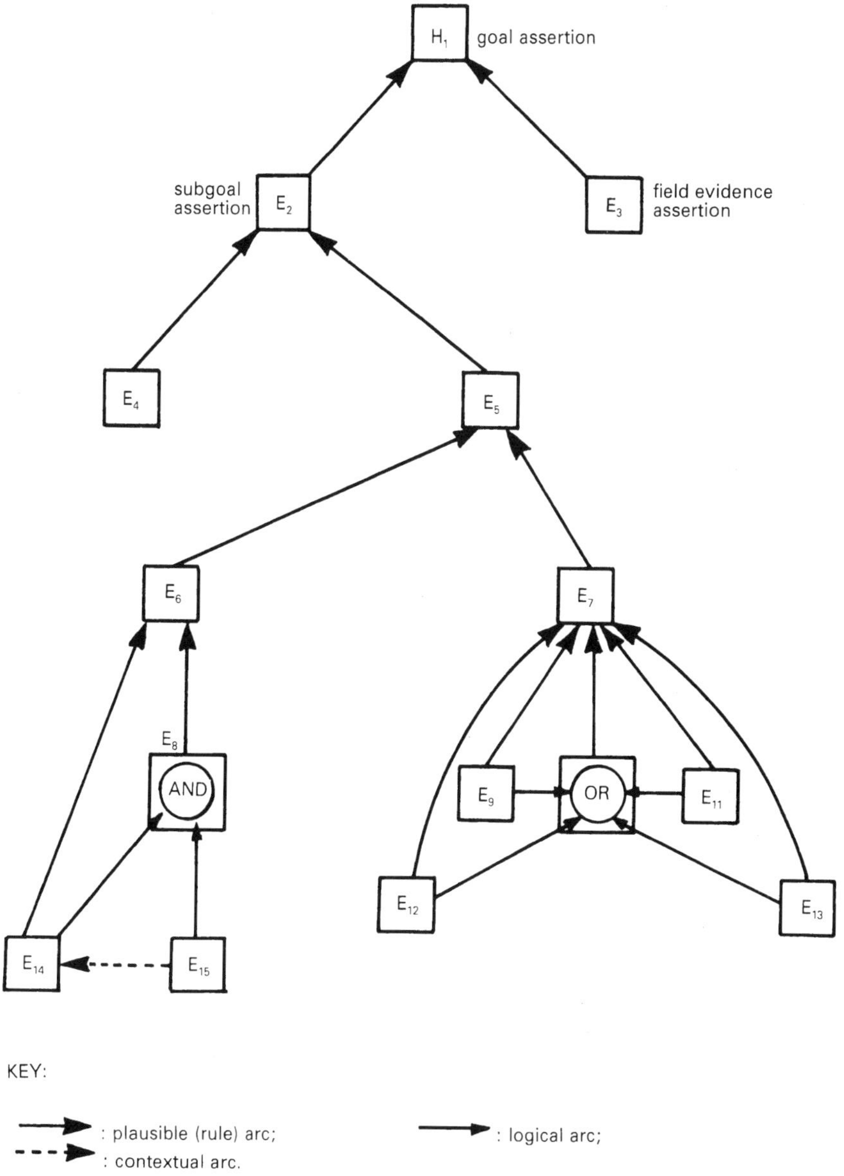

FIGURE 1 A simple inference network in PROSPECTOR (after Johnson and Keravnon).

bearing on several different hypotheses. Rules can also be linked implicitly through the element-subset "chains" e.g. when the antecedent of one rule is a restriction on the antecedent of another rule having the same hypothesis. A simple inference network representing the model of some ore-deposit is a hierarchical structure of assertions, linked through rule and logical arcs. The principal or top-level assertion of an inference network is the assertion that the available evidence matches that particular model. It is therefore the model's goal. The terminal assertions correspond to field evidence required by the user. Every assertion is assigned an *a priori* probability. There are also contextual links which are used to specify the order in which the relevant assertions are to be considered, when arbitrary ordering is meaningless.

In the dynamics of PROSPECTOR assertions corresponding to terminal nodes of the inference networks constitute direct evidence, assertions corresponding to intermediate nodes constitute both intermediate geological hypotheses and 'circumstantial' evidence for higher level assertions and assertions corresponding to the topmost nodes constitute the ultimate goal(s). The objective of the system is to determine the ore deposits likely to be present in the given situation context and recommend drilling sites. This is done by consultation with the user. The validity of every assertion in the given situation context is initially undetermined. The validity of assertions corresponding to pieces of evidence is determined by the user whilst the validity of intermediate and goal assertions is determined by the system. An assertion is therefore determined when its degree of truth (its *a posteriori* probability) in the given situation has been fully established. Thus the determined status can be refined into a whole sequence of status ranging from confirmed to denied.

When a consultation starts the user can volunteer any observations (evidence) considered significant. Such observations are used to update the *a priori* probabilities of the goal assertions by forward chaining from the terminal assertions. At every subsequent stage of the diagnostic process the system attempts to establish the most likely goal assertion.

A goal assertion is pursued by backward chaining: All the rules that end the assertion are determined, and the antecedent of the rule judged to be the one to most influence the current probability of the pursued assertion. Thus a rule chain, leading to a terminal assertion is gradually linked. When the hypothesis is to be pursued next corresponds to a piece of evidence then the user is asked about it. The effect of the answer is then put through the inference networks until the probability of every goal assertion reachable from the given terminal node has been updated. If by the end of this stage, the current goal assertion is still the most likely one then back-chaining resumes from where it had been interrupted. Otherwise back-

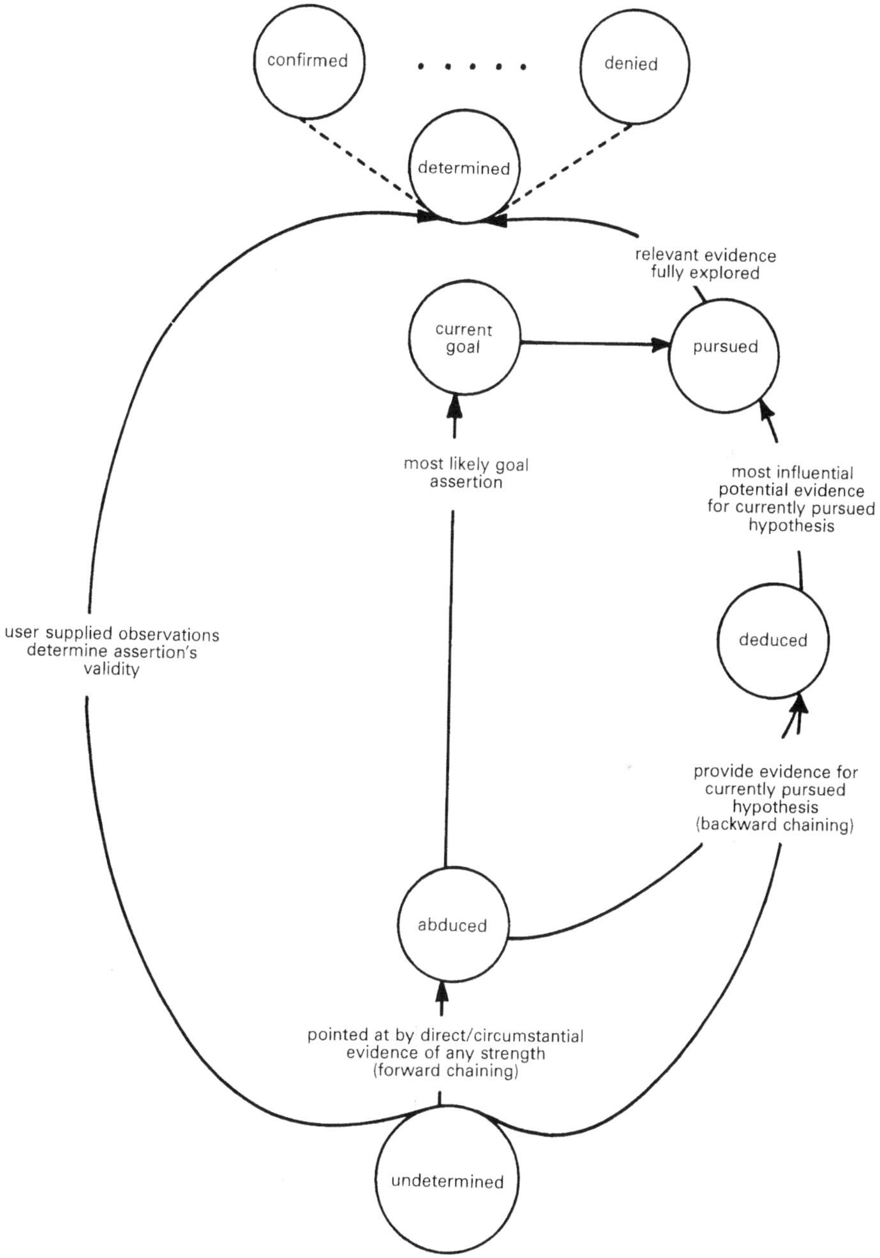

FIGURE 2 Assertion status transition diagram in PROSPECTOR (after Johnson and Keravnou).

chaining starts from the new most likely goal assertion. The diagnostic process terminates when every sufficiently promising model has been fully investigated.

User observations are entered in PROSPECTOR as simple declarative sentences accompanied with "certainty factors" (−5 to +5) denoting the user's degree of belief in the sentences' truthness. The system converts such sentences into their associative network representations and matches them against the knowledge-base assertions. A user observation either does not match with any assertion (in which case it is ignored) or it yields matches with some assertions. The match between a sentence referring to a user observation and a knowledge-base assertion is classified as one of *identity*, *restriction* (or *generalisation*) (the taxonomies of concepts play an important role in determining whether a sentence is a generalisation/restriction of another sentence, or overlapping, which means a match between some of the primitive component sentences of the two assertions occurs. A rule whose antecedent is either identical to, or a generalisation of, some user observation can be applied. However this is not so for a rule whose antecedent is either a restriction of or overlaps with some user observation. In such cases additional information needs to be elicited from the user before the relevant rules are rendered applicable.

The designers of PROSPECTOR believe that the representation scheme of associative networks provides the basis for building a mechanism for detecting inconsistencies in the evidence provided by the user. PROSPECTOR's model of inexact reasoning that dictates how to derive the degree of belief in a conclusion from the degrees of belief in the antecedents is probablistic, based on Bayes Rule. A detailed description of the model is given in Duda *et al.* (1979), but we can briefly say that the diagnostic process deals with two types of uncertainties:

i) uncertainties associated with the rules, and
ii) uncertainties associated with the evidence.

A PROSPECTOR production (inference) rule is of the format:

If E *then* (to degrees S, N) H

S is the sufficiency condition and N the necessity conditions; both have numeric values that specify the strength of association between E and H.

They are calculated from

$$S = \frac{P(E/H)}{P(E/\sim H)}$$

where S represents the degree of sufficiency of E in establishing H. N represents the degree of necessity of E in establishing H. If N approaches zero then E is *necessary* for H. The above conditional probabilities are not objective, i.e. they are not calculated from statistical samples, but they are subjective probabilities derived from the experts.

The inference networks' assertions are preassigned subjective *a priori* probabilities suggested by the experts, they are eventually converted into certainty factors. In general, the user cannot specify whether a piece of evidence is definitely present or absent, but only indicate a likelihood. From Bayes' Rule we can combine uncertainties in the following way:

$$P(H/E) = \frac{P(E/H)\,P(H)}{P(E)}$$

the following two equations can be deduced:

$$O(H/E) = \frac{P(H/E)}{P(\sim H/E)} = \frac{P(E/H)}{P(E/\sim H)} * \frac{P(H)}{P(\sim H)} = S * O(H) \qquad (1)$$

$$O(H/\ E) = \frac{P(H/\sim E)}{P(\sim H/\sim E)} = \frac{P(\sim E/H)}{P(\sim E/\sim H)} * \frac{P(H)}{P(\sim H)} = N * O(H) \qquad (2)$$

where: O(H) denotes the prior odds on H being true,
O(H/E) denotes the posterior odds on H being true given that E is observed to be present, and
O(H/ E) denotes the posterior odds on H being true given that E is observed to be absent.

Probabilities can be recovered from their odds by the simple formula:

$$P = \frac{0}{0+1}$$

Equation (1) updates the probability on H when E is observed to be present. This updating is based on S, the sufficiency factor. Equation (2) updates the probability on H when E is observed to be absent. This updating takes into consideration N, the necessity factor. These updating formulae can be extended to accommodate uncertainty in the evidence, but there are further means which will not be described here (Duda *et al.* 1979).

It often happens that several pieces of evidence bear on the same hypothesis. In other words there are rules with the same consequent condition but different antecedent conditions. By assuming that the E_i's are conditionally independent under both H and H the following formula can be used for updating the probability of H:

$$O(H/E_1, E_2, \ldots, E_n) = \overset{n}{\underset{i=1}{}} \;{}_{i}\, O(H)$$

where $_i$ denotes the odds multiplier corresponding to E_i.

PROSPECTOR's diagnostic process involves forward or data-driven reasoning; the user volunteers information whenever desired. Any information submitted at the beginning of a consultation is used to constrain the system's focus of attention to the most likely deposit models. At every diagnostic stage the most likely model is pursued. When the diagnostic process is a reasoning backwards from the model under investigation the following "focusing" heuristics are employed:

i) If the currently pursued hypothesis is a disjunction (conjunction) of assertions then the component assertion with the largest (smallest) probability is selected as the next hypothesis to be pursued.

ii) Every untried rules having the currently pursued hypothesis as a consequent is scored according to how heavily it may influence the hypothesis' likelihood. The highest scoring rule is selected. The heuristic scoring function is:

$$S_o(Ei) = abs(log(Si))P(Ei) + abs(log(Ni))\,(1\text{-}P(Ei))$$

where: Ei is the antecedent of the ith applicable rule, and
Si/Ni are the sufficiency/necessity factors assigned to the rule.
i is the odds-multiplier corresponding to E_i.

When the antecedents are unlikely a priori, the heuristic favours the rules with small necessity factors, and as they become more likely it favours the rules with large sufficiency factors.

The drilling sites selection mechanism depends upon the first stage of the consultation. This determines whether there is sufficient evidence to believe in the presence of ore deposits. If this is so PROSPECTOR goes to the second stage of recommending drilling sites. During this stage the system derives its inputs from digitised maps of geological characteristics, and produces as output a colour-coded graphic display of the favourability of each cell on a grid corresponding to the input map.

PROSPECTOR provides a number of explanatory facilities, most important amongst these being the WHY (why a given question was asked) and HOW (how a given conclusion was reached) explanations. The *Knowledge Acquisition System* (KAS) (Reboh, 1981) guides the experts during the several stages of elaboration, refinement and revision required to construct prospect-scale models. Finally it should be said that PROSPECTOR is coded in INTERLIS, and makes direct use of Hendrix and Slocum's semantic net package.

Our next example of an expert system is INTERNIST 1, a medical system, whose principal researchers are J.D. Meyers and H.E. Pople, of the University of Pittsburgh, and the function of INTERNIST 1 is the diagnosis of internal medicine.

The work of the INTERNIST/CADUCEUS (Pople, 1982) project has concentrated on the investigation of heuristic methods for imposing what might be called a differential diagnostic task structure on the clinical decision making problems. An aspect of this investigation is to devise knowledge structures that aggregate groups of diseases and pathological states into a taxonomy. This taxonomy may then be used either to select or to rule out groups of diseases on the basis of an answer to a question directed at a common characteristic. In INTERNIST-1 (Pople, 1975 and Miller *et al.*, 1982) the taxonomy is in the form of strict hierarchy which is organised around the concept of organ system involvement. It has been found that a strict hierarchy can not be used effectively to develop suitable foci during the course of a consultation. The approach os using only a taxonomy of diseases turns out to be deficient, relative to the precision found in a causal model when assessing the findings with respect to particular diseases. Current work on CADUCEUS is aimed at investigating the conceptualisation of the differential diagnostic problem in both causal and approximately hierarchical terms. The knowledge-base of INTERNIST is of two basic types: diseases and manifestations in the form of case histories, symptoms, physical signs and laboratory findings. The knowledge-base has been structured so that abnormal findings are used to abduce disease hypotheses directly. The manifestations of the various pathological states associated with each disease, are part of the disease's profile. The exceptions are various well established states of clinical significance such as heart failure.

Each (pathological) manifestation defines a set of diseases by means of data structure called EVOKES. This structure records, for each such manifestation the list of diseases in which the manifestation has some likelihood of occurring, the strength (0 to 5) by which the manifestation is linked to the disease is contained in the data structure. Another data structure, MANIFEST, profiles each disease with a list of manifestations of the disease and an estimate (1 to 5) of their *frequency*. The causal, temporal and other associations by which various diseases and pathological states are interrelated, incorporating weighing factors like those in EVOKES and MANIFEST (above) are contained in relational statement. One important auxiliary relation, IMPORT, expresses (1 to 5) the global importance of a manifestation.

Initially patient data are entered. In order to assess the attribution of a finding to a particular disease, the program uses a scoring procedure that awards "marks" to a disease on the basis of its "explanatory power", while frequency of occurrence weights, of the manifestations expected, but not found, count against.

From the ordered list of disease hypotheses a new task is then constructed. The highest order hypotheses can be considered to be mutually exclusive if they can individually explain as many findings as they could taken collectively. If there is only one element in the set of highly ranked alternatives then the program necessarily pursues this hypothesis seeking confirmatory data. Where there are a number of highly ranked alternatives the program looks for data that will discriminate between them and hence make a choice possible, sometimes a degree of "juggling" is needed. Concluded hypotheses are then entered on a list, and manifestations explained by them are marked as no longer in need of explanation.

Because of causal, temporal and other interrelationships, certain disease combinations are more likely to occur than others; hence on confirmation of a disease hypothesis, hypotheses linked to it are given additional weight and thus may themselves require consideration. The cycle is repeated until all problems present in the case have been revealed and their solution (hopefully) found.

In the static aspect of INTERNIST-1, it has a hierarchically organised knowledge-base which is built around the concept of a disease profile (a cluster of manifestations). The word 'manifestation', in INTERNIST-1 is used ambiguously to denote either a finding (historical item, symptom, physical sign, laboratory abnormality, etc.), a predisposing factor, or a disease related to a disease process.

The basic conceptual structure of the system's knowledge-base is given in terms of the following relationships (depicted in Figure 3)

EVOKES relates the domain of manifestations to the domain of diseases categories. A manifestation M is related to a specified degree to some disease D under EVOKES which denotes the likelihood that the observation of manifestation M being indicative of disease D. This degree is referred to as M's evocative association (strength) for D, and is represented as an integer from the set 0 – 5. These strengths of association are *subjective estimates* made on the basis of extensive clinical experience.

The list of diseases related to a manifestation M, under the EVOKES data structure forms the "differential diagnosis list" of M. This is achieved by data-driven reasoning operating from manifestations hypotheses which may be abduced. The other data structure MANIFEST relates the domain of disease categories to the domain of manifestations. A disease D is related to some manifestation M under MANIFEST to a specified degree

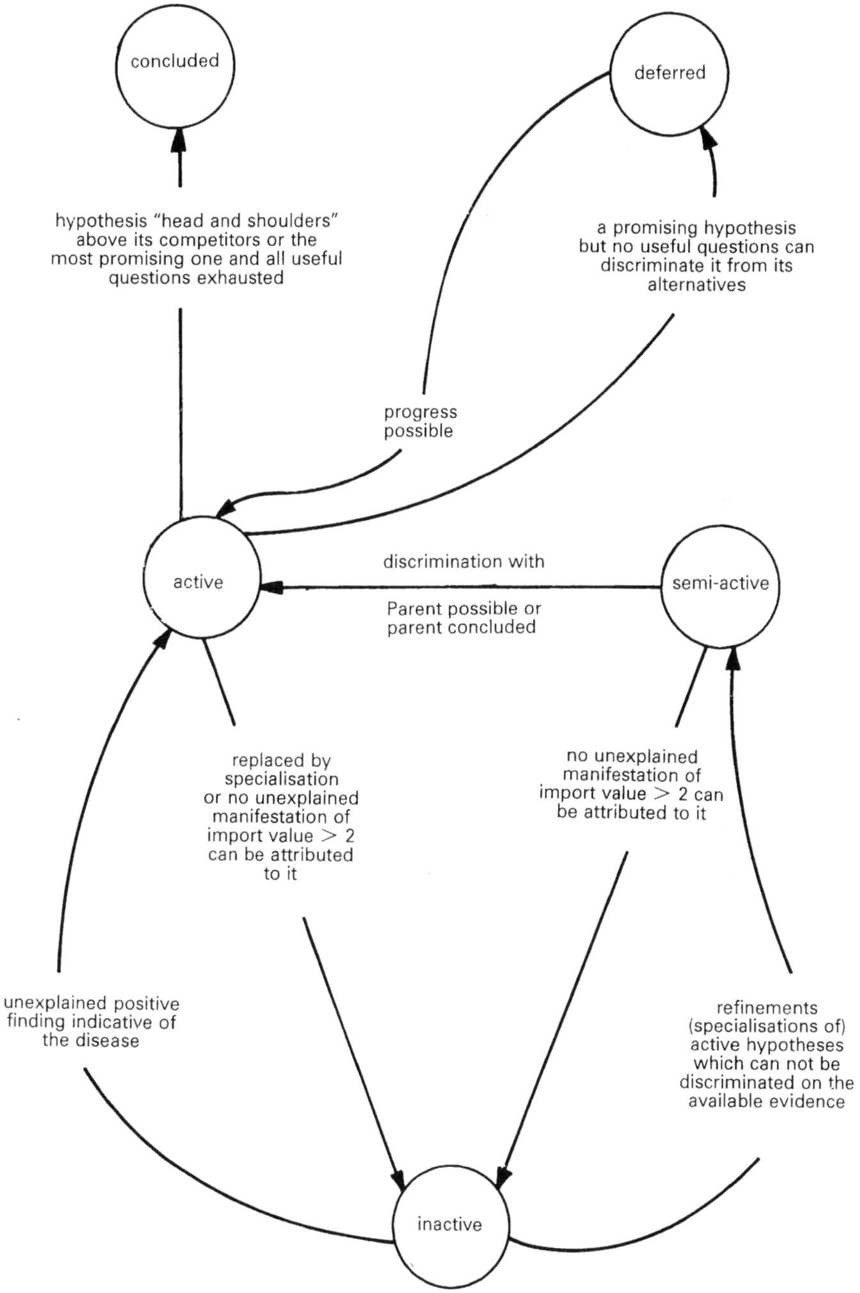

FIGURE 3 Hypothesis status transition diagram for INTERNIST-I (after Johnson and Keravnon).

denoting how often M is associated with instances of M. This degree of association is so-called frequency of occurrence of M in D and is given by the usual integer from 1 to 5. Such estimates are supported by data obtained from a review of the relevant medical literature and to this extent can be more objectively based.

FORM-OF relates disease categories to their underlying specialisations. FORM-OF (D1, D1.1) represents the fact that D1.1 is a form (specialisation) of disease category D1. The manifestations for a disease category are those common to each of its specialisations (for the disease category the evocative association and frequency of occurrence of each manifestation, is, respectively, the maximum evocative association and minimum frequency of occurrence of that manifestation among the specialisations).

IMPORT is a disease independent attribute associated with manifestations. The IMPORT, expressed as an integer from 1 to 5 of a manifestation denotes the global importance of the manifestation, and thus the extent to which one is compelled to explain its presence in any patient. Knowledge of how the presence or absence of a manifestation may influence the presence or absence of other manifestations is also included in the knowledge-base.

The domain of internal medicine is large and diverse.

The dynamic aspect of INTERNIST employs abductive (data-driven) and deductive (hypothesis-driven) reasoning in order to establish the presence of particular diseases in the patient. Manifestations constitute the evidence and disease categories the hypotheses. Initially all hypotheses are inactive. A hypothesis is activated (evoked) when at least one unexplained finding which signifies the disease under EVOKES, is observed in the paticnt.

The disease taxonomy is an important mechanism for controlling the proliferation of active hypotheses during the diagnostic process and a sufficiently promising active hypothesis is concluded either if it has no serious competitors. The conclusion of a hypothesis causes all observed manifestation explained by it to be removed from future consideration; subsequent observations are marked as explained when a previously concluded hypothesis can account for them. Concluding a disease category means that the observed manifestations explained by it can only be subsequently attributed to specialisations of it — intuitively the conclusion of a disease category would cause the activation of its underlying semi-active specialisations. The most promising active hypothesis and its competitors and transferred into the deferred status when the level of questioning, permitted for the given set of alternatives has been exhausted, and the set's resolution has not been possible. An active hypothesis is inactivated when no unexplained manifestation be accounted for by the hypothesis.

At the beginning of a consultation with INTERNIST-1, the user enters all positive (observed) and negative (not observed) findings considered significant. Findings are expressed as precise sequences in terms in a controlled vocabulary. The system alternates between data- (abductive) and hypothesis- (deductive) driven reasoning until every positive finding, with a global import value of at lest 3 has been attributed to one of its potential causes. Thus every positive finding instigates an elementary diagnostic task, for the attribution of the finding to a disease that explains it.

Data-driven reasoning abduces hypotheses from manifestations whose presence in the patient has not yet been explained. *Hypothesis-driven reasoning* is also used to confirm the deductions that can be drawn from active promising hypotheses.

Active hypotheses are evaluated using unexplained manifestations and negative findings. The competitors of the most promising hypothesis are dynamically determined by a partitioning heuristic. The most promising hypothesis and its competitors form the system's current focus of attention or the current problem area to be resolved. If the configuration of the problem area does not permit the conclusion of the most promising hypothesis, the system attempts to elicit additional useful items of information from the user.

The INTERNIST-1 diagnostic strategy involves the repeated scoring and partitioning of active hypotheses in the light of new evidence. Hence the system's focus of attention could switch from one problem area to another if questioning in the first area is not helpful. The INTERNIST-1 *focusing mechanism* determines the system's current focus of attention or problem area by: firstly scoring the active hypotheses, secondly temporarily discarding those active hypotheses whose scores fall below the most promising hypothesis. Finally the partitioning of the remaining hypotheses into competitors and non-competitors of the most promising hypothesis occur. The most promising hypothesis and its competitors form the current problem area.

Four lists are maintained for the scoring of each active hypothesis:

l_1 — list of (unexplained) positive findings matching the disease profile, i.e. manifestations potentially explained by the disease hypothesis;

l_2 — list of findings which are part of the disease profile but are currently missing from the patient (possibly these are findings yet to come depending on the state of the disease reached, but as mentioned earlier, no such knowledge is held in the knowledge-base;

l_3 — list of (unexplained) findings which are present in the patient but not explained by the disease hypothesis (possibly explained by a coexistent disease?);

1_4 list ~~of~~ findings which are part of the disease's profile but about which nothing is known (this list is used in determining which questions to ask next).

The initial score of an active hypothesis is computed using the *match* and *mismatch* between the hypothesis' expectations and the currently unexplained positive findings. The score of the hypothesis is then completed by adding the bonuses awarded by it being the antecedent of concluded diseases. The hypothesis with the highest score is the most promising one. The details of the INTERNIST-1 scoring procedure are given below:

The score of the active hypothesis H_i, $S(H_i)$ say, is given by:

$$S(H_i) = P(H_i) - N(H_i) + \text{BONUS}(H_i)$$

where: $P(H_i)$ is the likelihood in the presence of H_i derived from direct evidence.

$N(H_i)$ is the likelihood in the absence of H_i derived from direct evidence, and

BONUS (H_i) is the likelihood in the presence of H_i derived from circumstantial causal evidence.

$P(H_i)$ is given by:

$$P(H_i) = \sum_{j=1}^{1_{1i}} W_e(Ej)$$

where: j ranges over the elements of the 1_1 list for hypothesis H_i, 1_{1i},

E_j denotes the evocative association between the jth element of 1_{1i} and H_i, and

W_e is the discrete weight function analysed in Table 1.1

$N(H_i)$ is given by:

$$N(H^i) = \sum_{j=1}^{1_{2i}} w_m(Fj) + \sum_{j=1}^{1_{3i}} w_u(Ij)$$

where: j ranges over the elements of the $1_2/1_3$ list for hypothesis

H_i, $1_{2i}/1_{3i}$,

F_j denotes the frequency to which the jth element of 1_{2i} occurs with instances of H_i,

I_j denotes the global clinical importance value of the jth element of 1_{3i}, and

w_m and w_u are discrete weight functions analysed, respectively, in tables 1.2 and 1.3.

BONUS (H_i) is given by:

$$\text{BONUS}(H_i) = \textstyle\sum_j 20 * F_j$$

where: j ranges over the established consequences of H_i, and

F_j denotes the frequency to which the concluded disease H_j occurs with instances of H_i.

The partitioning of the attractive hypotheses is based on the following heuristic (Miller *et al.*, 1982, p. 471):

> "Two diseases are competitors if the items not explained by one disease are a subset of the items not explained by the other, otherwise they are alternatives (and may possibly coexist in the patient). To paraphrase, if disease A and disease B, taken together, explain no more observed manifestations than either one does when taken alone, the diseases are classified competitors".

The leading hypothesis and its competitors constitute the system's focus of attention for the given stage of the consultation.

If the configuration of the problem area does not permit the conclusion of the leading hypothesis, the system employs an *information acquisition strategy*, the choice of which depends on the number of competing hypotheses and their relative promises. The following strategies are used for resolving problem areas:

The RULEOUT strategy is employed when there are five or more diseases within 45 points of the leading disease. This strategy restricts the questioning to findings obtainable via history or physical examination, and which are expected on the competing hypotheses to high degree (reflected by high frequency of occurrence values). Negative responses are welcomed since they will remove (rule out) some diseases from contention.

The DISCRIMINATE strategy is employed if there are two to four diseases within 45 points of the leading disease. This strategy formulates questions that serve to support one hypotheses at the expense of another; more costly procedures may be called for in order to achieve this objective;

i.e. the questions may refer to findings obtainable via laboratory tests.

The PURSUE strategy is employed if the second best contender is 46-89 points behind the leading disease. This strategy formulates questions that serve to establish the leading disease. The level of questioning is unconstrained, so that questions about biopsies (if useful) can be asked, or other specialised procedures capable of providing pathognomonic data (findings with evocative associations of 5).

The application of an information acquisition strategy results in the formulation of a question which is subsequently put to the user.

The explanatory facilities of INTERNIST-1 do not include diagnostic reasoning. As to teaching the EXAMINER system (Oleson, 1977) teaches the INTERNIST-1 knowledge to students. It presents the student with a list of manifestations from a case in internal medicine and then elicits the student's classification of the disease (processes) present in the case.

INTERNIST-1 is *implemented* on a PDP-10 under the TENEX operating system. It takes about 800 mbytes. The primary implementation language is INTERLIS with interfaces to the knowledge-base coded in assembly language. Program execution times for INTERNIST-1 typically range from three to seven minutes of CPU time for reasonably complex case analyses.

It is to be hoped that this brief summary of PROSPECTOR and INTERNIST-1 will provide a certain air of familiarity with the sort of structure and function which are depicted in working expert systems. It is reasonably certain that this is one field of Artificial Intelligence that is likely to progress most quickly in the immediate future.

This finally ends our survey of the context in which AI operates.

References

Addis, T.R. (1980). Towards an 'expert' diagnostic system. *ICL Technical Journal*, 73-105

Amarel, S. (1962). An approach to automatic theory formation. In *Principles of Self Organisation.* (Eds. H. von Foerster & G.W. Zopf). Pergamon Press, Oxford.

Amarel, S. (1965). Problem solving procedures for efficient syntactical analysis. ACM 20th National Conference.

Andrew, M. (1983). *Artificial Intelligence.* Abacus Press, Tunbridge Wells.

Arbib, M.A. (1965). *Brains, Machines and Mathematics.* McGraw-Hill, New York.

Armstrong, D.M. (1973). *Belief, Truth and Knowledge.* Cambridge University Press.

Ashby, W.R. (1953). *Design for a Brain.* Methuen, London.

Ashby, W.R. (1960). *Introduction to Cybernetics.* Methuen, London.

Austin, J.L. (1962). *How to do Things with Words.* (Ed. J. Ormson). Oxford University Press.

Ayer, A.J. (1968). *The Origins of Pragmatism*, Macmillan, London.

Ayer, A.J. (1973). *Questions of Philosophy.* Macmillan, London.

Baker, G.P. & Hacker, P.M.S. (1980). *Analytical Commentary on Wittgenstein's "Philosophical Investigations".* Basil Blackwell, Oxford.

Banrji, R. (1962). A language for description of concepts. *General Systems Yearbook*, **5**.

Berliner, H. (1980). Backgammon computer program beats world champion. *Artificial Intelligence*, **14** (2) 205-220.

Blumm, M. (1960). Properties of a neuron with many inputs. *Bionics Symposium.* (Wright-Patterson Air Force Base). Off. Tech. Serv. US Dept. of Comm. Washington.

Bobrow, D.G. (1964). Natural language input for a computer problem solving system. In *Semantic Information Processing* (Ed. M. Minsky). MIT Press, Cambridge, Mass.

Bobrow, D.G. (1966). METEOR: a LISP interpreter for string manipulation. *The Programming Language LISP: Its Operations and Applications.* MIT Press, Cambridge, Mass.

Bobrow, D.G. & Winograd, T. (1977). An overview of KRL, a knowledge representation language, *Cognitive Science*, **1**.

Bowden, M.A. (1977). *Artificial Intelligence and Natural Man.* Harvester Press.

Brady, J.M. (1981). The changing face of computer vision. *Artificial Intelligence*, **17**, 1-15.

Braithwaite, R.B. (1953). *Scientific Explanation.* Cambridge University Press.

Brouwer, L.E.J. (1913-14). *Intuitionisme en Formalisme.* Groningen 1912. (English Translation in *Bull. Am. Math. Soc.*, **20**).

Buchanon, B.G. and Feigenbaum, E.A. (1978). DENDRAL and META-DENDRAL: Their applications dimension. *Artificial Intelligence*, **11** (1-2), 5. 24.

Bundy, A. (1979). Will it reach the top? Prediction in the mechanics world. *Development of Artificial Intelligence.* Research Report 31. University of Edinburgh.

Bundy, A., Byrd, L., Leiger, G., Mellish, C. & Palmer, M. (1979). Solving mechanics problems using meta-level inference. In *Expert Systems in the Micro-electronics Age.*, (Ed. Michie, D.). Edinburgh University Press.

Burstall, R.M. (1966). A heuristic method for a job scheduling problem. Experimental Programming Unit, Edinburgh.

Carnap, R. (1937). Testability and Necessity. *Phil. Sci.* **3**, pp. 419-77; **4**, pp. 1-40.
Carnap, R. (1937). Testability and meaning. *Phil. Sci.* **3**, pp. 419-71; **4**, pp. 1-40.
Carnap, R. (1942). *Introduction to Semantics.* Harvard University Press. Cambridge, Mass.
Carnap, R. (1943). *Formalisation of Logic.* Harvard University Press. Cambridge, Mass.
Carnap, R. (1947). *Meaning and Necessity.* Chicago University Press.
Carnap, R. (1948). *Meaning and Necessity.* Chicago University Press.
Chandler, W.J. (1984). *The Science of History.* Gordon and Breach, London and New York.
Chapman, B.L.M. (1959). A self organising classifying system. *Cybernetics,* **2** (2), pp. 152-61.
Chomsky, N. (1953). Systems of syntactic analysis. *J. Symb. Log.*, **18**, pp. 242-265.
Chomsky, N. (1955). *Logical Structure of Linguistic Theory.* Microfilm, MIT Library, Cambridge, Mass.
Chomsky, N. (1956). *Syntactic Structures,* The Hague, Mouton.
Chomsky, N. (1957). *Syntactic Structures.* Mouton, Holland.
Chomsky, N. (1961). Explanatory Models in Linguistics. In *Logic, Methodology and the Philosophy of Science.* (J. Norgel, P. Suppes and A. Tarski, Eds.). Stanford University Press. Stamford, Calif.
Clowes, M.B. (1967). Perception, picture-processing and computers. *Machine Intelligence* **I**. (Eds. Collins, N.L.X. Michie, D.). Oliver and Boyd, Edinburgh 181-198.
Clowes, M.B. (1969). Picture relationships — a syntactic approach. *Machine Intelligence* (Eds. B. Meltzur & D. Michie) pp. 361-384.
Cohen, E. (1962). A recognition algorithm for a grammar model. *Rep. 7885 Nat. Bur. Stand.* Washington, D.C.
Colby, K.M. (1964). Experimental treatment of neurotic computer programs. *Arch. Gen. Psychiatry,* pp. 220-227.
Colby, K.M. (1975). *Artificial Paranoia.* Pergamon Press, Oxford.
Colby, K.M. (1976). Clinical implications of a simulation model of the paranoid processes. *Arch. Gen. Psychiatry* **33**, pp. 854-857.
Cook, J.W. (1969). Human beings. In *Studies in the Philosophy of Wittgenstein.* (Peter Winch, Ed.) Routledge & Kegan Paul, London.
Coombs, A.W.M. (1969). On the construction of an efficient feature space for optical character recognition. In *Machine Intelligence,* B. Meltzer and D. Michie (Eds.), Edinburgh University Press.
Cowan, J. (1962). Many valued logics and reliable automata in Principles of Self-Organisation. (H. von Foerster and G.W. Zopf, Eds.) Pergamon Press, Oxford.
Clarkson, G.P.E. (1963). A model of the trust investment process. In *Computers and Thought.* E.A. Feigenbaum and J. Fieldman (Eds.), McGraw-Hill, New York.
Clowes, M.B. (1971). On seeing things, *Artificial Intelligence.* **2**, pp. 79-116.
Culbertson, J.T. (1950). *Consciousness and Behaviour.* Brown.
Culbertson, J.T. (1952). *Hypothetical Robots.* Rand Project.
Culbertson, J.T. (1956). Some uneconomical robots, in *Automata Studies.* (C.E. Shammon and J. McCarthy, Eds.) Princeton University Press, Princeton, N.J.
Darlington, J.L. (1969). Theorem proving and information retrieval. In *Machine Intelligence* **4**, B. Meltzer and D. Michie (Eds.).
Davis, M. (1958). *Computability and Unsolvability.* McGraw-Hill, New York.
Davis, R. and Buchanon, B.G. (1977). Meta-level knowledge overview and applications. Proc. 5th International Joint Conference on Artificial Intelligence. MIT Cambridge, Mass.
Darlington, J.L. (1964). A COMIT program for the Davis-Putnam algorithm. *Res. Lab. Electron Mech. Transl. Gyp.* MIT, Cambridge, Mass.
Da Fonseca, J. (1966). *Neuronal Models.* Centre de Estudos egas monig.
Deutsch, J.A. (1954). A machine with insight. *Quarter J. Exp. Psychol;* **6**, pp. 6-11.

Draper, S.W. (1981). The use of gradient and dual space in line-drawing interpretations. *Artificial Intelligence.*

Deutsch, J.A. (1955). A theory of shape recognition. *Brit. J. Psychol.* **46**, pp. 30-37.

Dreyfuss, H.L. (1965). *Alchemy and Artificial Intelligence.* P-3244. Rand Corporation, Santa Monica, California.

Dreyfuss, H.L. (1972). *What Computers Can't Do: A Critique of Artificial Reason.* Harper & Row, New York.

Duda, R., Gasching, J. & Hart. P. (1979). Model design in the PROSPECTOR consultant system for mineral exploration. In Michic, D. (Ed.). *Expert Systems in the Micro-electronic Age.* Edinburgh University Press. pp. 153-167.

Evans, T.G. (1968) A program for the solution of a class of geometric analogy intelligence-test questions. In Muisky, M. (Ed.) *Semantic Information Processing.* MIT Press, Cambridge, Mass. pp. 271-353.

Fahlman, S.E. (1974). A planning system for robot construction tasks: *Artificial Intelligence,* **5**, pp. 1-50.

Fahlman, S.E. (1979). Representing and using realworld knowledge. In *Artificial Intelligence: An MIT perspective.* (Eds. P.H. Winston and R.H. Brown).

Feigenbaum, E.A. & J. Feldman (Eds) (1963). *Computers and Thought.* McGraw-Hill, New York.

Feigenbaum, E.A. (1974). Artificial Intelligence research. what is it? what has it achieved? where is it going? *Symposium on Artificial Intelligence.* Canberra, Australia.

Feigenbaum, E.A. (1977). *The Art of Artificial Intelligence 1: themes and case studies of knowledge engineering.* Rep. STAN-CS-77-61. Stanford University, Stanford.

Feigenbaum, E.A. (1979). Themes and case studies of knowledge engineering. In *Expert Systems in the Micro-electronic Age* (D. Michie, Ed.) 3-25. Edinburgh University Press.

Feigenbaum, E.A., Buchanan, B.G. & Lederberg, J. (1971). On generality and problem solving: a case study using the DENDRAL program. In *Machine Intelligence* **6** Edinburgh University Press.

Feigenbaum, E.A. & McCorduck, P. (1983). *The Fifth Generation,* Michael Joseph.

Foundos, S. (1980). Several notes have appeared in the form of memos from the founder of testrolog.

Gabor, D. (1954). Communication theory and cybernetics. *Proc.* IRE CT-1, **19**.

Deutsch, J.A. (1954). A machine with insight. *Quarter J. Exp. Psychol;* **6**, pp. 6-11.

Gasching, J. (1982). PROSPECTOR: An expert system for mineral exploration. In Michie, D. (Ed.) *Introductory Readings in Expert Systems.* Gordon & Breach, London & New York, pp. 47-64.

Gelb, J.P. (1971). Experiments with a natural language problem solving system. In *Second International Joint Conference on Artificial Intelligence.*

Gelerntner, H. (1963). Realization of a geometry-theorem proving machine. In *Computers and Thought.* (Eds. E.A. Feigenbaum & J. Feldman). McGraw-Hill.

George, F.H. (1956). Pragmatics, *J. Phil. Phen. Res.*, **17**, pp. 226-235.

George, F.H. (1957). Logical networks and probability. *Bull. Math. Biophys.*, **18**, pp. 337-48.

George, F.H. (1958). Probalistic machines. *Automation Progress,* **3**, pp. 19-21.

George, F.H. (1961). *The Brain as a Computer.* Pergamon Press. (Ed. 2, 1973), Oxford.

George, F.H. (1962a). Minds, machines and Godel: Another reply to Mr Lucas. *Philos.*, **37**, 62-63.

George, F.H. (1962b). *Cognition.* Methuen.

George, F.H. (1962c). *Simple Adaptive Programs for Computers.* Cybernetics Conference, UCLA, California.

George, F.H. (1965). *Cybernetics and Biology.* Oliver & Boyd, Edinburgh.

George, F.H. (1966). Hypothesis-confirmation on a digital computer. Paper read at Conference of Biomics, Dayton, Ohio pp. 739-798.
George, F.H. (1967). The current state of artificial intelligence NATO Conference of Artificial Intelligence.
George, F.H. (1970a). *Cybernetics in Management.* Pan Books, London.
George, F.H. (1970b). *Models of Thinking.* George Allen & Unwin, London.
George, F.H. (1974). *The Anatomy of Business.* A.B.P. and Wiley-Halstead, London.
George, F.H. (1977a). *Machine Takeover.* Pergamon Press. Oxford.
George, F.H. (1977). *Precision, Language and Logic.* Pergamon Press, Oxford.
George, F.H. (1979). *Philosophical Foundations of Cybernetics.* Abacus Books, Tunbridge Wells.
George, F.H. (1980). *Problem Solving.* Duckworth, London.
George, F.H. (1981) *Science of Philosophy.* Gordon & Breach, New York & London.
George, F.H. (1982). *The Science of Philosophy.* Gordon & Breach, London and New York.
George, F.H. (1984). *The Science of Investment.* Abacus Press. Tunbridge Wells.
George, F.H. & Handlon, J.H. (1955). Towards a general theory of behaviour. *Methods,* **1**, pp. 25-44.
George. F.H. & Handlon, J.H. (1957). A language for perceptual analysis. *Psychol. Rev.,* **64**, pp. 14-25.
George, F.H. & Johnson, L. (1984). Man-computer Interaction: a cognitive approach. Abacus Press.
Gilmore, P.C. (1960). A proof method for quantification theory, IBM J. Res. Devel. **4**.
Goldstein, I.P. (1975). Summary of MYCROFT: A system for understanding simple picture programs. In *Artificial Intelligence,* **6**, pp. 249-288.
Goldstein, I.P. & Miller, M.L. (1976). Structured planning and debugging: a linguistic theory of design. MIT AI Lab. Memo 384.
Good, I.J. (1982). A five year plan for Automatic Chess. Michie, D. (Ed.) In *Machine Intelligence* **2** pp. 89-118.
Green, B.E., Wolf, A.K., Chomsky, C. & Laughery, K. (1963). Baseball: an automatic question and answer. In *Computers and Thought.* (Eds. Feigenbaum & Feldman). McGraw-Hill, New York.
Guzman, A. (1968). Decomposition of a visual scene into three-dimensional bodies. *Proc. Fall Joint Computer.*
Halliday, M.A.K. (1970). Functional diversity in language as seen from a consideration of modality and mood in English. *Foundations of Language,* **6**, pp. 322-361.
Hamlyn, D.W. (1961). *Sensation and Perception: A History of the Philosophy of Perception.* Routledge & Kegan Paul, London.
Hayek, S.A. (1952). *The Sensory Order.* University of Chicago.
Hays, D.G. (1962). Automata language data processing in *Computer Applications in the Behavioural Sciences.* (H. Bosko, Ed.), Prentice Hall, Englewood Cliffs, N.J.
Hebb, D.O. (1949). *The Organisation of Behaviour.* Wiley, New York.
Hendrix, G.G. (1979). Encoding knowledge in partitioned networks. In Findler, N.V. (Ed.) *Associative Networks: Representation and Use of Knowledge by Computers. Academic Press,* New York. pp. 51-92.
Hesse, M.B. (1956). *Models and Analogies in Science.* University of Notre Dame Press.
Hewitt, C. (1972). Planner: A Language for Proving Theorems in Robots. I CAI-69, Washington DC, 295-302.
Hewitt, C. (1979). Design of the APIARY for VLSI support of Knowledge-Based Systems. MIT AI Lab Working Paper 186.
Hilditch, C.J. (1969). An application of graph theory in pattern recognition in *Machine Intel-*

ligence 3. (Ed. D. Michie) pp. 325-350.

Horn, B.K.P. (1977). Understanding image intensities. *Artificial Intelligence*, **8**, pp. 201-281.

Horn, B.R.P. (1979). Kinneatics, studies and dynamics of two-dimensional manipulators. In *Artificial Intelligence* (Eds. P.H. Winston & R.H. Brown) MIT Press, Cambridge, Mass., pp. 273-310.

Horn, B.K.P. & Bachman, B.L. (1978). Using synthetic images to register real images with surface models. *Comm ACM* **21**, pp. 914-924.

Horn, B.K.P. & Bachman, B.L. (1979). Registering real images using synthetic images. In *Artificial Intelligence: AN MIT perspective.* (Eds. P.H. Winston & R.H. Brown). MIT Press, Cambridge, Mass.

Hubel, D.H. & Wiesel, T.N. (1962). Binocular interaction and function architecture in the cat's visual cortex. *J. Physiol.*, **148**, pp. 579-591.

Hubel, D.H. & Wiesel, T.N. (1965). Receptive field and single neurons in the cat's striate cortex. *J. Physiol.*, **195**, pp. 215-243.

Hunt, E.B. & Hovland, C.E. (1960). Programming a model of human concept formulation. *Proc. Western Joint Computer Conf.*, pp. 145-155.

Ikeuchi, K. & Horn, B.K.P. (1981). Numerical shape from shading and occluding boundaries. *Artificial Intelligence*, **17**, pp. 141-184.

Kirsch, R.A. (1964) Computer interpretation of English test and picture patterns. *IEE Trans. on Electronic computers*, **13**, pp. 363-376.

Kleene, S.C. (1952). *Introduction to Metamathematics.* Van Nostrand. New York.

Kling, R.E. (1971). A paradign for reasoning by analogy. In *Second International Joint Conference on Artificial Intelligence*, pp. 568-585.

Kowalski, R. and Hayes, P.J. (1969). Semantic trees in automatic theorem-joining. In *Machine Intelligence*, 4, (Eds. B. Meltzer & D. Michie, University of Edinburgh Press pp. 87-102

Klirst, K. (1934). *Gehirnpathologic*, Barth, Leipzig.

Kochen, M. (1960). Experimental Study of hypothesis formation. *Proc. London Synopos. on Information Theory* (Ed. Colin Cherry) 377-403, Butterworths, London.

Koenig, E.C. & Schultz, J.V. (1972). Analysis of general logical discourse for man-machine interaction — Part I. *Kybernetics*, **1**, pp. 231-241.

Koenig, E.C. and Schultz, J.V. (1972). Analysis of a general logical discourse for man-machine interaction — Part I, *Kybernetics*, pp. 231-241.

Kohler, W. (1949). *Dynamics in Psychology.* Liveright, New York.

Korner, S. (1959). *Conceptual Thinking.* Dover publications, New York.

Korzybski, A. (1933). *Science and Sanity.* Science Press, Lancaster, Pa.

Kowalski, R. & Hayes, P.J. (1969) Semantic trees in automatic theorem-proving. *Machine Intelligence*, **4**. (Eds. B. Meltzer & D. Michie) pp. 87-102.

Ledley, R.S. (1964). High speed automatic analysis of biomedical pictures. *Science*, **146**, pp. 216-223.

Lerner, Y. (1972). *The Fundamentals f Cybernetics.* Chapman and Hall, London.

Lettvin, J.Y., Maturana, H.R., Pitts, W., and McCulloch, W.S. (1959). What the frog's eye tells the frog's brain. *Proc. Inst. Radio Engineers.* **47**, pp. 1940-1959.

Lin, Shen (1965). Computer solutions of the travelling salesman problem. *Bell System Tech. J.*, **44**, pp. 2245-2269.

Lindsy, (1963). Inferential memory as the basis of machines which understand natural language. In *Computers and thought.* A Feigenbaum and J. Feldman (Ed) McGraw-Hill.

Lofgren, L. (1942). Automata of high complexity and methods of increasing their reliability and redundancy. *Inf. and Control.*, **1**, pp. 127.

Lofgren, L. (1962). Kinematic and Tessallation models of self-repair, in *Biological Rototypes and Synthetic Systems.* (Eds. R.E. Bernard and M.R. Cane). Plenum Press, New York.

Longuet-Higgins, H.C. (1968a). A holograph model of temporal recall. *Nature*, **217**, pp. 104.
Longuet-Higgins, H.C. (1968b) The non-local storage of temporal information. *Proc. Ro. Soc.*
Luckham, D. (1968). Some tree-paring strategies for theorem proving. *Machine Intelligence* **3**, Edinburgh University Press, pp. 95-112.
Luria, A.R. (1971). Memory disturbances in local brain lesions. *Neuropsychologia*, **9**.
Luria, A.R. (1973). *The Working Brain.* Penguin Books, Harmondsworth.
Luria, A.R. and Tsvetkava, L.A. (1967). *Les troubles de la resolution des problemes analyse neuropsychologic.* Gautier Villar, Paris.
Marcus, M.P. (1979). A theory of syntactical recognition for natural language. In *Artificial Intelligence* (Eds. P.H. Winston & R.H. Brown) MIT Press, Cambridge, Mass., pp. 191-229.
Marr, D. (1974). *An Essay on the Primal Retinal.* MIT AI Memo 296.
Marr, D. (1975). *Early Processing of Visual Information.* MIT AI Labs.
Marr, D. (1979). Representing and computing visual information. In *Artificial Intelligence an MIT perspective.* (Eds. P.H. Winston and R.H. Brown). MIT Press, Cambridge, Mass.
Marr, D. (1982) *Vision* W.H. Freeman, San Francisco.
Marshall, W.H. and Talbot, S.A. (1942). Recent evidence for neural mechanisms in vision leading to a general theory of sensory activity. In (Ed. H. Klurer *Visual Mechanisms* Biology Symposium **7**, pp. 117-164.
Mayhew, J.E.W. and Frisby, J.P. (1981). Psychophysical and computational studies towards a theory of human stereosis. *Artificial Intelligence*, **17**, pp. 349-385.
McCulloch, W. and Pitts, W. (1943). A logical calculus of the ideas imminent in nervous activity. *Bi. Maths. Biophys*, **5**, pp. 115-133.
McNaughton, R. (1961). The theory of automata, a survey. *Advances in Computers*, **2**, pp. 379-421.
Meletis, C.P. (1978). *Concepts and Analogies in Cybernetics.* Ph.D. Thesis. Brunel University.
Meltzer, B. (1966). Theorem proving for computers: some results on resolution and renaming. *Comput. J.*, **8**, pp. 341-3.
Meltzer, B. (1974). The programming of deduction and induction. In *The Robots are Coming.* (Eds. F.H. George & J.D. Humphries) NCC Publications.
Michie, D. (Ed.) (1974). *On Machine Intelligence.* Edinburgh University Press.
Michie, D. (Ed.) (1982). *Introductory Readings in Expert Systems*, Gordon & Breach, London and New York.
Miller, G.A. Galanter, E. and Pribram, K.H. (1960). *Plans and the Structure of Behaviour.* Itolt, Rinehart & Winston, New York.
Miller, G.A. (1956). The magical number seven; plus or minus two: some limits on our capacity for processing information. *Psychol. Reve.*, **63**, pp. 81-97.
Miller, M.L. & Goldstein, I.P. (1979). Planning and debugging in elementary programming. In *Artificial Intelligence An MIT Perspective.* (Eds. P.H. Winston and R.H. Brown. MIT Press, Cambridge, Mass.
Miller, R.A., Pople, H.E. & Myers, J.D. (1982). INTERNIST-I An experimental computer-based diagnostic consultant for general internal medicine. *New England J. of Medicine*, **37** (*8*), pp. 468-476.
Millikin, C.H. and Darley, F.L. (1967). *Brain Mechanisms Underlying Speech and Language.* Grune and Stratton.
Milner, P. (1957). The cell assembly: Mark II. *Psychol. Rev.*, **64**, pp. 242-252.
Minsky, M. (1967). *Computation: Finite and Infinite Machines. Prentice-Hall.*
Minsky, M. and Papert, S. (1969). *Perceptrous*, MIT Press, Cambridge, Mass.
Mountcastle, V.B. (1975). The view from within pathways to the study of perception. *The John Hopkins Med. J.* **136**, pp. 109-31.

Moore, G.E. (1953). *Some Main Problems of Philosophy.* Unwin, London.
Murray, N.V. (1982). Completely non-clausal theorem proving. *Artificial Intelligence,* **18**, pp. 67-85.
Narasimhan, R. (1966). Syntax-directed interpretation of classes of pictures. *Communs. Ass. Computer Mach.*, **9**, pp. 166-173.
Newell, A. Shaw, J.C. and Simon, H.A. (1958). Chess playing programs and the problem of complexity. *IBM Jl. of Res and Dev.* **2**, pp. 320-355.
Newell, A., Shaw, J.C. and Simon, H.A. (1958). Elements in a theory of human problem solving. *Psychol. Rev.*, **65**, pp. 151-166.
Newell, A., Shaw, J.C. and Simon, H.A. (1963). The Theorem proving machine. In *Computers and Thought* (Eds. E. Feigenbaum and J. Feldman). McGraw-Hill, New York.
Newell, A. and Simon., H.A. (1972). *Human problem solving.* Prentice-Hall, Englewood Cliffs, N.J.
Nillson, N.J. (1971). *Problem-solving Methods in Artificial Intelligence.* McGraw-Hill, New York.
Oettinger, A.G. (1952). Programming a digital computer to learn. *Phil. Mag.*, **1** (43), pp. 1243-63.
Oleson, C.E. (1977). Examiner: A system using contextual knowledge for analyses of diagnostic behaviour. *Proc. IJcai-77,* pp. 814-818.
Osgood, C.E. and Heyer, A.W. (1952). A new interpretation of figural after-effects. *Psychol. Rev.*, **59**, pp. 98-118.
Palm, G. (1982). *Neural Assemblies.* Springen-Verlag, Holland.
Papert, S. (1971). *The Artificial Intelligence of Humbert L. Dreyfus.* AI Memo 154, MIT AI Lab Cambridge, Mass.
Papert, S. (1973). Theory of knowledge and complexity in *Process Models for Psychology.* (Ed. G.J. Dalenoort), pp. 1-49. Rotterdam University Press.
Pastre, D. (1978). Automatic theory proving in set theory. *Artificial Intelligence,* **10**, pp. 1-28.
Peirce, C.S. (1931-35). *Collected papers 1931-5.* Harvard University Press, Cambridge, Mass.
Penfield, W. and Rasmussen, T. (1950). *The Cerebral Cortex of Man.* Macmillan.
Pereira, L.M., Pereira, F. and Warren, D.H.D. (1978). Users guide to D.E.C. System — 10 Prolog Dept. of Artificial Intelligence, University of Edinburgh.
Pople, H.E. (1975) DIALOG: A model of diagnostic logic for internal medicine. *Proc. IJCAI-75,* pp. 848-855.
Pople, H.E. (1982). Heuristic methods for imposing structure on ill-structured problems the structuring of medical diagnosies. In Szolovits, P. (Ed.) *Artificial Intelligence in Medicine,* AAAS Symposium Service, Boulder Colorado, Western Press, pp. 119-185.
Post, E.L. (1943). Formal reductions of the general combinational decision problem. *Amer. J. Math.*, **65**, pp. 197-268.
Pribram, K.H. (1967). The limbic systems, efferent control of neural inhibition and behaviour. In (Eds. Adey, W.R. and Tokizane, T.) *Progress in Brain Research,* **27**, pp. 318-336. Elsevior Publishing Co., Amsterdam.
Pribram, K.H. (1971). *Languages of the Brain.* Prentice-Hall Englewood Cliffs, N.J.
Price, H.H. (1953). *Thinking and Experience.* Hutchinson, London.
Quillian, M.R. (1968). Semantic memory. In *Semantic Information Processing.* M. Minsky (Ed.) MIT Press, Cambridge, Mass.
Quine, W.V.O. (1953). *From a Logical Point of View.* Harvard University Press, Cambridge, Mass.
Quine, W.V.O. (1975). Mind and verbal dispositions. In *Mind and Language.* (Ed. S. Guttenplan). Oxford University Press.
Quinlan, J.R. (1982). Fundamentals of the knowledge engineering problem. In *Introductory*

Readings in Expert Systems (Ed. D. Michie) pp. 33-46. Gordon Breach, London and New York.

Ramsey, F.P. (1931). *The Foundations of Mathematics.* Kegan Paul, French, Toubrea and Co., London.

Rankin, B.K. (1961). A programmatic grammar for a fragment of English for use on information retrieval system *Rep. T352, Nat. Bur. Stand.* Washington, D.C.

Raphael, B. (1964). SIR: a computer program for Semantic Information Retrieval. Ph.D. thesis, MIT, Cambridge, Mass.

Rapoport, A. (1950a). Contribution to the probabilistic theory of neural nets I *Bull. Math. Biophys.*, **12**, pp. 109-121.

Rapoport, A. (1950b). Contribution to the probabilistic theory of neural nets II *Bull. Math. Biophys.* **12**, pp. 187-197.

Raporport, A. (1950c). Contribution to the probabilistic theory of neural nets III *Bull. Math. Biophys.*, **12**, pp. 317-325.

Rapoport, A. (1950d). Contribution to the probabilistic theory of neural nets IV *Bull. Math. Biophys.*, **12**, pp. 327-337.

Rapoport, A. (1955). Applications of information network to a theory of visions. *Bull. Math. Biophys.*, **17**, pp. 15-33.

Reboh, R. (1981). Knowledge engineering techniques and tools of expert systems. *Linkoping Studies in Science and Technology.* Dissertation No. 71. Software Systems Research Center, Linkoping University, S-581 83 Linkoping, Sweden.

Reiter, S. (1980). An expert system using plausible inference. Machine Intelligence Reserve Group, University of Edinburgh.

Reichenbach, H. (1938). *Experience and Prediction.* University of Chicago Press.

Reichenbach, H. (1947). *Elements of Symbolic Logic.* New York.

Rescher, N. and Brandon, R. (1980). *The Logic of Inconsistency.* Basil Blackwell, Oxford.

Roberts, L.G. (1965). Machine perception of three-dimensional solids. In *Optical and Electro-Optical Processing.* (Eds. J.T. Tippett, D.A. Berkowitz, L.C. Clapp, C.J. Koester, and Alexander Vanderburgh, pp. 159-198. MIT Press, Cambridge.

Robinson, J.A. (1965). A machine oriented logic based on the resolution principle. Jl. A.C.M. **12**, pp. 23-41.

Robinson, J.A. (1967). A review of automatic theorem-proving. *Arrival symposia in applied mathematics XIX, Providence, Rhode Island.* American Mathematical Society.

Robinson, J.A. (1979). The logical basis of programming by assertion and query. In *Expert Systems in the Micro-electronic Age.* (Ed. Michie, D.) Ediburgh University Press.

Robinson, J.A. (1982). Problems and Trends for the future of logic programming. In *Introductory Readings in Expert Systems.*

Rosenberg, M.J. (1983). *The Cybernetics of Art: Reason and the Rainbow.* Gordon & Breach, London and New York.

Rosenblatt, F. (1958). The perception — a theory of statistical separability in cognitive systems. Cornell Aerolab. Report No. VG-1196-G-1.

Rosenblatt, F. (1962). *Principles of Neurodynamics.* Spartan Books.

Rosenbleuth, A., Wiener, N. & Bigelow, J. (1943). Behavior, purpose and teleology. *Phil. Sci.*, **10**. pp. 18-24.

Sacerdoti, E.D. (1979). Problem-solving tactics. Proc. 6th IJCA Conf. Tokoyo.

Sampson, J.R. (1976). *Adaptive Information Processing.* Springer-Verlag, New York.

Samuel, A.L. (1963). Some studies in machine learning, using the game check. In *Computers and Thought.* E.A. Feignebaum and J. Feldman (Eds.) McGraw-Hill.

Sarker, P. and George, F.H. (1969). LIP: *A Study in National Language Programme.* BIS — memo.

Schank, R. (1973). *The Fourteen Primitive Actions and their Inferences.* Stanford Artificial Intelligence Memo. AI M-183.

Schank, R.C. & Colby, K.M. (Eds) (1973). *Computer Models of Thought and Language.* Freeman.

Searle, J.R. (1969). *Speech Acts,* Cambridge University Press.

Searle, J.R. (1979). *Expression and Meaning.* Cambridge University Press.

Searle, J.R. (1982). Minds, brains and programs. *The Behav. and Brain Sci.,* **3**, pp. 417-457

Selfridge, O. (1959). Pandemonium: a paradigon for learning. In *Mechanisation of Thought Processes.* NPL Symposium.

Shannon, C.E. Programming a computer for playing chess *Phil. Mag.,* pp. 256-275.

Shannon, C.E. and Weaver, W. (1949). *The Mathematical Theory of Communication.* Univer. of Illinois Press.

Shimble, A. (1955). Some elementary considerations of neural models. *Bull. Math. Biophys.* **14**, pp. 68-71.

Sillars, W. (1963). An algorithm for representing English sentences in a formal language. *Rep. 7884 Nat. Bur. Stand.* Washington, D.C.

Simmons, R.F. (1962). Answer English questions by computer: a survey. *Communication of the A.C.M.,* **8** (*1*), p. 53.

Simmons, R.F.S., Klein, S. and McConlogue, K. (1964). Indexing and dependency logic for answering English questions. *American Documentation,* **15** (3), pp. 196-204.

Simmons, R.F. & Bruce, B.C. (1971). Some relations between predicate calculus and semantic net representations of discourse. Second International Joint Conference of Artificial Intelligence, pp. 524-529.

Slagle, J.R. (1971). Artificial Intelligence: *The Heuristic Programming Approach.* McGraw-Hill, New York.

Sommerhoff, G. (1974). *Logic of the Living Brain.* Wiley, London.

Stamm, J.S. and Rosen, S.G. (1973). The locus and crucial time of implication of prefrontal cortex in the delayed response task. In *Psycho-physiology of the Frontal Lobes.* K.H. Pribram and A.R. Luria (Eds.) Academic Press, New York.

Stevens, Kent (1979). Representing and analyzing surface orientation. In Artificial Intelligence: An *MIT perspective.* (Eds. P.H. Winston and R.H. Brown) MIT Press, Cambridge, Mass.

Stockwell, R.P. (1965). The transformational model of generative or predictive grammar in *Natural Language and the computer.* (P. Garvin, Ed.) McGraw-Hill, New York.

Strank, R.H.D. (1983). *Management Principles and Practice: A Cybernetic Approach.* Gordon & Breach, London and New York.

Sussman, G.J. (1975). The virtuous nature of bugs. AISB-1, pp. 224-237.

Sutherland, N.S. (1959). Stimulus analyzing mechanisms. In *Mechanisation of Thought Processes.* NPL symposium.

Tomkins, S.S. and Messick, S. (Eds.) (1963). *Computer simulation of Personality Frontier of Psychological Research.* Wiley, New York.

Tonge, F.M. (1963). Summary of a heuristic line balancing procedure. In *Computers and Thought* (Eds. A.A. Feingenbaum and J. Feldman.) McGraw-Hill. New York.

Turing, A.M. (1936). On computable numbers, with an approach to the Entscheidings problem. *Proc. Lond. Math. Soc.,* **42**, pp. 230-265.

Turing, A.M. (1951). Computing machinery and intelligence, MND, **59**, pp. 433-460.

Uhr, L. and Vossler, C. (1961). A pattern recognition program that generates, evaluates and adjusts its own operators. In *Pattern Recognition,* L. Uhr (Ed.) Wiley, New York.

Uhr, L. & Vossler, C. (1966). *Pattern Recognition,* Wiley.

Ullman, S. (1979). *The Interpretation of Visual Motion,* MIT Press, Cambridge, Mass.

Uttley, A.M. (1954). The classification of signals in the nervous system. *Electroenceph. Clin. Neurophysiol.*
Uttley, A.M. (1955). *The conditional probability of signals in the nervous system.* PRE Mem. No. 1109.
Uttley, A.M. (1958). Conditional probability computing in the nervous system. Symposium on *Mechanisation of Thought Processes,* Nat. Phys. Lab.
Uttley, M. (1966). The transmission of information and the effect of local feedback in theoretical and neuron networks. *Brain Research,* **2**. pp. 21-50.
Verbeck, L. (1960). On error minimising neural nets. In *Principle of Self-Organization.* (Eds. H. von Foerster and G.W. Zopf) Pergamon Press, Oxford.
von Neumann, J. (1951). *Protabilistic Logic,* California Inst. Tech. pp. 4-15.
Walter, W.G. (1953). *The Living Brain.* Duckworth, London.
Wang, H. (1960). Towards mechanical mathematics, *IBM Journal of Res. and Dev.,* pp. 42-22.
Warnock, G.L. (Ed.) (1967). *The Philosophy of Perception,* Oxford University Press.
Weyrauch, R.W. (1979). Prolegomena to a theory of mechanised formal reasoning. RWW. Note 8. Stanford University.
Weizenbaum, J. (1966). ELIZA-A computer program for the study of natural language communication between man and machine. CACM, **9**, pp. 36-45.
Wiener, N. (1948). *Cybernetics.* MIT Press, Cambridge, Mass.
Wilks, Y. (1976). *Natural Language Understanding System Within the AI Paradigm.* Edinburgh University AI Dept.
Winograd, T. (1973). *Understanding Natural Languages.* Academic Press, New York.
Winograd, T. (1974). *Five lectures on Artificial Intelligence.* Stanford Artificial Intelligence Memo. AIM-246.
Winston, P.H. (1975). Learning structural descriptions from examples, in *The Psychology of Computer Vision,* P.H. Winston (Ed.).
Winston, P.H. & Brown, R.H. (Eds) (1979). *Artificial Intelligence: MIT Perspective* 2 Vols. MIT Press, Cambridge, Mass.
Wittgenstein, L. (1922). *Tractatus Logico Philosophicas.* Routledge and Kegan Paul, London.
Wittgenstein, L. (1953). *Philosophical Investigations.* Basil Blackwell, Oxford.
Woodger, J.H. (1937). *The Axiomatic Method in Biology.* Cambridge University Press.
Woodger, J.H. (1939). *The Technique of Theory Construction.* Encyclopeodia of Unified Sciences, **2** (5), Chicago.
Woodger, J.H. (1952). *Biology and Language,* Cambridge University Press. MIT Press, Cambridge, Mass.
Woodham, R. (1979). Analyzing curved surfaces using reflective map techniques. In Winston P.H. & Brown, R.H. (Eds). *Artificial Intelligence: An MIT Perspective.* MIT Press, Cambridge, Mass. pp. 161-184.